Arduino Programming for Absolute Beginners

First Edition

By Sarful Hassan, MechatronicsLAB

Preface

Welcome to the First Edition of *Arduino programming for beginners*. This edition builds upon the foundation laid in the first, with expanded content, deeper insights into advanced Arduino programming concepts, and a greater focus on real-world applications. Whether you're just starting out or looking to elevate your skills, this edition will provide the knowledge you need to succeed in Arduino programming.

Who This Book Is For

This edition is perfect for:

- **Beginners and Enthusiasts**: People new to Arduino who want a clear, step-by-step approach to learning the platform.
- **Engineers and Designers**: Professionals aiming to use Arduino for prototyping and building systems.
- **Educators**: Teachers looking for structured instructional material for Arduino courses.
- **IoT and Automation Experts**: Individuals exploring Arduino for use in robotics, automation, and Internet of Things (IoT) projects.

No prior experience with electronics or programming is required. All you need is curiosity and a willingness to experiment!

How This Book Is Organized

This second edition has been reorganized and enhanced with practical projects, in-depth explanations, and more advanced topics. Here's a quick look at the new structure:

- **Introduction to Arduino**: Gain a solid understanding of Arduino basics and how to set up your environment.
- **Arduino IDE**: Explore the IDE in detail and learn to write and upload code.
- **Input/Output Functions**: Dive deeper into essential functions like `digitalRead()`, `digitalWrite()`, `analogRead()`, and `analogWrite()`, with practical projects.

- **Control Structures and Flow**: Learn advanced techniques for using loops, conditionals, and functions to enhance your program's efficiency.
- **Sensors and Actuators**: Get hands-on experience integrating sensors and actuators for real-world applications.

What Was Left Out

While this edition expands into advanced topics, certain areas such as complex data structures, low-level programming, and highly specific hardware configurations are not covered in detail. Once you master the material here, you'll be well-equipped to explore these areas independently.

Code Style (About the Code)

The code presented in this book is written in a clean and structured manner. Each example is accompanied by comments that explain key steps, ensuring that it's easy for beginners to follow. The second edition emphasizes best practices for readability, maintainability, and optimization.

Arduino Platform Release Notes

This edition is updated to include the latest changes to the Arduino platform as of 2024. You'll find new functions, features, and supported boards integrated throughout the book. Be sure to visit the Arduino website for future updates that may impact your projects.

Notes on the First Edition

The first edition focused on providing a solid foundation for beginners, with easy-to-follow lessons on Arduino basics, functions, and simple projects. It helped introduce new users to the world of microcontrollers.

Using Code Examples

Feel free to use, modify, and share the code examples provided in this book. The best way to master Arduino programming is through experimentation, so don't hesitate to adapt the code to fit your needs or projects.

MechatronicsLAB Online Learning

Visit www.mechatronicslab.net for additional resources, tutorials, and learning materials. Whether you're looking for extra guidance or new project ideas, our online platform is here to support your Arduino journey.

How to Contact Us

We encourage feedback and are happy to answer any questions you may have. Please contact us at:

- **Email**: mechatronicslab@gmail.com
- **Website**: www.mechatronicslab.net

Thank you for choosing *Arduino Programming Essentials*, and we hope you enjoy learning from this second edition.

Copyright

Disclaimer

- **Control Structures and Flow**: Learn advanced techniques for using loops, conditionals, and functions to enhance your program's efficiency.
- **Sensors and Actuators**: Get hands-on experience integrating sensors and actuators for real-world applications.

What Was Left Out

While this edition expands into advanced topics, certain areas such as complex data structures, low-level programming, and highly specific hardware configurations are not covered in detail. Once you master the material here, you'll be well-equipped to explore these areas independently.

Code Style (About the Code)

The code presented in this book is written in a clean and structured manner. Each example is accompanied by comments that explain key steps, ensuring that it's easy for beginners to follow. The second edition emphasizes best practices for readability, maintainability, and optimization.

Arduino Platform Release Notes

This edition is updated to include the latest changes to the Arduino platform as of 2024. You'll find new functions, features, and supported boards integrated throughout the book. Be sure to visit the Arduino website for future updates that may impact your projects.

Notes on the First Edition

The first edition focused on providing a solid foundation for beginners, with easy-to-follow lessons on Arduino basics, functions, and simple projects. It helped introduce new users to the world of microcontrollers.

Using Code Examples

Feel free to use, modify, and share the code examples provided in this book. The best way to master Arduino programming is through experimentation, so don't hesitate to adapt the code to fit your needs or projects.

MechatronicsLAB Online Learning

Visit www.mechatronicslab.net for additional resources, tutorials, and learning materials. Whether you're looking for extra guidance or new project ideas, our online platform is here to support your Arduino journey.

How to Contact Us

We encourage feedback and are happy to answer any questions you may have. Please contact us at:

- **Email**: mechatronicslab@gmail.com
- **Website**: www.mechatronicslab.net

Thank you for choosing *Arduino Programming Essentials*, and we hope you enjoy learning from this second edition.

Copyright

Disclaimer

Table of Contents

Chapter-1 Introduction to Arduino

Overview of the Arduino Platform

Arduino is an open-source electronics platform based on simple, user-friendly hardware and software, designed to make electronics accessible to a wide range of users, from beginners to advanced professionals. The platform consists of a physical programmable circuit board, often referred to as a microcontroller, and a software component called the Arduino Integrated Development Environment (IDE). The IDE is used to write and upload code to the board. Programs for Arduino are written in a language based on C/C++, but it also uses a simplified Arduino library that makes creating interactive projects much easier.

The platform's hardware comes in various models, each featuring different specifications, like the Arduino Uno, Arduino Mega, and others. These boards can be connected to sensors, actuators, motors, and other components, making them suitable for building anything from simple LED light displays to sophisticated IoT applications.

History and Evolution of Arduino

The Arduino platform was created in 2005 by a group of engineers, including Massimo Banzi, as a tool for students at the Interaction Design Institute Ivrea, Italy. The intention was to develop an affordable, open-source tool that would make it easier for students and artists to work with technology in creative ways.

Arduino quickly gained popularity, driven by its simplicity, affordability, and the vast opportunities it offered for learning and experimentation. Over the years, the Arduino platform has evolved, introducing a wide range of boards to meet the needs of different projects. The evolution included developing boards like Arduino Uno for general purposes, Arduino Mega for projects needing more input/output pins, and specialized versions like the Arduino Nano and Arduino Pro Mini for compact projects. The platform also supports wireless communication with versions such as Arduino MKR and the Arduino Nano 33 IoT, aimed at making IoT prototyping easy.

Why Arduino is Popular for Beginners and Professionals
Arduino has gained widespread popularity due to its unique ability to appeal to both beginners and professionals alike.

Beginner-Friendly:

- Easy to use with a plug-and-play experience.
- Simple programming language based on C/C++.
- Lots of tutorials, sample codes, and a helpful community.

Great for Professionals:

- Flexible prototyping environment.
- Open-source, allowing customization of hardware and software.
- Ideal for creating prototypes and testing new ideas quickly.

Moreover, Arduino's ecosystem includes various shields—hardware add-ons that extend the capabilities of the basic board, like adding WiFi, motor control, or GPS. This modularity, combined with the compatibility of the software and easy integration with third-party tools and sensors, makes Arduino ideal for building everything from simple DIY projects to more advanced automation and IoT systems. The presence of libraries that support integration with different components saves time, which is crucial for professionals working under time constraints.

Overall, Arduino's popularity stems from its affordability, simplicity, scalability, and a large support community that caters to both beginners starting their learning journey and professionals looking to build and prototype efficiently.

Understanding the Arduino Board

Arduino boards are designed to be accessible for both absolute beginners and professionals, with a structure that is easy to understand and versatile for a wide variety of projects. Let's break down the details to highlight the main components, types of boards, and power supply/pin configurations, explaining their relevance to both beginners and experienced users.

Main Components of the Arduino Board

An Arduino board consists of several key components that work together to create an easy-to-use and versatile microcontroller platform:

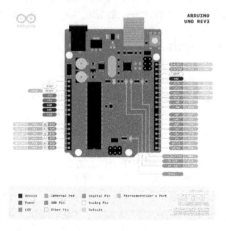

Pinout Diagram , Image source arduino.cc

Component	What It Is	Example	Pin Numbers
Microcontroller	The "brain" of the board that runs the code you upload.	Like a tiny computer that follows your commands, such as making an LED blink or running a motor.	N/A
Digital Pins	Pins that can turn things on or off, or check if something is on or off.	You can use these pins to make an LED blink or detect if a button is pressed.	D0-D13

Analog Pins	Pins that measure changing signals, such as light or temperature.	Use these pins to read a light sensor or measure the room temperature.	A0-A5
Power Supply	How the board gets power, either through a USB cable from your computer or from a battery.	You can power the board by plugging it into your computer or by using a battery for portable projects.	USB, Vin, GND, 5V, 3.3V
Reset Button	A button to restart the board and run your code again from the beginning.	Press this button to reset your project if something isn't working.	N/A
ICSP Header	Special pins that advanced users can use to program the board directly.	Beginners don't usually need this, but it's useful for advanced programming.	6 ICSP pins
LED Indicators	Small built-in lights that show if the board is powered or if your code is working.	There's an LED on pin 13 that you can use to test simple projects by turning it on or off with code.	Pin 13, Power LED

Different Types of Arduino Boards

There are various types of Arduino boards, each suited to different project requirements. Here are some of the most popular models:

Arduino Board	Microcontroller	Digital I/O Pins	Analog Pins	PWM Pins	Operating Voltage	Flash Memory	Clock Speed
Arduino Uno	ATmega328P	14	6	6	5V	32 KB	16 MHz
Arduino Mega 2560	ATmega2560	54	16	15	5V	256 KB	16 MHz
Arduino Nano	ATmega328P	14	8	6	5V	32 KB	16 MHz
Arduino Leonardo	ATmega32u4	20	12	7	5V	32 KB	16 MHz
Arduino Micro	ATmega32u4	20	12	7	5V	32 KB	16 MHz
Arduino Due	ATSAM3X8E	54	12	12	3.3V	512 KB	84 MHz
Arduino Pro Mini	ATmega328P	14	8	6	5V or 3.3V	32 KB	16 MHz (5V) / 8 MHz (3.3V)

Arduino Zero	ATSAMD21G18	14	6	10	3.3V	256 KB	48 MHz
Arduino MKR1000	ATSAMW25	8	7	12	3.3V	256 KB	48 MHz
Arduino MKR Zero	ATSAMD21G18	8	7	12	3.3V	256 KB	48 MHz
Arduino Nano 33 IoT	SAMD21 Cortex-M0+	14	8	8	3.3V	256 KB	48 MHz

How to Choose the Right Arduino Board for Beginners

Arduino Board	Why Choose It?	Best For
Arduino Uno	Most popular board for beginners, easy to find tutorials.	Learning basics, small projects like blinking LEDs.
Arduino Nano	Similar to Uno but smaller, fits into breadboards easily.	Compact projects, beginners needing a smaller board.
Arduino Mega	Has many more pins for complex projects.	Projects with lots of sensors or components.
Arduino Leonardo	Can act as a computer keyboard or mouse.	Projects needing direct USB communication (e.g., keyboards).

Arduino Micro	Very small, also acts like a keyboard or mouse.	Tiny projects, wearable tech, USB projects.
Arduino Due	More powerful, but uses 3.3V (be careful with components).	Advanced projects needing more processing power.
Arduino Pro Mini	Tiny, low power consumption, perfect for portable projects.	Small projects where size and low power are important.

Power Supply and Pin Configuration

1. **Power Supply**: Arduino boards can be powered in multiple ways:
    - **USB Port**: This is the most common way to power an Arduino while uploading and testing code. It provides 5V and is convenient for beginners.
    - **DC Barrel Jack**: An external power supply of 7-12V can be used to power standalone projects.
    - **VIN Pin**: This pin can be used to supply voltage to the Arduino when an external power source is used.

Setting Up the Arduino IDE

The Arduino Integrated Development Environment (IDE) is a crucial tool for programming Arduino boards. Below is a beginner-friendly guide to downloading, installing, and getting started with the IDE, while also providing additional details that will be useful for professionals.

How to Download and Install the Arduino Integrated Development Environment (IDE)

1. **Downloading the Arduino IDE**:
    - Go to the official Arduino website.
    - You'll see several options to download the Arduino IDE for different operating systems (Windows, macOS, Linux).
    - For Windows users, there's an option to download an installer or a zip file. Beginners can simply download the installer, which makes installation easier.

2. **Installation Steps**:
   - ○ **Windows**: After downloading, run the installer and follow the instructions. It will ask for permissions to install USB drivers—make sure to accept these, as the drivers are necessary for communication with your Arduino board.
   - ○ **macOS**: Download the .dmg file, drag the Arduino app to the Applications folder, and you're done.
   - ○ **Linux**: The IDE is available as a .tar file. You need to extract the contents and run the installation script. Professionals familiar with the Linux terminal may prefer using package managers to simplify the process.

For beginners, installing the Arduino IDE is very straightforward with simple on-screen prompts. Professionals appreciate that it's available on multiple platforms and can be customized according to individual preferences.

Overview of the Arduino IDE Interface

The Arduino IDE is designed to be user-friendly, and it features several key components to help users write, compile, and upload code to their Arduino boards.

Image source:arduino.cc

1. **Code Editor**:
   - ○ The main area is where you write the code (called sketches). It's simplified to avoid overwhelming beginners, with features like basic syntax highlighting to help differentiate various code components.

- o Professionals can take advantage of extensions and plugins to add more functionality, such as code linting or integration with external version control systems.

2. **Menu Bar**:
   - o The **File** menu allows you to create, open, and save sketches. You can also find built-in example codes here—perfect for beginners wanting to learn how to use sensors or control LEDs.
   - o The **Tools** menu gives you options for board selection, port selection, and other settings needed to upload the code, allowing professionals to configure advanced settings.

3. **Buttons in the Toolbar**:
   - o **Verify** (checkmark icon): This button checks your code for any errors. It helps beginners ensure their code is correct before uploading.
   - o **Upload** (arrow icon): After verifying, click this button to upload the code to your board. This is one of the first steps beginners learn.
   - o **New, Open, Save**: These buttons make managing your sketches easy, just like in other text editors.
   - o **Serial Monitor**: This button opens a window that allows you to see real-time data from the Arduino. Beginners often use this to display sensor values, while professionals use it extensively for debugging.

4. **Status Area**:
   - o Below the code editor is a status bar that shows information like compilation errors or successful uploads. For beginners, this area helps in identifying issues, while professionals use the detailed output to troubleshoot their projects effectively.

5. **Examples and Libraries**:
   - o Arduino provides many built-in examples in the IDE. Beginners can learn basic functionality like blinking an LED or reading sensor data by going to **File > Examples**.
   - o Professionals can include external libraries using **Sketch > Include Library**, enabling advanced functionalities like networking, communication, and more complex hardware interaction.

How to Connect Your Arduino to the Computer

Physical Connection:

- o Use a **USB cable** (usually Type-A to Type-B for boards like Arduino Uno) to connect your Arduino board to your computer. Once connected, the power LED on the Arduino board should turn on, indicating that it is receiving power.
- o This is a simple plug-and-play process, which makes it extremely beginner-friendly. Professionals, however, may also use other methods like FTDI adapters for more compact boards.

Selecting the Board and Port:

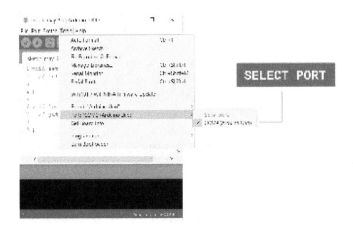

- o After connecting the Arduino to the computer, open the Arduino IDE.
- o Go to **Tools > Board** and select the type of Arduino you are using (e.g., Arduino Uno, Mega, Nano).
- o Then, go to **Tools > Port** and select the port your Arduino is connected to. On Windows, this may appear as "COM3" or another number, while on macOS/Linux, it might show as "/dev/cu.usbmodemXXX". For beginners, this step is crucial as it ensures that the IDE knows which device to communicate with.

Uploading Your First Sketch:

- ○ Open an example sketch by going to **File > Examples > Basics > Blink**.
- ○ Click **Verify** to check for any errors in the code.
- ○ Click **Upload** to upload the code to your Arduino board. If successful, you will see the onboard LED start blinking. This step helps beginners understand the complete process from writing code to seeing its effects in the real world, while professionals use it to verify that the board and IDE setup are correct.

Writing Your First Program (The "Hello World" of Arduino)

The "Hello World" equivalent for Arduino is typically the **LED blink** program, which is a great starting point for absolute beginners and provides a solid foundation for understanding the basics of how an Arduino sketch works. Here's a beginner-friendly guide with a professional structure, explaining the structure of an Arduino sketch, writing your first LED blink program, and how to upload it to the Arduino board.

Explanation of the Structure of an Arduino Sketch (setup() and loop())

An Arduino program is called a **sketch**, and every sketch contains two main functions: setup() and loop(). These functions are essential to the way Arduino works and make it approachable for both beginners and professionals:

1. **setup() Function**:
   The setup() function is called once when your Arduino board is powered on or reset. It is used to initialize variables, pin modes, or to start using libraries. This function sets the stage for everything that follows in your project.
   - Example: If you want to control an LED connected to a specific pin, you would use pinMode() to declare whether that pin will act as an input or output inside setup().

2. **loop() Function**:
   The loop() function runs continuously after setup(). This is where the main logic of your program goes, allowing the Arduino to perform tasks repeatedly. For beginners, this is where they will add commands to make things happen repeatedly, like blinking an LED.
   - Example: To blink an LED, you will turn it on, wait for some time, turn it off, and then wait again. This sequence runs over and over inside loop(), making it perfect for repeated actions like blinking.

Writing a Simple LED Blink Program
Let's write a basic LED blink program. Most Arduino boards (like the Uno) have a built-in LED on **pin 13**. Here's how to write the sketch:

```
// Define the pin number for the LED
int ledPin = 13;
// The setup function runs once when you press reset or power the board
void setup() {
  // Set the digital pin as output
  pinMode(ledPin, OUTPUT);
}
// The loop function runs over and over again
void loop() {
  // Turn the LED on (HIGH is the voltage level)
  digitalWrite(ledPin, HIGH);
  // Wait for a second
  delay(1000);
  digitalWrite(ledPin, LOW);
  delay(1000);
```

}

Explanation:

- `int ledPin = 13;` declares a variable called `ledPin` and assigns it the value 13, representing the pin connected to the LED.
- `pinMode(ledPin, OUTPUT);` in the `setup()` function tells the Arduino that pin 13 will be used as an **output**, meaning it will send electrical signals.
- Inside the `loop()`, `digitalWrite(ledPin, HIGH);` turns on the LED by sending a HIGH signal (5V) to pin 13.
- `delay(1000);` pauses the program for **1000 milliseconds (1 second)**.
- `digitalWrite(ledPin, LOW);` turns off the LED.
- `delay(1000);` again pauses for 1 second before repeating the process.
- For more complex timing, professionals might prefer using non-blocking code techniques (like `millis()`) instead of `delay()`, which stops all other processes in the sketch during the wait period.
- This sketch is a great foundation, but it can be expanded by adding more LEDs, creating patterns, or incorporating other components like buttons.

Uploading Your First Sketch to the Arduino Board

1. **Connect the Arduino Board**:
   - Use a USB cable to connect your Arduino board to your computer. Ensure that the correct port and board are selected in the Arduino IDE. Go to **Tools > Board** and select your board type (e.g., Arduino Uno), then go to **Tools > Port** to select the appropriate port.
2. **Upload the Sketch**:
   - **Verify** your code by clicking the checkmark button at the top left of the Arduino IDE. This checks the code for errors.
   - Once verified successfully, click the **Upload** button (arrow icon) to upload the code to your Arduino board.
   - After uploading, you should see the LED connected to pin 13 blinking on and off at 1-second intervals.

Tips

- The onboard LED (labelled **L** on many boards) is connected to pin 13, making it an excellent first experiment since no additional components are needed.
- If you encounter errors, check that you selected the correct board and port in the Tools menu, and ensure your code doesn't have typos.
- If working on more advanced projects, you may want to use `Serial.begin(9600);` in `setup()` to begin serial communication, allowing you to print messages to the Serial Monitor for debugging.
- Consider using other pins to connect multiple LEDs or even writing custom functions to organize the code better as your projects grow in complexity.

Overview of Common Arduino Libraries

Libraries are an important part of the Arduino ecosystem, providing pre-written code that simplifies complex operations, making it easier to work with different components and sensors. Here's a guide to understanding what libraries are, why they're essential, how to add them to the Arduino IDE, and some of the most commonly used libraries.

Introduction to Libraries and Why They Are Important

Arduino libraries are collections of code that allow you to easily control hardware like sensors, displays, and actuators. They abstract away the technical complexities, making it much simpler to get components working with minimal effort.

For beginners, libraries are crucial because they enable quick learning and experimentation without needing a deep understanding of low-level hardware programming. For professionals, they speed up prototyping and allow complex projects to be created with less repetitive coding. Libraries come with pre-defined functions that are tested, reducing the potential for errors and allowing users to focus on the creative aspects of their projects.

How to Add Libraries in Arduino IDE

Adding libraries to the Arduino IDE can be done in several ways:

1. **Using the Library Manager**:
   o Open the Arduino IDE.
   o Go to **Sketch > Include Library > Manage Libraries...**.
   o The **Library Manager** window allows you to browse and search for available libraries.
   o Click on the desired library and click **Install**.
2. This method is very straightforward and highly recommended for beginners since it helps ensure compatibility and provides updates.
3. **Adding a ZIP Library**:
   o Download the library as a .zip file from a trusted source.
   o In the Arduino IDE, go to **Sketch > Include Library > Add .ZIP Library...**.
   o Browse to the location of the ZIP file and select it.
4. This method is useful when you need to add a library that's not available through the Library Manager.
5. **Manual Installation**:
   o Copy the library folder into the **libraries** folder in your Arduino sketch directory.
   o Restart the Arduino IDE if it's open.
6. This approach is useful for advanced users who may be modifying or creating custom libraries.

Common Arduino Libraries

1. **Wire Library** (Wire.h):
   The **Wire library** is used for I2C communication, a protocol that allows multiple devices to communicate over just two wires (SCL and SDA). It's commonly used with sensors and displays, making it ideal for building sensor networks and reading data from different modules.
2. **Servo Library** (Servo.h):
   The **Servo library** allows you to control servo motors with ease. This library is widely used in robotics and automation projects to create precise movement control, such as for robotic arms or pan-tilt systems.

3. **LiquidCrystal Library** (LiquidCrystal.h):
   The **LiquidCrystal library** is used to control LCD displays. It enables displaying text or data on 16x2 or 20x4 character LCDs, which is useful for providing information or creating a simple interface for your projects.

Chapter 2: Arduino Variables and Data Types

Chapter explores variables and data types in Arduino, which are fundamental to storing and manipulating data in your programs. Variables are named storage locations, while data types determine the kind of data these variables can store, such as `int` for whole numbers, `float` for decimal numbers, `bool` for true/false values, and more. Choosing the correct data type is crucial for efficient memory use and optimal program performance, especially in a memory-constrained environment like Arduino. This chapter also introduces arrays, advanced data types, and constants, helping you write effective, optimized, and easy-to-understand code.

Syntax Table: Arduino Variables and Data Types

Topic Name	Syntax	Simple Example
Declaring an Integer Variable	`int varName = value;`	`int count = 10;`
Declaring a Boolean Variable	`bool varName = true/false;`	`bool isOn = true;`
Declaring a Byte Variable	`byte varName = value;`	`byte ledBrightness = 150;`
Declaring a Long Variable	`long varName = value;`	`long duration = 1000000;`
Declaring a Float Variable	`float varName = value;`	`float temperature = 23.75;`
Declaring a Double Variable	`double varName = value;`	`double pi = 3.1415926535;`
Declaring a Character Array (String)	`char arrayName[] = "text";`	`char greeting[] = "Hello";`

Declaring a String Object	String varName = "text";	String message = "Arduino";
Declaring an Unsigned Char Variable	unsigned char varName = value;	unsigned char redValue = 255;
Declaring a Constant Variable	const dataType varName = value;	const int ledPin = 13;

1. Introduction to Variables and Data Types in Arduino

1.1 What are Variables and Data Types?

What are Variables and Data Types?
Variables are **named storage locations** that hold information in a program. A variable has a **data type**, which defines what kind of data it can store, such as numbers, characters, or boolean values. For example, an **int** is used for whole numbers, and a **float** is used for decimal numbers. The data type determines how much memory the variable will use and how the information will be processed by the Arduino.

Why are they important?
Selecting the correct **variable** and **data type** is essential for efficient programming in Arduino. Using the wrong data type can waste memory or cause the program to run inefficiently. For instance, using an **int** to store true/false values wastes memory when a **bool** would be more appropriate. Proper data types ensure that your program uses memory and processing power wisely, which is especially important for devices with limited resources like Arduino.

1.2 Key Concepts and Terms (Glossary)

What is a Variable?
A variable is a **named place** in memory where the program can store data that may change during execution.

What is a Data Type?
A data type defines what kind of **data** a variable can hold, such as integers, floating-point numbers, characters, or boolean values.

Why is it important to choose the right data type?
Using the correct data type is important because it ensures **efficient memory usage** and **accurate data processing**. For example, using a **float** when you only need an **int** wastes memory, while using a **bool** for true/false values minimizes memory use.

1.3 Overview of Core Data Types

What are the Common Data Types?
Some of the most common data types in Arduino are:

- **int**: for whole numbers like 10 or -3.
- **float**: for decimal numbers like 3.14.
- **char**: for storing single characters like 'A'.
- **bool**: for storing true/false values.

These data types allow you to manage different types of information in your programs, from simple numbers to more complex data like text or boolean logic.

Why are they important?
Choosing the right data type ensures **efficient memory usage** and helps your program run smoothly. Using an **int** for whole numbers, for example, saves space compared to using a **float**. A **char** is used when dealing with text or individual characters, while a **bool** is perfect for handling logical decisions. Correctly choosing these types optimizes the performance of your Arduino projects.

Quiz: Test Your Understanding of Variables and Data Types

1. What is the maximum value an **int** can store on Arduino UNO? (Multiple Choice)
2. How do you define a **bool** data type? (Short Answer)

2. Arrays in Arduino

2.1 Introduction to Arrays

What is an Array?
An array is a **collection of variables** stored in a single **data structure**, all sharing the same **data type**. Instead of creating multiple individual variables, an array groups them under one **name**, with each element accessed by an **index number**. For example, you can use an array to store multiple sensor readings or manage multiple LED states in a project. Arrays make handling multiple values **easier** and **efficient** in Arduino.

Why are Arrays important?
Arrays are crucial when you need to manage **multiple values** efficiently. Instead of creating many variables, you can store related data, like sensor readings, in an array. This simplifies the code, reduces memory usage, and helps with tasks like **iterating** over values in loops. Arrays also make it easier to **modify** or update groups of values simultaneously.

Syntax

```
dataType arrayName[arraySize];
```

This is how you declare an array. The **dataType** specifies what type of data the array holds, such as **int** or **float**.

Syntax Explanation
In dataType arrayName[arraySize], the **arraySize** defines how many elements the array can hold, and the **arrayName** is used to reference it. Arrays in Arduino are **zero-indexed**, meaning the first element is accessed with index **0**.

Usage
Arrays are used to **group related data**, like storing multiple **sensor readings** or managing multiple LED outputs. By accessing elements via their **index**, you can loop through the array and perform tasks on each value, making arrays useful in complex projects.

Code Example

```
int sensorReadings[5] = {0, 100, 200, 300, 400};
Serial.println(sensorReadings[2]);  // Outputs the third value in the
array
```

This example declares an array of **five integers** and prints the third value, which is stored at index **2**.

Notes
Remember that arrays in Arduino start at **index 0**. Accessing elements outside the array's bounds can lead to **unexpected behavior**.

Warnings
If you try to access an index that is **out of bounds**, the program may crash or return **undefined results**, leading to potential errors.

Troubleshooting Tips
If your array isn't behaving as expected, check the **array size** and ensure you're not accessing elements outside its bounds. Use the **Serial Monitor** to debug the values stored in the array.

2.2 Working with Arrays

Accessing Array Elements
Array elements are accessed using the **index number** inside square brackets. The first element is always at index **0**, the second at **1**, and so on. For example, array[0] accesses the first element, while array[3] accesses the fourth element.

Looping through Arrays
To perform actions on each element of an array, use a **for loop**. Looping through arrays is useful for tasks like reading multiple sensor values or turning on LEDs. You can access and modify each element inside the loop by using the **index variable**.

Array Bounds
Array bounds refer to the **limits** of the array. If an array is declared with size 5, its valid indexes range from **0 to 4**. Accessing an index outside these bounds (like array[5] for a 5-element array) will lead to errors.

Code Example

```
for (int i = 0; i < 5; i++) {
  Serial.println(sensorReadings[i]);  // Prints each value in the array
}
```

This code loops through an array and prints each element using the **index variable** i.

Notes
Use loops to handle arrays efficiently. This helps when you need to **perform repeated actions** on each element, such as calculations or outputs.

Warnings
Always ensure you stay within the **array bounds** while looping or accessing elements, as accessing out-of-bounds elements can lead to crashes or **unexpected behavior**.

Troubleshooting Tips
If you encounter array issues, check your loop limits and ensure you're not exceeding the array size. Print array values to the **Serial Monitor** to help track issues with individual elements.

Quiz: Check Your Understanding of Arrays

- How do you declare an array? (Multiple Choice)
- What happens if you access an array element out of bounds? (Fill in the Blank)

3. Basic Data Types

3.1 The bool Data Type

What is bool?
The bool data type represents a **boolean value**, which can only be

true or **false**. It is commonly used in Arduino programs to make **decisions**. For example, if a sensor detects a certain condition, a bool can store **true** if the condition is met and **false** otherwise. This type is ideal for scenarios where you need to store **binary logic**, such as whether a button is pressed or an LED is on.

Why is it important?
bool is important because it provides a simple way to handle **yes/no** decisions or logical operations in your code. Using a bool helps to **minimize memory usage** since it only stores one bit of information, compared to other data types like int. It is especially useful in projects where you are checking conditions, such as monitoring if a sensor has triggered a response.

Syntax

```
bool varName = true;
```

This defines a bool variable named varName and sets its initial value to **true**. You can also set it to **false**.

Syntax Explanation
In bool varName = true;, varName is the name of the boolean variable. The value can either be **true** or **false**, depending on the condition being evaluated in the program. For example, you might use bool buttonPressed = false; to store whether a button has been pressed.

Usage
You typically use bool for conditions that need **true/false** responses, such as whether a sensor is activated or a button is pressed. In **if statements**, bool variables help control the flow of the program based on whether a condition is met.

Code Example

```
bool buttonPressed = false;
if (digitalRead(buttonPin) == HIGH) {
  buttonPressed = true;
}
if (buttonPressed) {
  digitalWrite(ledPin, HIGH);  // Turn on the LED
```

```
}
```

This code checks if a button is pressed and updates the bool variable. If the button is pressed, the LED turns on.

Notes
Use bool for **binary decisions** like true/false or on/off. It simplifies code where conditions need to be checked frequently.

Warnings
bool can only store **true** or **false** values. Attempting to store other types of data, like numbers, will result in **unexpected behavior**.

Troubleshooting Tips
If your program isn't working as expected, check the bool variables using Serial.print(). This will help you see whether they are correctly set to **true** or **false** during execution, making it easier to find and fix problems.

3.2 The byte Data Type

What is byte?
The byte data type stores an **8-bit unsigned number**, meaning it can hold values between **0 and 255**. It is a great choice when you know your values will be small and positive, such as when storing **sensor readings, RGB color values**, or **LED brightness levels**. byte is more efficient in memory usage compared to larger data types like int, making it useful in projects where memory is limited.

Why is it important?
Using byte is important for **memory-efficient programming**, especially in Arduino devices where memory is limited. When working with values that stay between **0 and 255**, using byte saves memory compared to using int. This is crucial in projects where you need to handle many small values, such as **lighting effects** or **communication protocols**.

Syntax

```
byte varName = 255;
```

This declares a `byte` variable called `varName` and assigns it the value **255**. It can hold any value between 0 and 255.

Syntax Explanation
In `byte varName = 255;`, `varName` is the name of the variable, and **255** is the value assigned to it. `byte` can store any number between **0** and **255**, which makes it perfect for storing data like sensor values, where larger data types would be **inefficient**.

Usage
`byte` is often used in situations like controlling the **brightness** of an LED using **PWM** or representing **color values** for RGB lights. It is also useful when working with **binary data** and communicating with external devices using protocols that require small numbers.

Code Example

```
byte brightness = 150;
analogWrite(ledPin, brightness);  // Set LED brightness to 150
```

This example uses `byte` to control the brightness of an LED using **analogWrite()**, where the value is limited to 0-255.

Notes
Use `byte` to store small positive values between **0 and 255**. This is ideal for controlling things like **LED brightness** or storing **RGB color data**.

Warnings
If you assign a value greater than **255** to a `byte`, it will **overflow**, causing unexpected results. Ensure that your values stay within the allowed range.

Troubleshooting Tips
If a `byte` variable behaves unexpectedly, check that the value doesn't exceed **255**. Use `Serial.print()` to debug and verify the value being stored in the `byte`. If it exceeds the limit, you will need to correct it.

3.3 The int Data Type

What is int?
The int data type is used to store **16-bit signed integers**, meaning it can hold values ranging from **-32,768 to 32,767**. This is the most commonly used data type in Arduino for storing **whole numbers**, such as sensor readings, counters, and loop iterations. int is versatile and provides enough range for most general-purpose tasks.

Why is it important?
int is important because it handles **most common integer values** needed in Arduino programs. It strikes a good balance between memory efficiency and value range, making it perfect for storing values like **sensor data** or **counting loops**. Unlike byte, it can store both positive and negative numbers, making it versatile for a wide range of applications.

Syntax

```
int varName = 1000;
```

This declares an int variable called varName and assigns it the value **1000**.

Syntax Explanation
In int varName = 1000;, varName is the variable name, and the value assigned is **1000**. int can store values between **-32,768 and 32,767**, making it suitable for tasks that require a wide range of positive and negative values.

Usage
int is commonly used to store **sensor readings**, **loop counters**, and **mathematical calculations**. It is flexible enough for most general-purpose tasks that require whole numbers, whether positive or negative.

Code Example

```
int temperature = 25;
Serial.println(temperature);  // Print the temperature value to the
Serial Monitor
```

This example declares an int variable to store a **temperature** value and prints it to the **Serial Monitor** for debugging or display purposes.

Notes

Use int for most general-purpose whole number storage, as it provides a good balance between **memory efficiency** and **range**.

Warnings

Do not use int for values greater than **32,767** or less than **-32,768**. Exceeding these limits will cause **overflow errors**, resulting in incorrect values.

Troubleshooting Tips

If your int values are incorrect, check to ensure they fall within the valid range. Use Serial.print() to monitor values in real time and verify they are being stored correctly. If overflow occurs, consider using a larger data type like long.

Quiz: Test Your Knowledge of Basic Data Types

- How does the bool data type work? (Multiple Choice)
- What range of values can be stored in int

4. Advanced Data Types

4.1 The long Data Type

What is long?

The long data type is used to store **32-bit signed integers**, meaning it can hold values from **-2,147,483,648 to 2,147,483,647**. It's perfect for handling **large numbers** that int cannot store, such as counting **milliseconds** in timers or storing **large sensor readings**. Unlike int, which is limited to smaller values, long can handle big numbers, making it useful in projects where you need to track **large ranges** of data.

Why is it important?
long is essential when you need to work with numbers that exceed the range of int. For example, to track the **time** since your program started, long is used to store the **millisecond count** over long periods. Without long, trying to store these values in int would cause **overflow**, leading to inaccurate data and program crashes.

Syntax

```
long varName = 100000;
```

This defines a long variable called varName and assigns it the value **100000**.

Syntax Explanation
In long varName = 100000;, varName is the name of the variable, and **100000** is the value assigned. The long data type can store values much larger than int, making it useful for **high-range counting** or storing big numbers, like long time intervals.

Usage
Use long to store values that go beyond what int can handle. For example, it is great for **time tracking** in milliseconds, **large cumulative totals**, or reading **high-range sensors**. The ability to store large numbers ensures you can track events over **long periods** without overflow.

Code Example

```
long duration = 1000000;
if (duration > 500000) {
  Serial.println("Long value exceeded half a million");
}
```

This code creates a long variable to store a **large value** and checks if the value exceeds **500,000**. It then prints a message if the condition is met.

Notes
Use long when you need to store numbers bigger than what int can handle. It is commonly used for **timing functions** or any task involving **large numerical values**.

Warnings
Beware of **overflow** with long if your number exceeds its limit. Values over **2,147,483,647** or below **-2,147,483,648** will cause **errors** and result in incorrect values.

Troubleshooting Tips
If your long variable produces incorrect results, check for **overflow** by ensuring values stay within the valid range. Use Serial.print() to monitor the variable's value during execution and verify that it doesn't exceed the allowed limits.

4.2 The float Data Type

What is float?
The float data type is used to store **32-bit floating-point numbers**, which means it can handle numbers with **decimal points**. This makes it ideal for **precise measurements** and calculations involving real numbers, such as **sensor data** like temperature, distance, or voltage. Unlike int, which only handles whole numbers, float can handle fractions, providing more **accuracy** for scientific and mathematical computations.

Why is it important?
float is crucial for handling **real-world measurements** that involve decimals, such as when working with **temperature sensors**, **distance sensors**, or **voltage calculations**. Without float, you would lose **precision**, and your program would round off important values, leading to inaccurate results. It is essential for **any application** that requires detailed, **non-integer data**.

Syntax

```
float varName = 3.14;
```

This declares a float variable called varName and assigns it the value **3.14**.

Syntax Explanation
In float varName = 3.14;, varName is the name of the variable, and **3.14** is a **decimal number**. The float type allows you to work with numbers that have **decimal precision**, making it perfect for **scientific calculations** or storing sensor data.

Usage
float is used for tasks requiring **decimal accuracy**, such as reading data from a **temperature sensor** or **voltage meter**. It's also useful in **engineering** or **scientific projects** where you need to track **precise measurements**.

Code Example
```
float temperature = 23.75;
Serial.println(temperature);   // Prints the value 23.75 to the Serial
Monitor
```

This example creates a float variable to store a **temperature** value and prints it with **decimal precision** to the Serial Monitor.

Notes
Use float when you need to handle **decimal numbers** or **precision measurements**. It's often used in **sensor readings** where exact values are important.

Warnings
float uses more **memory** than int or byte, so avoid using it unnecessarily. Overusing float in memory-constrained programs can **slow down** your Arduino's performance.

Troubleshooting Tips
If you notice errors with float values, check that your **calculations** are accurate and that you're not losing precision during **type**

conversions. Use `Serial.print()` to display the `float` value and ensure the number is being stored correctly.

4.3 The `double` Data Type

What is `double`?
The `double` data type is like `float`, but it offers **64-bit floating-point precision**, allowing for greater accuracy with **decimal numbers**. On most Arduino boards, `double` behaves just like `float`, but on platforms that support `double`, it can handle **higher precision** calculations. This makes it useful for **scientific** or **engineering projects** where precise calculations are needed.

Why is it important?
`double` is essential for situations that require **high precision** beyond what `float` can offer. It is often used in **advanced scientific** and **engineering calculations** where even small decimal inaccuracies can lead to large errors. Although on most Arduino boards `double` behaves like `float`, for supported platforms, it offers **more precise calculations**.

Syntax

```
double varName = 3.14159;
```

This declares a `double` variable called `varName` and assigns it the value **3.14159**.

Syntax Explanation
In `double varName = 3.14159;`, `varName` stores a **64-bit floating-point number**. Even though Arduino treats `double` like `float` on many boards, using `double` ensures more **decimal places** are considered in calculations when the hardware supports it.

Usage
`double` is used in applications that require **highly precise measurements**, such as **scientific sensors** or **mathematical**

simulations. It is especially useful in projects where small **decimal inaccuracies** can lead to major **calculation errors**.

Code Example

```
double pi = 3.1415926535;
Serial.println(pi);   // Prints 3.1415926535 to the Serial Monitor
```

This code shows how to use double to store and print a highly precise value of **pi**.

Notes
Use double when **precision is critical** for your project. In most cases on Arduino, double behaves like float, but use it if your hardware supports **higher precision**.

Warnings
Be cautious when using double in memory-limited devices, as it consumes more **resources**. Only use it when **extra precision** is absolutely necessary to avoid wasting memory.

Troubleshooting Tips
If you notice issues with double precision, check whether your hardware supports **64-bit floating-point numbers**. Use Serial.print() to verify that values are being stored and processed accurately.

Quiz: Test Your Advanced Data Types Knowledge

1. How is long different from int? (Multiple Choice)
2. When should you use float or double? (Short Answer)

5. Strings in Arduino

5.1 Using char Arrays for Strings

What is a char array?
A char array is a **collection of characters** that is used to store text data, such as words or phrases. Each character in the array is represented by an **ASCII value**, and the array must include a **null**

terminator (¥0) to indicate the end of the string. This method is a **low-level approach** to string manipulation, giving you full control over how memory is used and how data is handled in Arduino.

Why use char arrays?
char arrays are more **memory-efficient** than using the String object. They give you precise control over **memory usage** and string manipulation, which is critical in **resource-limited environments** like Arduino. This is important when you need to **manipulate strings manually** for tasks such as **serial communication**, reading from sensors, or managing text input/output.

Syntax

```
char str[] = "Hello";
```

This declares a char array named str and assigns it the value "Hello", with the **null terminator** automatically added.

Syntax Explanation
In char str[] = "Hello";, the array str holds five characters plus a **null terminator** (¥0) to mark the end of the string. This is required to properly manage memory and ensure the string is handled correctly by functions that process text.

Usage
Use char arrays when you need to store **fixed-length strings** or when performance and memory efficiency are critical. This is often used in **low-level communication protocols**, **embedded systems**, or programs that require precise control over how text is processed.

Code Example

```
char greeting[] = "Arduino";
Serial.println(greeting);  // Outputs "Arduino" to the Serial Monitor
```

This code defines a char array containing the word "Arduino" and prints it to the Serial Monitor. The **null terminator** is automatically added to the array to mark the end of the string.

Notes
Ensure that your char array has enough space to include the **null terminator** (¥0). If the null terminator is missing, string functions may fail or produce incorrect results.

Warnings
If you attempt to store a string that exceeds the size of the char array, it will overwrite memory, causing **unpredictable behavior**. Always allocate enough memory for both the string and the null terminator.

Troubleshooting Tips
If your char array isn't behaving as expected, check that the **null terminator** is in place. Use Serial.print() to display the string and verify that it ends correctly. If the string doesn't terminate properly, the program might crash or output unexpected characters.

5.2 The String Object in Arduino

What is the String object?
The String object in Arduino is a **higher-level abstraction** for handling strings. Unlike char arrays, String objects automatically manage **memory allocation, resizing**, and **concatenation**. This makes it easier to manipulate strings without worrying about memory management. The String class is ideal for more complex operations like handling **user input, parsing data**, or dynamically changing strings in real-time.

Why is it important?
The String object simplifies **text manipulation** in Arduino, making it easier to work with strings that may change in size. It eliminates the need to manually handle **memory allocation**, and its built-in functions for concatenation, comparison, and conversion make it

highly versatile for projects involving **serial communication**, **text processing**, and **dynamic data handling**.

Syntax

```
String str = "Hello";
```

This declares a String object named str and assigns it the value "Hello".

Syntax Explanation
In String str = "Hello";, str is an object that holds the string "Hello". Unlike char arrays, you don't need to worry about manually handling the **null terminator** or the string's length, as the String object manages this automatically.

Usage
Use the String object when working with **dynamic strings** that may change size during program execution, such as when reading **user input**, processing **sensor data**, or manipulating **text files**. The String object simplifies handling these tasks, though it uses more **memory**.

Code Example

```
String greeting = "Hello";
greeting += " Arduino";  // Concatenates " Arduino" to the existing string
Serial.println(greeting);  // Outputs "Hello Arduino"
```

This example demonstrates how to concatenate strings using the String object and print the result to the Serial Monitor.

Notes
The String object is easier to use than char arrays, but it consumes more **memory**. Be cautious when using it in memory-constrained environments like Arduino.

Warnings
Overusing the String object in memory-limited projects can lead to **memory fragmentation**, causing the program to slow down or crash over time. Monitor memory usage carefully.

Troubleshooting Tips
If your program using the `String` object behaves unexpectedly, use `Serial.print()` to monitor **free memory**. Memory fragmentation can be a problem, especially if strings are frequently resized. Switching to **char arrays** may help in memory-constrained projects.

Quiz: Check Your Understanding of Strings

1. How is `String` different from a char array? (Multiple Choice)
2. When would you use a `String` object over a char array? (Short Answer)

---

6. Unsigned Variables in Arduino

6.1 The `unsigned char` Data Type

What is `unsigned char`?
The `unsigned char` data type is similar to the char type but can only store **positive values**. It uses **8 bits** to store numbers from **0 to 255**. Since it doesn't need to account for negative numbers, it can store larger positive values compared to a signed char, which ranges from **-128 to 127**. This makes `unsigned char` useful for storing **binary data**, **RGB values**, or **sensor readings** that don't involve negative values.

Why is it important?
`unsigned char` is important for **memory optimization** in projects where only positive values are needed. It allows you to store a **wider range** of positive numbers compared to a signed char, making it more efficient when dealing with **limited memory**. It is often used in situations where negative values are irrelevant, like in **color codes** or **bitwise operations**.

Syntax

```
unsigned char varName = 255;
```

This declares an unsigned char variable named varName and assigns it the maximum value of **255**.

Syntax Explanation

In unsigned char varName = 255;, the variable varName is assigned a value between **0 and 255**. Unlike a signed char, which can store negative numbers, unsigned char is strictly for positive values. This allows for more **efficient storage** of data in applications where negative numbers are unnecessary.

Usage

Use unsigned char for storing small **positive numbers** like **RGB color values**, **sensor data**, or **communication protocols** that require binary data. This data type is efficient when working with values that don't need to represent negative numbers.

Code Example

```
unsigned char redValue = 255;
analogWrite(redPin, redValue);  // Set the red LED to full brightness
```

This code demonstrates how to use unsigned char to store the brightness value of an LED in an RGB system, which ranges from 0 to 255.

Notes

Use unsigned char when working with **positive-only data** to optimize memory usage. It's ideal for handling **small numerical values**, such as **sensor inputs** or **bitwise operations**.

Warnings

If you try to assign a value greater than **255** to an unsigned char, the value will overflow, causing unexpected behavior. Be mindful of the range when working with this data type.

Troubleshooting Tips

If your unsigned char variables are behaving unexpectedly, check for **overflow** issues. Use Serial.print() to ensure that the values remain between **0 and 255** and are not exceeding the maximum range.

---

7. Constants in Arduino

7.1 The const Keyword

What is const?
The const keyword is used to define **constant variables** in Arduino. These are variables whose values **cannot be changed** after being initialized. This is useful when you need to define values that remain **fixed** throughout the program, such as **pin numbers, thresholds**, or **configuration settings**. Declaring constants improves **code clarity** and **prevents errors** by ensuring critical values are not accidentally modified.

Why is it important?
Using const is essential for ensuring that **fixed values** in your code remain unmodified. This makes the program more **stable** and **easier to debug** because you can guarantee that certain variables won't be accidentally altered during execution. It also helps improve **code readability**, making it clear which values are constant.

Syntax

```
const int ledPin = 13;
```

This declares a constant integer ledPin with the value **13**. This value cannot be changed later in the program.

Syntax Explanation
In const int ledPin = 13;, const ensures that the value of ledPin remains fixed throughout the program. Once defined, ledPin will always represent **13**, which makes it useful for **pin numbers** or settings that don't change.

Usage
Use const when working with values that should not change during program execution, such as **pin numbers, sensor thresholds**, or **configuration constants**. This prevents errors caused by accidental modification and ensures **stability** in your program.

Code Example

```
const int ledPin = 13;
```

```
pinMode(ledPin, OUTPUT);
digitalWrite(ledPin, HIGH);   // Turn on the LED connected to pin 13
```

This code demonstrates how to declare and use a constant for the
pin number controlling an LED. The const keyword ensures the pin
number is not changed accidentally.

Notes
Using const is good practice when dealing with values that should
remain **unchanged**, such as **hardware pin assignments** or
calibration settings. It helps prevent accidental changes.

Warnings
Once declared, a constant cannot be modified. If you attempt to
change the value of a const variable later in the program, it will
result in a **compilation error**. Ensure that you assign the correct
value when initializing.

Troubleshooting Tips
If you experience errors related to constants, ensure that you are not
trying to modify a const variable later in the program. Double-check
that the **initial value** is correct, as it cannot be changed after being
set.

8. Practical Projects for Mastering Variables and Data Types

8.1 Project 1: Controlling LEDs with Arrays

This project demonstrates how to control multiple **LEDs** using an
array to make your code more efficient and easier to manage.
Instead of controlling each LED individually, the pin numbers of the
LEDs are stored in an **array**, allowing you to use **loops** to control
them. This is particularly useful when working with many LEDs.

Components List:

- **Arduino**
- **5 LEDs**
- **Resistors** (220Ω recommended for each LED)
- **Wires**
- **Breadboard**

Circuit Diagram: The **circuit diagram** shows 5 LEDs connected to digital pins **2-6** on the Arduino. Each LED is connected in **series with a resistor** to limit the current. The other end of the LEDs is connected to **ground (GND)**.

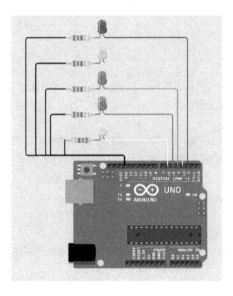

Circuit Connection:

1. Connect the **positive leg** (anode) of each LED to **digital pins 2-6** on the Arduino.
2. Connect a **220Ω resistor** between the **negative leg** (cathode) of each LED and **ground (GND)**.
3. Ensure each LED has its **own resistor** in series to prevent damage from excessive current.

Code:

```
int ledPins[] = {2, 3, 4, 5, 6};  // Array to store LED pin numbers
void setup() {
  for (int i = 0; i < 5; i++) {
    pinMode(ledPins[i], OUTPUT);   // Set each pin as output
  }
}
void loop() {
  for (int i = 0; i < 5; i++) {
    digitalWrite(ledPins[i], HIGH);  // Turn on LED
    delay(500);                      // Wait 500ms
    digitalWrite(ledPins[i], LOW);   // Turn off LED
    delay(500);                      // Wait 500ms before next LED
  }
}
```

Code Walkthrough:

1. **Array Initialization**: The array ledPins[] stores the **digital pin numbers** to which the LEDs are connected. This allows easy access to each LED.
2. **Setup Function**: Inside the setup() function, a **for loop** sets each pin in the array as an **OUTPUT** using pinMode().
3. **Loop Function**: In the loop(), a **for loop** iterates through the ledPins[] array. For each iteration:
   - The **current LED** is turned **on** using digitalWrite().
   - The code waits for **500ms**.
   - The same LED is then turned **off**, and the code waits another **500ms** before moving to the next LED.
4. This creates a **sequence effect**, where each LED turns on and off in order.

Challenge: Create a Blinking Pattern

Modify the code to create a custom **blinking pattern**. For example:

- Make **two LEDs blink together** at the same time.
- Create a **back-and-forth sequence**, similar to the **Knight Rider** light effect, where the LEDs light up in one direction and then reverse.

8.2 Project 2: Temperature-Based Fan Control using `float`

In this project, a **DC fan** is controlled based on temperature readings from a **sensor**. The temperature is stored in a **float** variable for precision, since sensor readings often contain decimal points. As the temperature increases, the fan speed is adjusted using **pulse-width modulation (PWM)** to control the fan speed. This demonstrates how to work with **float values** for hardware control and data processing.

Components List:

- **Arduino**
- **Temperature sensor** (e.g., LM35)
- **DC fan**
- **Transistor** (e.g., NPN type like 2N2222)
- **Diode** (e.g., 1N4007)
- **Resistor** (1kΩ for transistor base)
- **Wires**
- **Breadboard**

Circuit Diagram:

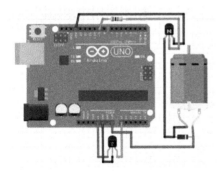

The **temperature sensor** is connected to an **analog pin** on the Arduino to read temperature data. A **transistor** is used to control the **DC fan**, with **PWM** from the Arduino adjusting its speed. A **diode** is placed across the fan's power terminals to protect the circuit from **back EMF** (voltage spikes) generated when the motor turns off.

Circuit Connection:

1. **LM35 Temperature Sensor**:
   - **VCC** → 5V on Arduino
   - **GND** → Ground
   - **Output** → Analog pin **A0**
2. **DC Fan**:
   - **Fan positive** → 12V power supply
   - **Fan negative** → **Collector** of NPN transistor
3. **Transistor**:
   - **Collector** → **Negative terminal** of the fan
   - **Emitter** → Ground
   - **Base** → **PWM pin 9** on the Arduino through a **1kΩ resistor**
4. **Diode**:
   - Place a **diode (1N4007)** across the fan's terminals to protect against **voltage spikes** caused by the fan turning off (back EMF).
   - **Cathode** to **positive** terminal of the fan, **anode** to **negative** terminal.

Code:

```
const int tempPin = A0;    // Temperature sensor pin
const int fanPin = 9;      // Fan control pin (PWM)
float temperature;         // Variable to store temperature

void setup() {
  pinMode(fanPin, OUTPUT);  // Set fan pin as output
  Serial.begin(9600);       // Start serial communication
}

void loop() {
  int sensorValue = analogRead(tempPin);  // Read analog value from
sensor
  // Convert analog value to temperature in Celsius
  temperature = (sensorValue * 5.0 * 100.0) / 1024.0;
  // Map temperature (20°C to 40°C) to fan speed (0 to 255)
  int fanSpeed = map(temperature, 20, 40, 0, 255);
  analogWrite(fanPin, fanSpeed);  // Control fan speed using PWM

  Serial.print("Temperature: ");  // Print temperature to Serial
Monitor
  Serial.print(temperature);
  Serial.println(" °C");
```

```
  delay(1000);  // Wait 1 second before reading again
}
```

Code Walkthrough:

1. **Temperature Reading**: The analogRead() function reads the voltage from the **LM35 sensor** connected to pin **A0**. The sensor output is proportional to temperature, with **10 mV/°C** sensitivity.
2. **Temperature Conversion**: The analog reading is converted to **Celsius** using the formula:
   - (sensorValue * 5.0 * 100.0) / 1024.0 converts the 10-bit analog value (0-1023) to a temperature in Celsius based on the **5V reference**.
3. **Fan Speed Control**: The map() function maps the temperature range **(20°C to 40°C)** to a **PWM value** range of **0 to 255**. This value is used to control the fan speed via **PWM** on pin **9**.
4. **Serial Output**: The current temperature is printed to the **Serial Monitor** to provide real-time feedback.

Challenge: Add an LED Indicator
Add an LED that lights up when the temperature exceeds **30°C** to provide a visual warning that the temperature is getting high.

8.3 Project 3: Measuring Distance Using long for Timing

This project measures the **distance** to an object using an **ultrasonic sensor** by calculating the time taken for sound waves to travel to the object and bounce back. The **long** data type is used to store the **timing data** because the sensor measurements involve **microseconds**, which require more memory than the **int** type can handle. This project demonstrates how **long** is crucial for **precise timing operations**.

Components List:

- **Arduino**
- **Ultrasonic sensor** (e.g., HC-SR04)
- **Wires**
- **Breadboard**

Circuit Diagram:

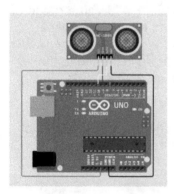

The **HC-SR04 ultrasonic sensor** has 4 pins:

- **VCC** → Connects to **5V** on the Arduino.
- **GND** → Connects to **Ground (GND)**.
- **Trig** → Sends the trigger signal to start the measurement.
- **Echo** → Receives the reflected signal to measure the time taken.

Circuit Connection:

1. **Trig Pin** → Connect to **digital pin 9** on the Arduino.
2. **Echo Pin** → Connect to **digital pin 10** on the Arduino.
3. **VCC** → Connect to **5V** on the Arduino.
4. **GND** → Connect to **GND** on the Arduino.

Code:

```
const int trigPin = 9;      // Trig pin
const int echoPin = 10;     // Echo pin
long duration;              // Variable to store the time of flight
int distance;              // Variable to store the calculated distance

void setup() {
  pinMode(trigPin, OUTPUT);  // Set the trig pin as output
  pinMode(echoPin, INPUT);   // Set the echo pin as input
  Serial.begin(9600);        // Initialize serial communication
}

void loop() {
  // Send the ultrasonic pulse
  digitalWrite(trigPin, LOW);
  delayMicroseconds(2);        // Wait for 2 microseconds
  digitalWrite(trigPin, HIGH); // Trigger the pulse
  delayMicroseconds(10);       // Wait for 10 microseconds
  digitalWrite(trigPin, LOW);  // Stop the pulse

  // Measure the time taken for the echo to return
  duration = pulseIn(echoPin, HIGH);  // Get the duration in
microseconds

  // Calculate the distance based on the speed of sound (0.034 cm per
microsecond)
  distance = duration * 0.034 / 2;

  // Display the distance in the Serial Monitor
  Serial.print("Distance: ");
  Serial.print(distance);
  Serial.println(" cm");

  delay(1000);  // Wait 1 second before repeating the measurement
}
```

Code Walkthrough:

1. **Pin Setup**:
   - The **Trig pin** is set as an **output**, and the **Echo pin** is set as an **input** to handle signals from the ultrasonic sensor.
2. **Sending the Ultrasonic Pulse**:
   - The `digitalWrite(trigPin, HIGH)` sends a **10-microsecond pulse** from the **Trig pin** to initiate the distance measurement.
3. **Measuring Time**:
   - The `pulseIn()` function measures the time it takes for the sound to travel to the object and reflect back to the **Echo pin**.
   - The time is stored in the `duration` variable, which is of type **long** because the time can be large, and **int** would not store the value correctly.
4. **Distance Calculation**:
   - The distance is calculated using the formula:
     - `distance = duration * 0.034 / 2`
     - **0.034 cm per microsecond** is the speed of sound, and the result is divided by 2 because the sound travels **to the object and back**.
5. **Displaying the Distance**:
   - The calculated distance is printed to the **Serial Monitor** for easy monitoring.
6. **Delay**:
   - A **1-second delay** is introduced to wait before the next measurement is taken.

Challenge: Display Distance on LCD
Add an **LCD display** to show the measured distance in centimeters. You can use the **LiquidCrystal** library to interface with the LCD.

8.4 Project 4: Displaying Text and Numbers Using char Arrays and String

This project demonstrates how to use both **char arrays** and **String objects** to display text in the **Serial Monitor**. It highlights the differences between the two methods, showing when to use each based on memory management and ease of use in Arduino programming.

Components List:
- **Arduino**
- **USB connection** (for serial communication via Serial Monitor)

Circuit Diagram:

No additional hardware is required for this project, as all interaction will happen through the **Serial Monitor**.

Circuit Connection:
No physical wiring is needed, simply connect your **Arduino** to the computer via USB.

Code:

```
// Using a char array and a String object
char name[] = "Arduino";   // Using char array
String greeting = "Hello";  // Using String object

void setup() {
  Serial.begin(9600);   // Initialize Serial Monitor communication

  // Display the String object in the Serial Monitor
  Serial.println(greeting);
  delay(2000);  // Wait for 2 seconds

  // Clear the Serial Monitor (optional)
  Serial.println("");

  // Display the char array in the Serial Monitor
  Serial.println(name);
}

void loop() {
  // Optionally add additional code for input or scrolling
}
```

Code Walkthrough:

1. **Serial Communication Setup**: The `Serial.begin(9600)` function initializes the **Serial Monitor** for communication at a baud rate of **9600**.
2. **Using String Object**: The **String object** `greeting` is printed using `Serial.println()`. String objects are easier to manipulate and offer dynamic memory usage, but they can lead to memory fragmentation in Arduino over time.
3. **Delay**: A **2-second delay** is added using `delay(2000)` to allow time for viewing the String object before printing the next value.
4. **Using Char Array**: The **char array** `name[]` is printed next. Char arrays are fixed-length strings, meaning they take up less memory and are more efficient, but require manual memory management and are less flexible than String objects.

Key Differences:

- **Char Array (`name[]`):**
  - **Fixed-length string**.
  - **Efficient** in terms of memory.
  - Requires **manual memory management**.
- **String Object (`greeting`):**
  - **Dynamic** and easier to manipulate.
  - Uses **more memory** and can cause **memory fragmentation** over time, especially in low-memory environments like Arduino.

Challenge: Add Scrolling Text Feature
Modify the project to make the text scroll across the LCD. You can use `lcd.scrollDisplayLeft()` or `lcd.scrollDisplayRight()` functions to scroll the text, either manually triggered by a button press or automatically in the `loop()` function.

9. Common Troubleshooting and Debugging Tips

9.1 Common Errors and How to Fix Them

What are common errors?
Some common errors in Arduino programming include **incorrect variable types**, **out-of-bounds array access**, and **overflow issues** when using certain data types like int or char. Another frequent error is failing to properly **initialize variables**, which can lead to unexpected behavior. String handling errors, such as missing **null terminators** in char arrays, can also cause problems with displaying or reading text.

Why do they happen?
These errors often occur due to **incorrect understanding of data types** or **memory management issues**. For example, if you declare a variable as int when it should be long, you might experience overflow errors when dealing with large numbers. Failing to allocate the right size for **arrays** or not including a **null terminator** can lead to memory corruption. **Improper debugging techniques** also make identifying these issues more difficult.

Use of Serial Monitor for debugging
The **Serial Monitor** is one of the most powerful tools in Arduino debugging. By using Serial.print() and Serial.println(), you can print **variable values**, **sensor readings**, or **error messages** to the monitor. This allows you to trace the program's flow and identify where things might be going wrong. For example, printing out **sensor data** at each step can help you detect calibration issues or faulty wiring.

9.2 Optimizing Code for Efficient Memory Usage
What is code optimization for memory efficiency?
Code optimization in Arduino involves reducing **memory usage** and improving **performance** by writing more efficient code. This is especially important because most Arduino boards have limited **RAM** and **flash memory**. By choosing the right data types, minimizing unnecessary string manipulations, and efficiently using memory for arrays and variables, you can optimize your program to run smoothly.

Why is it important?
Optimizing code is essential for making sure your program runs
without crashes or delays, especially in **memory-constrained
environments** like Arduino. Poor memory management can lead to
slow performance, **random resets**, or **program failures** due to
memory exhaustion. Efficient code ensures your program can
handle more **complex operations**, use **dynamic data** smoothly,
and work consistently over long periods of time.

Tips for performance and memory management
To optimize memory usage:

- Use **appropriate data types** (e.g., byte instead of int if the
  value is small).
- Avoid using **String objects** excessively; instead, use **char
  arrays** to handle text.
- Limit **global variables**, as they use memory for the duration
  of the program.
- Minimize unnecessary operations inside loops to improve
  execution speed.
- Use **F()** macro to store strings in **flash memory** instead of
  RAM.

10. Conclusion and Next Steps

10.1 Recap of Key Variables and Data Types

What have we learned?
Throughout this guide, we explored different types of **variables** and
data types in Arduino, including int, float, long, char arrays, and
String objects. We also discussed more advanced topics like
arrays, **unsigned variables**, and using const for constants.
Understanding how to choose the right data type is crucial for
optimizing **memory usage** and ensuring your program runs
efficiently. We applied these concepts in real-world projects such as
controlling LEDs, **measuring distances**, and **managing
sensors**.

Why is this important?
Mastering variables and data types allows you to write more
efficient, **flexible**, and **scalable** code. By choosing the appropriate
data type and managing memory carefully, you can ensure that your
projects perform well, even as they become more complex.

Chapter 4: Arduino Input/Output Functions

Chapter 4 covers how to use **Arduino's Input/Output (I/O) functions** to interact with external components like sensors, LEDs, and motors. It provides an understanding of both **digital and analog operations**—explaining how data is read from sensors (inputs) and how signals are sent to control devices (outputs). Core concepts such as **digital signals, analog signals,** and **Pulse Width Modulation (PWM)** are discussed, alongside I/O functions like `pinMode()`, `digitalRead()`, `digitalWrite()`, `analogRead()`, and `analogWrite()`. This chapter aims to equip readers with the foundational knowledge necessary for using Arduino to interface with physical hardware effectively.

Syntax Table: Arduino I/O Functions

Topic Name	Syntax	Simple Example
Set Pin Mode	*pinMode(pin, mode)*	*pinMode(13, OUTPUT);*
Read Digital Input	*digitalRead(pin)*	*int buttonState = digitalRead(2);*
Write Digital Output	*digitalWrite(pin, value)*	*digitalWrite(13, HIGH);*
Read Analog Input	*analogRead(pin)*	*int sensorValue = analogRead(A0);*
Write Analog Output	*analogWrite(pin, value)*	*analogWrite(9, 128);*
Set Analog Read	*analogReadResolution(bits)*	*analogReadResolution(12);*

Resolution		
Set PWM Resolution	`analogWriteResolution(bits)`	`analogWriteResolution(10);`

---

1. Introduction to Arduino Input/Output Operations

1.1 What is Input/Output in Arduino?

What is Input/Output?
In Arduino, **input** refers to receiving data from devices such as sensors, while **output** involves sending signals to control external devices like motors or LEDs. **Digital input/output** deals with binary values, either **HIGH** (on) or **LOW** (off). For example, you can turn an LED on by setting the pin to HIGH. **Analog input/output** involves continuous values, typically between 0 and 1023, and is used to read sensor data or control devices like dimming lights.

Why is it important?
Input/output operations are crucial because they enable the Arduino to interact with the outside world. Without I/O, the board wouldn't be able to read from sensors or control external devices like motors or LEDs. These operations allow you to monitor and control environments, such as reading temperature data or adjusting the brightness of an LED. It makes the Arduino capable of responding to the real world, making it essential for any project.

1.2 Key Concepts and Terms (Glossary)

Digital Signal (HIGH/LOW states)
A digital signal is a binary value: **HIGH** (on) or **LOW** (off). It is used to control devices like LEDs or to read button inputs.

Analog Signal (Continuous range of values)
Analog signals are continuous values, typically ranging from 0 to

1023, used to read sensors like potentiometers or temperature sensors.

PWM (Pulse Width Modulation)
PWM is a method of simulating analog output by rapidly switching between HIGH and LOW. It's often used to control motor speed or dim LEDs.

pinMode()
The pinMode() function sets a pin as either input or output. It tells the Arduino how to interact with external components like buttons or LEDs.

HIGH/LOW
HIGH and LOW are the two possible states in digital input/output. Setting a pin to HIGH means turning on a connected device, while LOW turns it off.

1.3 Overview of Core Functions

Core Arduino Functions
Arduino provides several core functions for I/O operations: digitalRead(), digitalWrite(), analogRead(), and analogWrite(). digitalRead() reads the state of a digital pin (HIGH or LOW). digitalWrite() sets a pin to either HIGH or LOW. analogRead() reads a value from an analog pin between 0 and 1023, while analogWrite() simulates analog output using PWM. pinMode() defines whether a pin is configured as input or output.

Syntax
Each function has a simple syntax. For example, digitalWrite(pin, value) sets a digital pin to HIGH or LOW, while analogRead(pin) returns a value between 0 and 1023 from an analog sensor.

Why are they important?
These functions are essential because they allow Arduino to interact with external devices. Whether reading sensor data or controlling motors and LEDs, these functions are the backbone of any Arduino project.

Quiz: Test Your Understanding of I/O Basics

What is the difference between digital and analog input/output?
A. Digital involves binary values (HIGH/LOW), while analog involves a continuous range of values. (Multiple Choice)

Define a digital signal in Arduino.
A. A digital signal is a binary signal that can either be HIGH (on) or LOW (off). (Short Answer)

What does PWM stand for?
A. PWM stands for **Pulse Width Modulation**. (Fill in the Blank)

2. Basic Digital Input/Output Functions

2.1 The digitalRead() Function: Reading Digital Inputs

What is digitalRead()?
The `digitalRead()` function in Arduino is used to read the state of a digital input pin. It returns **HIGH** if the pin is receiving a high voltage (usually 5V) or **LOW** if the pin is receiving low voltage (0V). This function is typically used with input devices like buttons or switches. For example, it can be used to check if a button is pressed.

Syntax

```
digitalRead(pin)
```

Where `pin` is the number of the digital pin you want to read.

Syntax Explanation
The `digitalRead()` function requires one parameter: the **pin number** from which you want to read the input. This pin must be configured as an **input** using the `pinMode()` function. The value returned will be either **HIGH** or **LOW**.

Usage
You can use `digitalRead()` to check the state of a button or switch in a project. For example, you might read a button's state to turn on an LED when pressed.

Code Example

```
int buttonState = digitalRead(2);  // Read pin 2
if (buttonState == HIGH) {
  // Do something, like turn on an LED
}
```

Notes
digitalRead() only works with pins set as **input**. You must use the pinMode() function to set the pin as input.

Warnings
Always use pull-up or pull-down resistors to prevent floating pins, which can lead to inconsistent readings.

Troubleshooting Tips
If your button doesn't seem to work, check for proper wiring, ensure the pin is set to **input**, and use resistors to stabilize the signal.

2.2 The digitalWrite() Function: Controlling Digital Outputs

What is digitalWrite()?
The digitalWrite() function is used to set a digital pin to either **HIGH** or **LOW**. This controls the output of devices like LEDs or relays. For example, you can turn an LED on by setting a pin to HIGH and turn it off by setting the same pin to LOW.

Syntax

```
digitalWrite(pin, value)
```

Where pin is the pin number, and value can be either **HIGH** or **LOW**.

Syntax Explanation
In digitalWrite(pin, value), pin is the pin number you are controlling, and value is either **HIGH** (to turn on the connected device) or **LOW** (to turn it off). Make sure the pin is configured as an **output** using pinMode().

Usage

You can use `digitalWrite()` to control an LED, motor, or other digital device. For example, turning an LED on/off by setting a pin HIGH or LOW.

Code Example

```
digitalWrite(13, HIGH);   // Turn on LED connected to pin 13
delay(1000);              // Wait 1 second
digitalWrite(13, LOW);    // Turn off the LED
```

Notes

This function is most commonly used to control devices like LEDs, motors, and relays. It can only be used with **output** pins.

Warnings

Make sure to use `pinMode()` to set the pin as **output** before using `digitalWrite()`. Otherwise, the pin may not work correctly.

Troubleshooting Tips

If the device doesn't respond, check the wiring, ensure the pin is set to **output**, and verify the device is properly connected to the Arduino.

2.3 The pinMode() Function: Configuring Pins for Input/Output

What is pinMode()?

The `pinMode()` function sets a pin as either **input** or **output**. It prepares the pin for interacting with external devices. For example, to read a button's state, you set the pin to input, and to control an LED, you set the pin to output.

Syntax

```
pinMode(pin, mode)
```

Where pin is the pin number, and mode can be INPUT, OUTPUT, or INPUT_PULLUP.

Syntax Explanation
The pinMode() function takes two parameters: the pin number you want to configure and the mode, which can be INPUT (for reading), OUTPUT (for controlling), or INPUT_PULLUP (for enabling an internal pull-up resistor).

Usage
You should always use pinMode() in the **setup()** function to configure the pins you are using in your project. For example, setting a pin as **output** to control an LED or as **input** to read a button.

Code Example

```
pinMode(13, OUTPUT);  // Set pin 13 as output for LED
pinMode(2, INPUT);    // Set pin 2 as input for button
```

Notes
Using INPUT_PULLUP can be very useful for avoiding the need for external pull-up resistors when reading buttons.

Warnings
Failing to set the correct **pinMode** can result in unpredictable behavior. Always ensure the pin is correctly configured.

Troubleshooting Tips
If the pin isn't behaving as expected, double-check the mode (input/output) and ensure proper wiring.

Quiz: Check Your Understanding of Basic Digital I/O

What does the digitalRead() function return?
A. It returns either **HIGH** or **LOW** depending on the state of the digital input pin. (Multiple Choice)

How do you set a pin as an output in Arduino?
A. Use `pinMode(pin, OUTPUT)` in the **setup()** function. (Fill in the Blank)

What is the correct syntax for using digitalWrite()?
A. The correct syntax is `digitalWrite(pin, value)`, where `value` is either **HIGH** or **LOW**. (Multiple Choice)

3. Analog Input/Output Functions

3.1 The analogRead() Function: Reading Analog Inputs

What is analogRead()?
The `analogRead()` function reads the voltage level from an analog pin and returns a value between 0 and 1023. This value corresponds to the input voltage, where 0 represents 0V and 1023 represents 5V (on most Arduino boards). It's commonly used to read analog sensors like potentiometers, temperature sensors, or light sensors.

Syntax

```
analogRead(pin)
```

Where `pin` is the number of the analog pin you want to read.

Syntax Explanation
The `analogRead()` function reads from one of the analog pins (typically labeled as A0, A1, etc.). It returns a value between 0 and 1023, which corresponds to the voltage level on the pin.

Usage
You can use `analogRead()` to gather data from sensors that provide variable output, like a light sensor or potentiometer. The function reads the voltage level and converts it to a digital value.

Code Example

```
int sensorValue = analogRead(A0);   // Read the value from pin A0
```

Notes
Analog input values range from 0 to 1023, corresponding to a voltage range of 0 to 5V. The accuracy depends on the board's resolution.

Warnings
Ensure the input voltage does not exceed 5V on a standard Arduino, as higher voltages could damage the board.

Troubleshooting Tips
If you're getting unexpected values, check that the sensor is wired correctly, the input voltage is within the correct range, and the correct pin is used in your code.

3.2 The analogWrite() Function: Controlling Outputs with PWM

What is analogWrite()?
The analogWrite() function outputs a **Pulse Width Modulation (PWM)** signal to a pin. This function simulates an analog output by switching the pin between HIGH and LOW very quickly. It's used for tasks like controlling the brightness of an LED or the speed of a motor. The value passed to analogWrite() can range from 0 (always off) to 255 (always on).

Syntax

```
analogWrite(pin, value)
```

Where pin is the PWM-capable pin, and value is between 0 and 255.

Syntax Explanation
In analogWrite(pin, value), pin must be a PWM-enabled pin (usually marked with a ~ symbol on the board). The value is a

number between 0 (off) and 255 (full on), controlling the duty cycle of the PWM signal.

Usage
analogWrite() is often used to control the brightness of an LED, the speed of a motor, or other devices requiring an analog-like output. For example, dimming an LED based on a sensor input.

Code Example

```
analogWrite(9, 128);   // Set PWM value of pin 9 to 50% brightness
```

Notes
Not all pins support PWM. Check your Arduino board's pin diagram to see which pins can be used with analogWrite().

Warnings
Make sure you are using a PWM-capable pin; otherwise, the analogWrite() function won't work.

Troubleshooting Tips
If you aren't getting the expected output, check that the pin supports PWM, and ensure the value parameter is within the 0-255 range.

Quiz: Test Your Analog I/O Knowledge

What value range does the analogRead() function return?
A. It returns values between 0 and 1023, corresponding to the voltage on the analog pin. (Multiple Choice)

How is PWM used to control LED brightness?
A. By adjusting the duty cycle of the PWM signal, which affects how long the LED stays on versus off. (Short Answer)

What is the correct syntax for using analogWrite()?
A. The correct syntax is analogWrite(pin, value), where value is between 0 (off) and 255 (full on). (Multiple Choice)

4. Advanced Input/Output Functions

4.1 The analogReadResolution() Function: Increasing Input Precision

What is analogReadResolution()?
The analogReadResolution() function allows you to change the precision of the analog-to-digital conversion by increasing or decreasing the number of bits. Normally, Arduino uses 10 bits, giving a range from 0 to 1023. By increasing the resolution to 12 bits, you get a range from 0 to 4095, which is helpful in applications requiring more detailed sensor readings, such as temperature or pressure sensors.

Syntax

```
analogReadResolution(bits)
```

Where bits is the number of bits for the resolution. The typical value is 10, but you can set it to 12 or more on supported boards.

Syntax Explanation
In analogReadResolution(bits), bits defines how many bits the Arduino should use for converting analog values into a digital number. For example, 12 bits give you more precise readings than 10 bits.

Usage
Use analogReadResolution() to improve the precision of sensor readings. For instance, if you're using a temperature sensor and need more accurate results, a higher resolution can help you detect smaller changes in temperature.

Code Example

```
analogReadResolution(12);  // Set resolution to 12 bits (0-4095)
int sensorValue = analogRead(A0);  // Read from pin A0
```

Notes
Not all boards support more than 10-bit resolution. Check your

Arduino's documentation to ensure your board can handle higher resolutions before using this function.

Warnings
Ensure that your sensors and components can provide meaningful results at higher resolutions. Some sensors may not benefit from increased precision.

4.2 The analogWriteResolution() Function: Finer Control Over PWM Signals

What is analogWriteResolution()?
The analogWriteResolution() function changes the resolution of the PWM signal from its default of 8 bits (values from 0 to 255). By increasing the resolution, you can achieve finer control over devices like motors or LEDs. For example, increasing it to 10 bits allows you to control the output more smoothly by using values from 0 to 1023. This is especially useful in projects that require smooth transitions, such as motor control.

Syntax

```
analogWriteResolution(bits)
```

Where bits represents the resolution, typically 8 or 10 bits.

Syntax Explanation
The analogWriteResolution(bits) function adjusts the resolution of the PWM signal. By increasing the bit depth, you provide smoother control for analog-like outputs. A higher resolution gives more granular control over outputs like LED brightness or motor speed.

Usage
Use analogWriteResolution() in projects where you need smooth control of outputs. For example, you can dim an LED more smoothly or control the speed of a fan or motor with greater precision using a higher resolution.

Code Example

```
analogWriteResolution(10);   // Set PWM resolution to 10 bits
analogWrite(9, 512);   // Set pin 9 to 50% brightness
```

Notes

Most Arduino boards use 8-bit PWM resolution by default. If you increase the resolution, make sure the pin you are using supports the new setting.

Warnings

Not all pins support higher PWM resolutions. Refer to your board's pinout to see which pins are capable of higher resolution.

Quiz: Advanced I/O Functionality Check

What is the default resolution of analogRead()?
A. The default resolution is 10 bits, returning values from 0 to 1023. (Multiple Choice)

How does changing the resolution of analogWrite() affect PWM?
A. Increasing the resolution provides finer control over the duty cycle, allowing smoother transitions in brightness or motor speed. (Short Answer)

What is the correct syntax for using analogWriteResolution()?
A. The correct syntax is analogWriteResolution(bits), where bits is the new resolution. (Multiple Choice)

5. Practical Projects for Mastering Input/Output

5.1 Project 1: Controlling an LED with a Push Button

Project Overview:

This project demonstrates how to control an LED using a **push button** connected to an Arduino. The LED turns **on** when the button is pressed and turns **off** when the button is released. This setup showcases the interaction between **digital input** (button) and **digital output** (LED).

Components List:

1. **Arduino** (e.g., Uno, Nano, etc.)
2. **Push Button** (momentary switch)
3. **LED**
4. **Resistor** (220 ohms for current-limiting the LED)
5. **Breadboard** and **Wires**

Circuit Diagram:

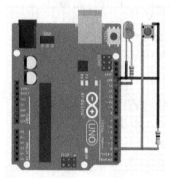

LED:

- The **LED** is connected to **pin 13** of the Arduino. The **long leg (anode)** connects to pin 13, and the **short leg (cathode)** connects to the ground through a **220-ohm resistor** to limit the current and prevent damage to the LED.

Push Button:

- The **push button** is connected to **pin 2** of the Arduino. One side of the button connects to **ground**, and the other side connects to pin 2. To ensure the button behaves reliably (avoiding floating states), you should use a **pull-down resistor** or configure an **internal pull-up resistor**.

Circuit Diagram Analysis:

1. **Power Supply**: The Arduino provides power to the button and LED through its pins.
2. **Push Button**: The button serves as an input device, allowing the user to control the state of the circuit.
3. **LED**: The LED serves as the output device, visually indicating whether the button is pressed or not.
4. **Resistor**: The 220-ohm resistor is placed in series with the LED to control the amount of current flowing through it, preventing the LED from burning out.

Code:

```
const int buttonPin = 2;   // Pin for the button
const int ledPin = 13;     // Pin for the LED
int buttonState = 0;       // Variable to hold the button state

void setup() {
  pinMode(ledPin, OUTPUT);    // Set LED pin as output
  pinMode(buttonPin, INPUT);  // Set button pin as input
}

void loop() {
  buttonState = digitalRead(buttonPin);   // Read the button state

  if (buttonState == HIGH) {        // If the button is pressed
    digitalWrite(ledPin, HIGH);     // Turn the LED on
  } else {
    digitalWrite(ledPin, LOW);      // If the button is not
pressed, turn the LED off
  }
}
```

Code Walkthrough:

1. **Global Variables**:

- o **buttonPin**: Pin 2 is used for the button input.
- o **ledPin**: Pin 13 is used to control the LED.
- o **buttonState**: This variable holds the state of the button, either HIGH (pressed) or LOW (not pressed).

2. **setup()**:
   - o **pinMode(ledPin, OUTPUT)**: Sets pin 13 as an output pin to control the LED.
   - o **pinMode(buttonPin, INPUT)**: Sets pin 2 as an input pin to read the state of the button.

3. **loop()**:
   - o **digitalRead(buttonPin)**: This reads the current state of the button (pressed or not pressed).
   - o **if (buttonState == HIGH)**: If the button is pressed, the button state is HIGH, and the LED is turned on by setting pin 13 to HIGH.
   - o **else**: If the button is not pressed (state is LOW), the LED is turned off by setting pin 13 to LOW.

Challenge: Debounce the Button
To prevent the button from reading multiple presses due to bouncing, modify the code to **debounce** the button for more accurate inputs.

5.2 **Project 2: Temperature-Based Fan Control**

This project demonstrates how to use a **temperature sensor** (such as the LM35) to control the speed of a **fan** using an Arduino. The fan speed increases as the temperature rises, utilizing **PWM (Pulse Width Modulation)** to adjust the fan's speed based on the temperature sensor's output.

Components List

1. Arduino (e.g., Uno, Nano)
2. Temperature Sensor (e.g., LM35 or similar)
3. Fan (small DC fan)
4. Transistor (e.g., NPN transistor like 2N2222 or TIP120)
5. Resistor (typically 220 ohms)
6. Diode (e.g., 1N4007)
7. Breadboard and wires

Circuit Diagram

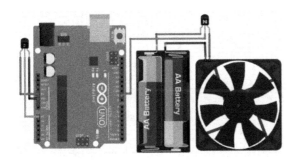

- **Temperature Sensor (LM35)**: Connect the VCC of the sensor to the 5V on the Arduino, the GND to the ground, and the analog output to the **A0** pin.
- **Fan and Transistor**: The fan is connected to the external 12V supply (or 5V, depending on your fan). The transistor drives the fan, with the base connected to **pin 9** (via a 220-ohm resistor). A **diode** is placed in parallel with the fan to protect the circuit from back EMF.

Circuit Diagram Analysis

1. The temperature sensor reads the ambient temperature and sends an analog signal to the Arduino.
2. The Arduino processes this signal and generates a PWM output based on the temperature, controlling the fan's speed.
3. The transistor allows the Arduino to control the higher current required by the fan, while the diode protects against back EMF spikes from the fan.

Code

```
int tempPin = A0;   // Pin for temperature sensor
int fanPin = 9;     // PWM pin for fan control
int tempValue = 0;  // Variable to store temperature sensor reading

void setup() {
  pinMode(fanPin, OUTPUT); // Set fan pin as output
}

void loop() {
  tempValue = analogRead(tempPin);        // Read the temperature sensor value
  int fanSpeed = map(tempValue, 0, 1023, 0, 255); // Map sensor reading to PWM value
  analogWrite(fanPin, fanSpeed);          // Control the fan speed using PWM
}
```

Code Walkthrough

1. **Global Variables**:
   - tempPin: Defines **A0** as the analog input pin for reading the temperature sensor.
   - fanPin: Defines **pin 9** as the PWM-capable pin for controlling the fan.
   - tempValue: Holds the temperature sensor's analog value (0–1023).
2. **setup ()**:
   - Configures **pin 9** as an output pin for the fan.
3. **loop ()**:
   - **analogRead (tempPin)**: Reads the temperature sensor's output.

- `map(tempValue, 0, 1023, 0, 255)`: Maps the temperature reading to the appropriate PWM range (0-255).
- `analogWrite(fanPin, fanSpeed)`: Uses the mapped value to control the fan speed based on the sensor's temperature reading.

Challenge: Add an LED Indicator

To extend this project, an **LED** can be added to indicate when the fan is running, meaning the temperature has reached a certain threshold.

5.3 Project 3: Analog Sensor-Controlled Motor Speed

In this project, a **potentiometer** is used to control the speed of a **motor**. The analog input from the potentiometer is read using the `analogRead()` function, and the speed of the motor is adjusted via **PWM (Pulse Width Modulation)** using the `analogWrite()` function. The motor's speed will vary based on the potentiometer's position.

Components List:

- Arduino
- Potentiometer
- Motor
- Motor driver (L293D or similar, to control motor speed and direction)
- Breadboard and wires

Circuit Diagram:

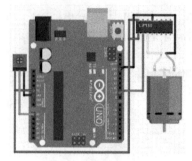

- **Potentiometer**: The potentiometer is connected to an analog input pin (A0). The middle pin of the potentiometer is connected to **A0**, one side to **5V**, and the other side to **GND**.
- **Motor**: The motor is connected to a **PWM-capable pin** on the Arduino via a **motor driver (L293D)**. The motor driver is necessary because the Arduino alone cannot supply enough current to drive the motor. The motor driver will allow the Arduino to control the motor's speed and handle the higher current requirements

Code:

```
int potPin = A0;      // Pin for the potentiometer
int motorPin = 9;     // Pin for the motor control (PWM)
void setup() {
  pinMode(motorPin, OUTPUT);  // Set motor pin as an output
}

void loop() {
  int potValue = analogRead(potPin);  // Read potentiometer value (0-
1023)
  int motorSpeed = map(potValue, 0, 1023, 0, 255);  // Map
potentiometer value to PWM range (0-255)
  analogWrite(motorPin, motorSpeed);  // Write PWM value to control
motor speed
}
```

Code Walkthrough:

1. **Global Variables**:
   - **potPin**: This defines **A0** as the input pin for the potentiometer.
   - **motorPin**: This defines **pin 9** as the PWM output pin to control the motor's speed.
2. **setup ()**:

- o `pinMode(motorPin, OUTPUT)`: Sets pin 9 as an output pin to control the motor.
3. `loop()`:
   - o `analogRead(potPin)`: Reads the analog voltage from the potentiometer, which ranges from 0 to 1023.
   - o `map(potValue, 0, 1023, 0, 255)`: Maps the potentiometer reading (0-1023) to a PWM range (0-255). This is necessary because the `analogWrite()` function accepts values from 0 to 255.
   - o `analogWrite(motorPin, motorSpeed)`: Outputs the PWM signal to the motor driver, adjusting the motor speed based on the potentiometer's position.

Challenge: Add Reverse Motor Control

To allow for reverse motor control, you can use an **H-bridge motor driver** like the **L293D**. This allows the motor to spin in both directions, depending on the potentiometer input.

Quiz: Test Your Understanding of Practical I/O Projects

- **How does the push button control the LED in the first project?**
  A. By reading the button state using `digitalRead()` and controlling the LED using `digitalWrite()` based on the button's state. (Multiple Choice)
- **What function is used to adjust the fan speed based on the temperature sensor?**
  A. `analogWrite()` is used to adjust the PWM output to the fan, controlling its speed. (Short Answer)
- **How is the potentiometer used in the motor speed control project?**
  A. The potentiometer provides an analog input that is mapped to control the motor speed through `analogWrite()`. (Multiple Choice)

6. Common Troubleshooting and Debugging Tips

6.1 Common Errors and How to Fix Them

- **Hardware Issues**
  One of the most common issues is loose or incorrect wiring. If your circuit isn't working, check all connections to ensure the components are securely plugged into the breadboard and connected to the correct Arduino pins. Another common hardware issue is **floating pins**, where input pins read random values because they aren't connected to a stable HIGH or LOW state. To prevent this, use **pull-up or pull-down resistors** to stabilize the input pin.

- **Software Issues**
  Incorrect syntax, undefined variables, and wrong logic are common programming errors. For example, forgetting to declare a variable or setting an incorrect pin number in your code can cause unexpected behavior. Always double-check the pin numbers in your code and ensure that the **pinMode()** is correctly set in the **setup()** function before using **digitalRead()**, **digitalWrite()**, or **analogRead()**.

- **Using the Serial Monitor for Debugging**
  The **Serial Monitor** is an essential tool for troubleshooting. Use Serial.print() and Serial.println() to display sensor values, button states, or other critical information from your code. By printing the values in real-time, you can identify if a sensor or a pin is functioning as expected. This makes it easier to pinpoint where the problem lies.

6.2 Optimizing Code for Performance and Accuracy

- **What is code optimization?**
  Code optimization involves improving the efficiency of your program by making it run faster or use less memory. In Arduino projects, this can be important when working with large programs, time-sensitive projects, or when resources are limited.

- **Why is it important?**
  Optimizing code improves performance and accuracy. For example, if you're controlling a motor or LED with **PWM**, minimizing the delay between sensor readings and output adjustments can create smoother transitions and more accurate responses. Similarly, reducing memory usage is

crucial for more complex projects that might run out of available memory.

- **Tips for improving performance**
  - ○ **Minimize delay usage**: Avoid using delay() whenever possible, as it blocks the program from executing other tasks. Instead, use the **millis()** function for non-blocking delays.
  - ○ **Optimize sensor readings**: If you don't need continuous updates, reduce the number of sensor readings by adding a timer to poll sensors less frequently.
  - ○ **Memory management**: Use smaller data types where appropriate (e.g., byte instead of int for values between 0 and 255). This conserves memory.

Quiz: Debugging and Optimization Knowledge Check

- **How can pull-up or pull-down resistors help with input pins?**
  A. They stabilize floating pins by pulling the input to a known HIGH or LOW state, preventing random readings. (Short Answer)
- **What tool can be used to print real-time data to help with debugging?**
  A. The **Serial Monitor** can be used to print real-time data, such as sensor values or button states. (Multiple Choice)
- **How can you improve the efficiency of your code?**
  A. By minimizing the use of delay() and optimizing sensor reading frequency, as well as managing memory usage effectively. (Multiple Choice)

7. Conclusion and Next Steps

7.1 Recap of Key Input/Output Functions

Throughout this chapter, you've learned about the essential input and output functions that make Arduino powerful for interacting with the real world. Key functions include:

- digitalRead(): Reads the state of digital input pins (HIGH or LOW).

- `digitalWrite()`: Controls digital output pins by setting them HIGH or LOW.
- `analogRead()`: Reads analog input values from sensors, returning values between 0 and 1023.
- `analogWrite()`: Simulates analog output using PWM, useful for controlling brightness, motor speed, and more.
- `pinMode()`: Configures pins as either input or output, a necessary step before using `digitalRead()`, `digitalWrite()`, or `analogRead()`.

You also explored more advanced functions such as `analogReadResolution()` and `analogWriteResolution()` to increase the precision and control of your input and output tasks. Understanding how to use these functions efficiently is key to building robust and responsive Arduino projects.

Quiz: Conclusion and Next Steps

- **What is the primary function of `digitalWrite()`?**
  A. It sets a digital pin to either HIGH or LOW, controlling devices like LEDs or relays. (Multiple Choice)
- **Where can you find official Arduino documentation for further learning?**
  A. On the official Arduino website, which includes tutorials, guides, and examples. (Short Answer)
- **Which advanced input/output function increases the resolution of PWM signals?**
  A. `analogWriteResolution()` is used to increase the resolution of PWM signals for finer control. (Multiple Choice)

Chapter 4: Timing Functions in Arduino Programming

Chapter 4 introduces the concept of timing in Arduino programming. Timing functions are essential for controlling when and how fast actions happen in your code. They help create delays, measure intervals, and synchronise tasks. This is crucial for operations like blinking an LED at regular intervals, reading sensors at specific time gaps, or controlling the speed of a motor. Core functions covered in this chapter include delay(), delayMicroseconds(), micros(), and millis(). Understanding these functions will allow you to create efficient programs that can manage multiple events without everything happening too quickly or inconsistently.

Syntax Table: Arduino Timing Functions

Topic Name	Syntax	Simple Example
Create Millisecond Delay	delay(milliseconds)	delay(1000); // Pause for 1 second
Create Microsecond Delay	delayMicroseconds(microseconds)	delayMicroseconds(500); // Pause for 500 µs
Measure Elapsed Time in Microseconds	micros()	unsigned long time = micros();
Measure Elapsed Time in Milliseconds	millis()	unsigned long time = millis();

1.1 What is Timing in Arduino?

- **What is Timing?**
  In Arduino, **timing** refers to controlling the sequence and speed of events within your code. Timing functions help to create **delays** between actions, measure intervals, and synchronize tasks. For instance, when blinking an LED, you need to turn it on and off at regular intervals using timing functions. Timing also helps with tasks like reading sensors at set intervals or controlling the speed of a motor. Timing is essential for ensuring that your Arduino program performs its tasks at the right moment. Without timing control, everything would happen instantly or inconsistently.
- **Why is it important?**
  Timing is crucial for keeping your Arduino projects **synchronized** and organized. For example, if you want to control an LED to blink every second, you need precise timing to ensure that it turns on and off at the correct intervals. Additionally, many sensors require timed readings to provide accurate data. By managing time correctly, you can ensure that motors, lights, and sensors work together seamlessly in a project. Without timing control, your program may execute tasks too quickly or not in the right order.

1.2 Key Concepts and Terms (Glossary)

What is delay()?
The delay () function pauses the program for a specified number of **milliseconds**, temporarily stopping all other operations. It is useful for creating pauses between actions like blinking an LED.

Why is delay() important?
It is important for controlling **timing** between tasks. Without a delay, the Arduino would execute actions continuously without waiting, causing problems like excessive sensor readings or rapid LED flashing.

What is delayMicroseconds()?
The delayMicroseconds () function allows for very short pauses, measured in **microseconds**. It's useful for tasks requiring precise control, such as handling high-speed signals.

Why is delayMicroseconds() important?
This function is critical for precise timing control in projects requiring

very short intervals. For example, it is often used in communication protocols or sensor interfaces that require millisecond-level accuracy.

What is micros()?
The micros() function returns the number of **microseconds** that have passed since the Arduino program started. It allows for precise time tracking in microsecond intervals.

Why is micros() important?
It is crucial for tasks requiring high-resolution time measurements, such as accurately tracking fast-changing events or controlling devices that need very specific timing.

What is millis()?
The millis() function returns the number of **milliseconds** that have passed since the Arduino started running. It's useful for timing tasks over longer intervals without blocking the program.

Why is millis() important?
It allows you to create **non-blocking delays**, where your program can continue running other tasks while waiting for a specific time interval to pass, unlike delay(), which pauses the entire program.

1.3 Overview of Core Timing Functions

What are Core Arduino Timing Functions?
The core Arduino timing functions include delay(), delayMicroseconds(), micros(), and millis(). delay() pauses the program for a given number of milliseconds, while delayMicroseconds() pauses it for very short intervals in microseconds. micros() returns the number of microseconds since the program began, allowing precise time measurement. millis() tracks the time in milliseconds, useful for non-blocking tasks. Together, these functions provide you with both short and long-term timing control, enabling you to manage various tasks like sensor reading, motor control, or LED blinking efficiently.

Why are they important?
These functions allow you to control the **timing** and flow of your Arduino projects. delay() is useful for simple pauses between tasks,

while delayMicroseconds() offers precision for fast processes. micros() is great for high-resolution timing, and millis() is essential for managing longer tasks without blocking other operations. Understanding when and how to use each function helps you create responsive, organized programs that handle both short-term and long-term events smoothly. Proper use of timing functions can prevent issues like program freezes or missed sensor data.

Quiz: Test Your Understanding of Timing Functions

What is the difference between delay() and delayMicroseconds()?
A. delay() pauses for milliseconds, while delayMicroseconds() pauses for microseconds. (Multiple Choice)

Define how millis() can be used to create a non-blocking delay.
A. millis() can track elapsed time without stopping the program, allowing other tasks to run while waiting for a specific time interval. (Short Answer)

2. Basic Timing Functions

2.1 The delay() Function: Pausing the Program

What is delay()?
The delay() function is used to pause the program for a set number of **milliseconds**. During this delay period, no other part of the code is executed. It's typically used in projects where you want to create a pause between two actions. For example, it can be used to blink an LED by pausing for one second between turning it on and off.

Why is it important?
The delay() function is important for simple tasks where waiting is required between actions. For example, it's used to control the timing between sensor readings or manage LED blinking at specific intervals. Without delay(), events could occur too quickly.

Syntax

```
delay(milliseconds)
```

Where milliseconds is the duration for which the program will pause.

Syntax Explanation
In the delay() function, the parameter **milliseconds** represents the number of milliseconds the program will pause. A value of 1000 means a 1-second pause. No other operations happen during this time.

Usage
You can use delay() in projects to create a timed pause between actions. For instance, waiting between sensor readings or creating a regular blink for an LED is easily done with delay().

Code Example

```
void loop() {
  digitalWrite(LED_BUILTIN, HIGH);   // Turn the LED on
  delay(1000);                       // Wait for 1 second
  digitalWrite(LED_BUILTIN, LOW);    // Turn the LED off
  delay(1000);                       // Wait for 1 second
}
```

Notes
delay() is a **blocking function**, meaning it stops all other code execution during the delay period. This can cause issues if you need other tasks to run simultaneously.

Warnings
Be cautious with long delays, as they can freeze your program and make it unresponsive. For tasks requiring frequent updates or simultaneous operations, delay() might not be the best choice.

Troubleshooting Tips
If your program seems to freeze, check for long delays that could be causing the issue. Try to reduce the delay duration or consider using

non-blocking alternatives like `millis()` for better control over timing without stopping other tasks.

2.2 The delayMicroseconds() Function: Precise Short Delays

What is delayMicroseconds()?

The `delayMicroseconds()` function is used to pause the program for a short duration, measured in **microseconds**. Unlike `delay()`, which works in milliseconds, this function is useful for tasks that require extremely precise timing. For example, it's commonly used in communication protocols or fast signal handling, where microsecond accuracy is critical.

Why is it important?

This function is important for tasks that require precise and short pauses, especially in high-speed operations like controlling communication protocols, generating precise signals, or handling fast sensors. In these cases, millisecond delays may be too long.

Syntax

```
delayMicroseconds(microseconds)
```

Where `microseconds` is the number of microseconds the program should pause.

Syntax Explanation

The `delayMicroseconds()` function takes a parameter `microseconds`, which determines how long the program will pause in microsecond units. For example, passing a value of 1000 would create a 1-millisecond pause.

Usage

Use `delayMicroseconds()` for tasks that need highly accurate timing, like generating PWM signals or controlling high-speed sensors. It provides greater precision than `delay()` for tasks requiring short intervals.

Code Example

```
void loop() {
  digitalWrite(LED_BUILTIN, HIGH);
  delayMicroseconds(500);   // Short delay
  digitalWrite(LED_BUILTIN, LOW);
  delayMicroseconds(500);   // Short delay
}
```

Notes
This function is often used in high-speed signal processing tasks, where timing precision is crucial. It is accurate for short delays but not suitable for long pauses.

Warnings
The precision of delayMicroseconds() can vary slightly depending on the Arduino board. It may not be as precise for very short delays on some boards.

Troubleshooting Tips
If the timing seems off, ensure that the microsecond value is appropriate for the task, and check the board's specifications for accuracy limits. For critical timing tasks, test the function's performance on your specific board.

2.3 The micros() Function: Measuring Microsecond Time Intervals

What is micros()?
The micros() function returns the number of **microseconds** that have passed since the program started running. It's used to measure time intervals with high precision. For example, it can be used to track short time periods in tasks that require accuracy, such as monitoring fast-changing events.

Why is it important?
This function is important because it allows you to measure very short time intervals, making it ideal for tasks where precision is required, such as in communication protocols or controlling devices that need microsecond-level accuracy.

Syntax

```
micros()
```

This function does not take any parameters and simply returns the elapsed time in microseconds since the Arduino program started.

Syntax Explanation
When `micros()` is called, it returns a number representing the number of microseconds since the Arduino was powered on or reset. It can be used to measure short time periods with high precision.

Usage
Use `micros()` when you need to measure short time intervals. For instance, it can be used to track the time between signal pulses in a sensor or communication protocol.

Code Example

```
unsigned long startTime = micros();  // Start time
// Some code here
unsigned long elapsedTime = micros() - startTime;  // Measure elapsed
time
```

Notes
`micros()` is accurate for up to about 70 minutes, after which it resets to zero. It provides high-resolution time measurement for tasks requiring precision.

Warnings
Keep in mind that `micros()` resets after about 70 minutes of continuous operation, which could affect long-running projects. Plan accordingly.

Troubleshooting Tips
If `micros()` returns unexpected values, ensure your program isn't running too long without reset, and double-check that you're measuring the right intervals. For long-duration tasks, consider using `millis()` instead.

What does the delay() function do?
A. It pauses the program for a specified number of milliseconds.
(Multiple Choice)

---

3. Advanced Timing Functions

3.1 Comparing delay(), delayMicroseconds(), micros(), and millis()

What are the differences?
The main difference between delay() and delayMicroseconds() is the precision. delay() pauses the program for milliseconds, while delayMicroseconds() provides much shorter pauses in microseconds. millis() and micros() measure the time since the program started, with millis() returning the time in milliseconds and micros() in microseconds. These functions allow for both blocking and non-blocking delays.

Why is it important to choose the right timing function?
Choosing the right timing function helps ensure your project performs optimally. If you need precise timing for fast tasks, use delayMicroseconds() or micros(). For longer intervals without blocking the program, use millis(). Selecting the wrong function could lead to missed data or blocked program execution.

Syntax and Usage
Here's a comparison table for core timing functions:

Function	Usage	Blocking/Non-blocking
delay()	Pauses for milliseconds	Blocking

delayMicroseconds ()	Pauses for microseconds	Blocking
millis ()	Measures milliseconds	Non-blocking
micros ()	Measures microseconds	Non-blocking

Code Example

```
unsigned long startTime = micros();  // Start time
// Some fast operation
unsigned long elapsedTime = micros() - startTime;  // Measure time
taken
if (elapsedTime > 1000) {
  // Do something if more than 1 millisecond passed
}
```

Notes
millis () and micros () are preferred for non-blocking tasks, where you need to measure time without halting the entire program.

Warnings
Mixing blocking (delay ()) and non-blocking (millis (), micros ()) functions can lead to issues in your program's timing and responsiveness. Use them carefully.

Troubleshooting Tips
If your program isn't performing as expected, check which timing function you are using. Blocking delays may cause your program to stop responding, while non-blocking timing lets other tasks continue.

Quiz: Advanced Timing Functionality Check

- **What's the key difference between millis() and delay()?**
  A. millis () allows other code to run while tracking time, while delay () pauses the entire program. (Multiple Choice)

- **Which function is best for high-speed signal control?**
  A. delayMicroseconds () provides the precision needed for fast tasks like signal handling. (Short Answer)

---

4. Practical Projects for Mastering Timing Functions

4.1 **Project 1: Button-Controlled LED with delay()**

This project demonstrates how to use a **push button** to control the on/off state of an **LED** with a simple timing mechanism using the delay () function. When the button is pressed, the LED turns on, stays on for a set period (1 second in this example), and then turns off. This project helps to introduce the concept of timing control using the delay () function in Arduino.

Components List:

1. Arduino
2. Push button
3. LED
4. Resistor (220 ohms for the LED)
5. Breadboard and wires

Circuit Diagram:

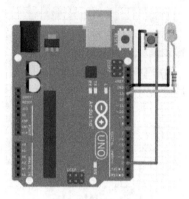

- **LED**: Connect the longer leg (anode) of the LED to pin 13 on the Arduino and the shorter leg (cathode) to **GND** through a 220-ohm resistor.
- **Push Button**: Connect the push button to pin 2 and **GND**. The button pin will read **HIGH** when pressed and **LOW** when released.

Code:

```
const int buttonPin = 2;   // Pin for the push button
const int ledPin = 13;     // Pin for the LED
int buttonState = 0;       // Variable to store button state

void setup() {
  pinMode(ledPin, OUTPUT);     // Set the LED pin as output
  pinMode(buttonPin, INPUT);   // Set the button pin as input
}

void loop() {
  buttonState = digitalRead(buttonPin);   // Read the button state

  if (buttonState == HIGH) {              // If the button is pressed
    digitalWrite(ledPin, HIGH);           // Turn the LED on
    delay(1000);                          // Keep the LED on for 1
second
    digitalWrite(ledPin, LOW);            // Turn the LED off
  }
}
```

Code Walkthrough:

Global Variables:

- buttonPin: Pin **2** is designated as the input pin for the push button.
- ledPin: Pin **13** is used to control the LED.
- buttonState: Stores the state of the push button (either HIGH when pressed or LOW when not pressed).

setup():

- **pinMode(ledPin, OUTPUT)**: Configures pin 13 as an output to control the LED.
- **pinMode(buttonPin, INPUT)**: Configures pin 2 as an input to read the push button's state.

loop():

- **digitalRead(buttonPin)**: Reads the state of the push button (either HIGH or LOW).
- **if (buttonState == HIGH)**: Checks if the button is pressed. When the button is pressed:
    - The LED is turned **on** using digitalWrite(ledPin, HIGH).
    - The delay(1000) function makes the program wait for **1 second**, keeping the LED on during this time.
    - After 1 second, the LED is turned **off** using digitalWrite(ledPin, LOW).

Challenge: Debounce the Button

Add a **debouncing** mechanism to prevent false readings caused by the button bounce. This will improve the reliability of the button press detection.

4.2 Project 2: Precise PWM Signal Generation with delayMicroseconds()

What is this project about?
This project generates a **precise PWM signal** to control the speed of a motor using the delayMicroseconds() function. This project demonstrates how to create fast timing intervals to control devices with microsecond-level precision.

Components List

- o Arduino
- o Motor
- o Transistor
- o Resistor

Circuit Diagram
Connect the motor to the Arduino through a transistor, using a PWM-capable pin like pin 9 for precise control.

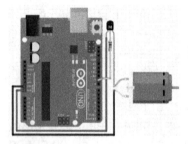

Code

```
int pwmPin = 9;     // PWM-capable pin
int pwmValue = 128; // Variable to store PWM value (50% duty cycle)
void setup() {
  pinMode(pwmPin, OUTPUT);  // Set the PWM pin as output
}
void loop() {
  analogWrite(pwmPin, pwmValue);  // Output the PWM signal using the
variable
  delay(1000);                     // Wait for 1 second

  pwmValue = 255;                  // Change PWM value to 100% duty
cycle
  analogWrite(pwmPin, pwmValue);  // Update the motor speed
  delay(1000);                     // Wait for 1 second
  pwmValue = 128;                  // Change PWM value back to 50% duty
cycle
}
```

Code Walkthrough
The code generates a PWM signal by alternating between **HIGH** and **LOW** signals with microsecond pauses, controlling the motor speed.

Challenge: Increase PWM Precision
Experiment with different microsecond values in the delayMicroseconds() function to achieve more precise motor control, adjusting speed based on timing.

---

5. Common Troubleshooting and Debugging Tips

5.1 Common Errors and How to Fix Them

What are common errors?
One common error is the misuse of **blocking** functions like delay() in time-sensitive programs. This can freeze the program and prevent it from responding to inputs like sensors. Additionally, using delayMicroseconds() with incorrect values can lead to inaccurate timing, especially in high-speed applications.

Why do they happen?
These issues usually occur when functions like delay() are used without considering the impact on program flow. Long delays can cause your program to miss important events, and incorrect use of timing functions like millis() can lead to bugs in timing calculations.

Use of Serial Monitor for debugging
The **Serial Monitor** is an effective tool for debugging timing issues. By printing out values from millis(), micros(), or sensor data, you can track whether timing is working as expected. This allows you to pinpoint where timing issues are occurring in the code.

6. Conclusion and Next Steps

6.1 Recap of Key Timing Functions

In this chapter, you've learned about the **key timing functions** in Arduino: `delay()`, `delayMicroseconds()`, `micros()`, and `millis()`. Each of these functions offers different levels of precision and blocking behavior, helping you manage time-sensitive tasks in your Arduino projects. Understanding when to use each function is essential for developing efficient programs, whether you're controlling an LED, measuring sensor data, or generating precise PWM signals. With these functions, you can effectively manage the timing of your Arduino applications.

Chapter 5: Control Structures

Control structures are fundamental programming commands that govern the flow of execution in a program. They enable decision-making and repetition, allowing the code to adapt to various conditions or perform tasks repeatedly. This chapter explores key control structures such as conditional statements (if, else, switch) and loops (for, while, do...while). These structures are essential in creating dynamic, interactive, and functional programs.

Syntax Table

Topic Name	Syntax	Simple Example
if Statement	`if (condition) { /* code */ }`	`if (x > 0) { Serial.println("Positive"); }`
if...else Statement	`if (condition) { /* code */ } else { /* code */ }`	`if (score >= 60) { Serial.println("Pass"); } else { Serial.println("Fail"); }`
switch Statement	`switch (variable) { case value1: /* code */ break; ... }`	`switch (day) { case 1: Serial.println("Monday"); break; }`
for Loop	`for (init; condition; increment) { /* code */ }`	`for (int i = 0; i < 5; i++) { Serial.println(i); }`
while Loop	`while (condition) { /* code */ }`	`while (x < 5) { Serial.println(x); x++; }`
do...while Loop	`do { /* code */ } while (condition);`	`do { Serial.println(x); x++; } while (x < 5);`

break Statement	`break;`	`for (int i = 0; i < 10; i++) {` `if (i == 5) break; }`
continue Statement	`continue;`	`for (int i = 0; i < 10; i++) {` `if (i % 2 == 0) continue; }`
return Statement	`return value;`	`int add(int a, int b) { return` `a + b; }`

goto Statement	`goto label; /*`
	`code */ label:`
	`/* code */`
		`goto end;`
		`Serial.println("Hello"); end:`
		`Serial.println("End");`

1. Introduction to Control Structures

1.1 What are Control Structures?

Define what control structures are
Control structures are commands in programming that dictate the flow of execution based on certain conditions or repetitions. They allow programs to make **decisions** (like if and switch statements) and **repeat** actions (using for and while loops). For instance, an if statement might execute a block of code only if a specific condition is met, while a for loop repeatedly executes a block of code a set number of times. Control structures are essential for creating dynamic and functional programs.

Explain why they are essential in programming
Control structures are **crucial** because they enable a program to handle different scenarios and automate tasks. They allow programmers to **create flexible and efficient** code by executing different code paths based on **conditions** and by repeating tasks as needed. Without control structures, programs would lack the ability to make decisions or loop through tasks, limiting their functionality. They are foundational for implementing **logic** and **complex behavior** in software, making them indispensable for developing any interactive or functional application.

1.2 Key Concepts and Terms (Glossary)

if
The if **statement** evaluates a condition and executes a block of code if the condition is true. It is used to implement **conditional logic**. Example: if (x > 0) { /* code */ }.

else
The else **statement** follows an if statement and executes a block of code if the condition in the if statement is false. It provides an **alternative path** of execution. Example: else { /* code */ }.

for
The for **loop** executes a block of code a specific number of times. It is used for **repetitive tasks** where the number of iterations is known. Example: for (int i = 0; i < 10; i++) { /* code */ }.

while
The while **loop** repeatedly executes a block of code as long as a condition is true. It is useful for **tasks with unknown iteration counts**. Example: while (x < 10) { /* code */ }.

switch
The switch **statement** allows the execution of different code blocks based on the value of a variable. It is useful for **multiple condition checks**. Example: switch (day) { case 1: /* code */ break; }.

1.3 Overview of Core Control Structures

Overview of decision-making structures
Decision-making structures such as if, else, and switch determine which code block to execute based on certain conditions. The if statement evaluates a condition and executes a block if true. The else statement provides an alternative if the if condition is false. The switch statement is used for **multiple possible values** of a variable, executing different code blocks based on the variable's value. These structures are essential for **branching logic** in programs, allowing for dynamic decision-making and control flow.

Overview of loops
Loops like for, while, and do...while are used for **repeating**

tasks. The for loop is ideal when the number of iterations is known, such as iterating through arrays. The while loop runs as long as a condition remains true, useful for **dynamic iteration counts**. The do. . . while loop executes a block of code at least once before checking the condition, ensuring that the code block runs **at least one time**. These loops are crucial for tasks that require repeated execution, such as processing data or automating repetitive tasks.

Quiz: Test Your Understanding of Control Structures

- What does the if statement do?
  A) Repeats code a set number of times
  B) Executes code based on a condition
  C) Handles multiple conditions
  Answer: B
- How does the for loop differ from the while loop?
  A) for loops execute at least once
  B) while loops execute based on a condition
  C) for loops use a known number of iterations
  Answer: C

2. Decision-Making Structures

2.1 The if Statement

What is the if statement?
The if **statement** allows a program to execute a block of code only if a specified **condition** is true. It's used to make decisions and control the flow of execution. For instance, if a sensor reading exceeds a certain threshold, an if statement can trigger an action. This helps in creating dynamic behaviors based on conditions.

Syntax

```
if (condition) {
   // code to execute if condition is true
}
```

Syntax Explanation
The if statement checks the **condition** in parentheses. If the condition evaluates to true, the **code block** inside the curly braces {} executes. If the condition is false, the code block is skipped. This basic structure is used to introduce **conditional logic** into a program, allowing for flexible execution paths.

Usage
Use the if statement to **perform actions** based on conditions, like turning on a light if it gets dark. It's essential for **branching** logic, where different code paths are executed based on different conditions. For example, you might use an if statement to check if a variable exceeds a threshold.

Code Example

```
int temperature = 25;
if (temperature > 20) {
  Serial.println("It's warm outside.");
}
```

In this example, if the temperature is greater than 20, the message "It's warm outside" is printed. This demonstrates how if checks a condition and executes code based on that check.

Notes
The if statement can be used with various **conditions**, including **comparisons** and **boolean expressions**. It is one of the most fundamental control structures in programming.

Warnings
Ensure that the **condition** is correctly written to avoid **logic errors**. For example, using = instead of == will result in incorrect behavior, as = is an assignment operator, not a comparison.

Troubleshooting Tips
If the if statement doesn't seem to work, check the condition for errors. Ensure there are no **syntax errors** and that the condition evaluates as expected. Use debugging tools to **inspect** variable values and verify that the condition is being met.

2.2 The if...else Statement

What is the if...else statement?

The if...else **statement** provides a way to execute one block of code if a condition is true, and a different block if the condition is false. It's used to handle **binary decisions**, where there are two possible outcomes. This allows a program to **choose between two paths** of execution.

Syntax

```
if (condition) {
    // code to execute if condition is true
} else {
    // code to execute if condition is false
}
```

Syntax Explanation

The if...else statement first evaluates the **condition**. If true, the code inside the first block runs. If false, the code inside the else block runs. This structure enables handling of **alternative scenarios**, ensuring that one of the two possible code paths is executed based on the condition.

Usage

Use if...else when you need to handle **two distinct outcomes**. For instance, you might use it to **check if a user is logged in** and provide different content based on their login status. It helps in **implementing different behaviors** for different conditions.

Code Example

```
int score = 85;
if (score >= 60) {
    Serial.println("Pass");
} else {
    Serial.println("Fail");
}
```

Here, if the score is 60 or above, it prints "Pass"; otherwise, it prints "Fail". This shows how if...else can be used to handle **binary decisions** based on a condition.

Notes

The if...else statement is useful for **making choices** between two possible actions. It is widely used in scenarios where **simple binary logic** is needed.

Warnings

Ensure the **condition** and **code blocks** are correctly written to avoid **unexpected behavior**. Incorrect conditions or misplaced braces can lead to **logic errors**.

Troubleshooting Tips

If the wrong block of code executes, double-check the **condition** for accuracy. Verify that the condition correctly reflects the logic you intend. Use print statements or a debugger to inspect the **flow** and ensure it matches your expectations.

2.3 The switch...case Statement

What is the switch...case statement?

The **switch...case statement** allows you to select one of many code blocks to execute based on the value of a variable. It is ideal for scenarios where you have multiple possible values and need to execute different code for each value. This structure simplifies **multiple conditional checks** compared to using a series of if statements.

Syntax

```
switch (variable) {
  case value1:
    // code to execute if variable == value1
    break;
  case value2:
    // code to execute if variable == value2
    break;
  default:
    // code to execute if variable doesn't match any case
}
```

Syntax Explanation
The `switch` statement evaluates the **variable** and matches it against case labels. If a match is found, the corresponding code block runs until a `break` statement is encountered. If no match is found, the `default` block (if present) executes. This structure provides a **clear way** to handle multiple possible values.

Usage
Use the `switch...case` statement when you need to handle multiple values of a variable, such as processing different **menu options** or handling various **error codes**. It's more organized and readable than multiple `if...else` statements.

Code Example

```
int day = 3;
switch (day) {
  case 1:
    Serial.println("Monday");
    break;
  case 2:
    Serial.println("Tuesday");
    break;
  case 3:
    Serial.println("Wednesday");
    break;
  default:
    Serial.println("Invalid day");
}
```

This code prints the day of the week based on the day variable. If day is 3, it prints "Wednesday". The `switch` statement simplifies handling multiple possible values.

Notes
The `switch...case` statement is useful for managing multiple **discrete values**. It enhances code readability and organization when dealing with a **limited set of options**.

Warnings
Ensure each `case` block ends with a `break` statement to prevent **fall-through** to the next case. Missing `break` statements can lead to unintended execution of multiple blocks.

Troubleshooting Tips
If the wrong case block executes, verify that the **variable** being switched matches the expected values. Check for missing break statements that could cause **fall-through**. Use debugging tools to **inspect** the variable's value and ensure it matches one of the case labels.

Quiz: Check Your Understanding of Decision-Making Structures

1. What does the if statement do?
   A) Executes code based on a condition
   B) Loops through code
   C) Switches between cases
   Answer: A
2. When should you use if...else instead of switch...case?
   A) When you have multiple conditions
   B) When handling multiple discrete values
   C) When you need binary choices
   Answer: C

3. Loop Structures

3.1 The for Loop

What is the for loop?
The **for loop** is a control structure that repeats a block of code a specified number of times. It's commonly used when the **number of iterations** is known beforehand. The loop has three parts: **initialization**, **condition**, and **increment/decrement**, which control the loop's execution. It's ideal for **iterating over arrays** or performing tasks that require a fixed number of repetitions.

Syntax

```
for (initialization; condition; increment/decrement) {
    // code to be executed
}
```

Syntax Explanation
The **initialization** part runs once before the loop starts. The **condition** is checked before each iteration, and if true, the code block executes. After each iteration, the **increment/decrement** updates the loop variable, and the process repeats. When the condition is false, the loop ends. This structure makes for loops efficient for **count-controlled repetition**.

Usage
Use the for loop when you need to repeat a task a known number of times, like **iterating through an array** or performing a calculation multiple times. It's especially helpful in tasks like **processing data sets** or generating **sequential values**.

Code Example

```
for (int i = 0; i < 5; i++) {
  Serial.println(i);
}
```

In this example, the for loop runs five times, printing the values from 0 to 4. The loop variable i is incremented by 1 after each iteration until the condition i < 5 is false.

Notes
The for loop is great for **fixed iteration counts**, making it ideal for tasks where you know how many times the loop will run, like processing an array.

Warnings
Be careful with the **loop condition** to avoid **infinite loops**. If the condition never becomes false, the loop will run indefinitely, potentially freezing the program.

Troubleshooting Tips
If the loop isn't working as expected, check the **initialization**, **condition**, and **increment/decrement** expressions. Make sure the loop variable is updated correctly to prevent infinite loops or incorrect iteration counts. Use print statements to check the loop's behavior.

3.2 The while Loop

What is the while loop?
The **while loop** repeatedly executes a block of code as long as a specified condition is true. Unlike the for loop, the **number of iterations** is not known in advance. The loop checks the condition before each iteration, making it ideal for **indefinite repetition** where the stopping point is determined by changing variables or external conditions.

Syntax

```
while (condition) {
    // code to be executed
}
```

Syntax Explanation
The condition is evaluated before each iteration. If the condition is true, the loop runs, and if false, the loop exits. The loop continues until the condition becomes false. This structure makes while loops suitable for tasks where the **exit condition** is determined dynamically, not at the beginning.

Usage
Use the while loop when you need to keep executing code until a condition changes, like waiting for user input or monitoring a sensor value. It's commonly used in **event-driven** programming.

Code Example

```
int x = 0;
while (x < 5) {
  Serial.println(x);
  x++;
}
```

In this example, the loop runs as long as x is less than 5. Each time, it prints x and increments the value of x. When x reaches 5, the loop stops.

Notes

The `while` loop is good for situations where the **end condition** isn't fixed and can change based on variables or events during runtime.

Warnings

Ensure that the loop's **condition** will eventually become false; otherwise, the loop will run indefinitely, causing the program to freeze.

Troubleshooting Tips

If the loop runs endlessly, check the **condition** and ensure the loop variable changes within the loop. Ensure that the condition is updated appropriately to eventually exit the loop. Debug with print statements to track the loop's progress.

3.3 The do. . . while Loop

What is the do. . . while loop?
The **do. . . while loop** is similar to the while loop but guarantees that the loop's code will run **at least once** before checking the condition. The condition is evaluated **after** the code block runs, making it useful for situations where the code must execute first, regardless of the condition.

Syntax

```
do {
   // code to be executed
} while (condition);
```

Syntax Explanation
The do block runs first, and then the **condition** is checked. If the condition is true, the loop repeats. If false, the loop exits. This ensures that the loop runs **at least one time**, regardless of the condition's initial value, making it unique among loop structures.

Usage
Use the do. . . while loop when you want the code to run **at least once**, such as prompting the user for input or initializing a system, before checking if further iterations are necessary.

Code Example

```
int x = 0;
do {
  Serial.println(x);
  x++;
} while (x < 5);
```

In this example, the loop prints the value of x and then checks the condition. The loop runs at least once, even if the condition is initially false.

Notes
The do...while loop is useful when you need the loop to **run at least once** regardless of the condition's initial value.

Warnings
Be cautious of loops running **unintentionally** if the condition never becomes false. Always ensure that the loop variable is updated properly.

Troubleshooting Tips
If the loop behaves unexpectedly, ensure the condition is checked after each iteration. Debug by printing the variable values inside the loop to verify the condition and track its changes.

Quiz: Test Your Knowledge of Loop Structures

1. What is the primary difference between a for loop and a while loop?
   A) for loop has a fixed number of iterations
   B) while loop has a fixed number of iterations
   C) for loop does not require a condition
   Answer: A
2. When does the code block in a do...while loop run?
   A) Only if the condition is true
   B) At least once, regardless of the condition
   C) Only if the condition is false
   Answer: B

---

4. Controlling Loops and Flow

4.1 The break Statement

What is the break statement?
The **break statement** is used to immediately **exit a loop or switch statement**. When encountered inside a loop, it stops further iterations, regardless of whether the condition is still true. It's

typically used to **interrupt** a loop when a certain condition is met, such as finding a specific value or handling an error.

Syntax

```
break;
```

Syntax Explanation
The break statement can be placed anywhere inside a loop or switch case. When the program encounters break, it **exits the loop** or switch statement and continues executing the code that follows. This is useful for **stopping execution** when a certain condition is met or to prevent unnecessary iterations.

Usage
Use break when you want to **terminate a loop early** or to exit a switch case after executing the desired code. It's essential for **optimizing loop performance** or handling **special cases**.

Code Example

```
for (int i = 0; i < 10; i++) {
  if (i == 5) {
    break;
  }
  Serial.println(i);
}
```

This loop prints values from 0 to 4, but exits when i equals 5. The break statement stops the loop early once the condition is met.

Troubleshooting Tips
If the break statement seems to exit too early, check the condition triggering it. Ensure the condition is accurate and placed correctly to avoid unintended exits. Use print statements to debug and verify that the break is executed at the right moment.

4.2 The continue Statement

What is the continue statement?
The **continue statement** skips the remaining code in the current
loop iteration and moves to the next iteration. Unlike break, it doesn't
exit the loop but allows you to **skip certain conditions** or values.
It's useful when you want to bypass specific situations within a loop
without stopping the loop entirely.

Syntax

```
continue;
```

Syntax Explanation
The continue statement is placed inside the loop. When the
program encounters continue, it **skips the current iteration** and
moves to the next one, ignoring the remaining code in the loop body
for that iteration. It's often used to **bypass unnecessary iterations**.

Usage
Use continue when you want to **skip specific conditions** within a
loop, such as avoiding even numbers or handling errors while
allowing the loop to continue. It's helpful for **filtering values** or
skipping steps.

Code Example

```
for (int i = 0; i < 10; i++) {
  if (i % 2 == 0) {
    continue;
  }
  Serial.println(i);
}
```

This loop prints only the odd numbers from 0 to 9 by skipping the
even numbers using the continue statement.

Quiz: Check Your Understanding of Loop Control

1. What does the break statement do in a loop?
   A) Skips to the next iteration
   B) Exits the loop immediately
   C) Skips even numbers
   Answer: B
2. When should you use the continue statement?
   A) To exit a loop
   B) To skip certain iterations
   C) To stop a program
   Answer: B

---

5. Functions and Program Flow

5.1 The return Statement

What is the return statement?
The **return statement** is used to **exit a function** and return a value to the calling code. It signals the end of a function and optionally passes data back to where the function was called. Without a return statement, functions can't provide results to the rest of the program.

Syntax

```
return value;
```

Syntax Explanation
The return statement is placed at the end of a function or when a value needs to be sent back to the calling code. The **value** provided after return is passed back, and the function **terminates**. If no value is returned, the function simply exits.

Usage

Use `return` when you want a function to **send back a result** or exit early based on a condition. It's essential for **modular programming**, where functions calculate values or handle tasks and return data to other parts of the program.

Code Example

```
int add(int a, int b) {
   return a + b;
}

void setup() {
   int sum = add(3, 5);
   Serial.println(sum);   // Outputs 8
}
```

In this example, the add function returns the sum of two numbers, which is printed to the Serial Monitor.

5.2 The goto Statement

What is the goto statement?

The **goto statement** transfers control to a labeled section of the code, **jumping** to a different part of the program. While it can simplify complex logic, it is generally discouraged because it can lead to **confusing and hard-to-maintain code**.

Syntax

```
goto label;
// code
label:
   // code to jump to
```

Syntax Explanation

The goto statement jumps to a **labeled section** of the code. The label must be defined elsewhere in the program. When goto is executed, control immediately transfers to the label, skipping any code between the goto and the label.

Usage

Use goto when you need to jump to another part of the program. However, it should be used **sparingly**, as it can make code difficult to follow. Structured alternatives like loops or functions are often better.

Code Example

```
int x = 0;
void loop() {
  x++;
  if (x == 5) {
    goto end;
  }
  Serial.println(x);
  end:
}
```

In this example, the goto statement jumps to the label end, skipping the Serial.println statement when x equals 5.

Quiz: Test Your Knowledge of Program Flow

1. What is the purpose of the return statement in a function?
   A) It ends the program
   B) It returns a value to the calling function
   C) It loops through the function
   Answer: B

2. Why should you avoid using the goto statement?
   A) It can lead to hard-to-read and maintain code
   B) It is slow
   C) It crashes programs
   Answer: A

6. Projects

6.1 Project 1: Smart Thermostat Control System

This project demonstrates how to build a **smart thermostat** using control structures like **if** and **else** statements to regulate the temperature of a room. The thermostat automatically turns on a **heater** when the temperature drops below a **set threshold** and turns it off once the desired temperature is reached. The system reads temperature data from a sensor, processes it, and controls a **relay module** connected to the heater.

Why is it important?
This project simulates the operation of real-world **smart thermostats**, automating climate control for a room. By using **if-else statements**, you create an intelligent system that manages the temperature efficiently without requiring manual intervention. This project provides hands-on experience with **sensor data** handling, control structures, and actuator management, all fundamental concepts in **home automation** and **smart home systems**.

Components List:

- **Arduino**
- **Temperature sensor** (e.g., LM35 or DHT11)
- **Relay module**
- **Heater** (or fan)
- **Jumper wires**
- **Resistors**

Circuit Diagram

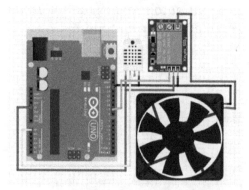

- The **temperature sensor's output** pin is connected to **analog pin A0** on the Arduino.
- The **relay module** is connected to **digital pin 9**, which controls the heater.
- The **heater** is powered through the relay, which acts as an electronic switch controlled by the Arduino.

Code

```
int temperature = 0;
int setTemp = 25;  // Desired room temperature

void setup() {
  pinMode(9, OUTPUT);    // Set pin 9 for relay control
  Serial.begin(9600);    // Initialize serial communication for debugging
}

void loop() {
  // Read the temperature sensor
  temperature = analogRead(A0);
  // Convert the sensor reading (0-1023) to Celsius (0-50°C range)
  temperature = map(temperature, 0, 1023, 0, 50);

  // Control the heater based on the current temperature
  if (temperature < setTemp) {
    digitalWrite(9, HIGH);   // Turn on heater
    Serial.println("Heater ON");
  } else {
    digitalWrite(9, LOW);    // Turn off heater
    Serial.println("Heater OFF");
  }

  // Wait 1 second before checking the temperature again
  delay(1000);
}
```

Code Walkthrough

Temperature Reading: The sensor data is read from **analog pin A0** using analogRead (A0), which provides a value between **0 and 1023**.

Mapping the Value: The map () function is used to convert the sensor value into a **Celsius** reading (0-50°C). The raw analog value is mapped to a temperature range that the sensor can measure.

Temperature Control:

- If the **temperature** is **below the set threshold** (25°C), the system turns on the heater by setting **pin 9** to **HIGH**.
- If the **temperature** reaches or exceeds the set point, the heater is turned **off** by setting **pin 9** to **LOW**.

Serial Output: The system sends a message to the **Serial Monitor** for debugging purposes, indicating whether the heater is ON or OFF.

Delay: A **1-second delay** is added to prevent rapid toggling of the heater and to give the system time to respond to temperature changes.

Challenge
Add a **cooling system** by incorporating a fan that turns on when the temperature exceeds a set threshold, using additional if...else logic.

6.2 Project 2: Automated LED Control Based on Temperature

This project automates the control of an **LED** based on **temperature readings** from a sensor. The LED will **turn on** when the temperature exceeds a certain threshold and **turn off** when the temperature drops below that threshold. The project demonstrates the use of **if...else statements** to control the state of the LED based on environmental conditions, specifically the room temperature.

Components List:

- **Arduino**
- **Temperature sensor** (e.g., LM35 or DHT11)
- **LED**
- **Resistors**
- **Jumper wires**

Circuit Diagram

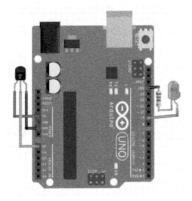

The **temperature sensor's output** pin connects to **analog pin A0** on the Arduino.
The **LED's positive leg** connects to **digital pin 9**, and the **negative leg** is connected to **ground** through a resistor.

Code

```
int temperature = 0;
int threshold = 30;  // Temperature threshold for LED

void setup() {
  pinMode(9, OUTPUT);   // Set pin 9 for LED control
  Serial.begin(9600);   // Initialize serial communication
}

void loop() {
  // Read the temperature from the sensor
  temperature = analogRead(A0);

  // Convert the analog reading (0-1023) to temperature in Celsius (0-
50°C)
  temperature = map(temperature, 0, 1023, 0, 50);

  // Control the LED based on the temperature
  if (temperature >= threshold) {
    digitalWrite(9, HIGH);   // Turn LED on
    Serial.println("LED ON");
  } else {
    digitalWrite(9, LOW);    // Turn LED off
    Serial.println("LED OFF");
  }

  // Delay for 1 second to prevent rapid changes
  delay(1000);
}
```

Code Walkthrough

- **Temperature Reading**: The temperature sensor's analog value is read using `analogRead(A0)`. The raw sensor value ranges between **0 and 1023**, representing the voltage output by the sensor.

Mapping Temperature: The `map()` function is used to convert the sensor's reading to a **Celsius** temperature value. The LM35 or DHT11 sensor is typically mapped to a temperature range from **0 to 50°C**:
```
temperature = map(temperature, 0, 1023, 0, 50);
```

- **LED Control**:
  - If the temperature exceeds the set **threshold** of **30°C**, the **LED turns on** by setting **pin 9** to **HIGH**.
  - If the temperature falls below **30°C**, the **LED turns off** by setting **pin 9** to **LOW**.

Serial Communication: The **Serial Monitor** is used to print out whether the LED is on or off, which helps with debugging:
```
Serial.println("LED ON");
```

- **Delay**: A **1-second delay** is added to prevent rapid toggling of the LED and to give the system time to stabilize between readings.

Challenge

Add a **buzzer** that sounds if the temperature exceeds a dangerous level (e.g., 40°C), demonstrating multiple control outputs based on different conditions.

6.3 Project 3: Smart Irrigation System with `if...else`

This project builds a **smart irrigation system** that automatically waters plants when the **soil moisture level** is too low and stops watering when the soil moisture reaches an adequate level. The system uses **if...else** statements to decide when to turn the **water pump** on or off based on the readings from a **soil moisture sensor**. This automation helps ensure plants receive the right amount of water without human intervention.

Components List:

- **Arduino**
- **Soil moisture sensor**
- **Water pump** (or **LED** for simulation)
- **Relay module** (to control the water pump)
- **Jumper wires**
- **Resistors**

Circuit Diagram

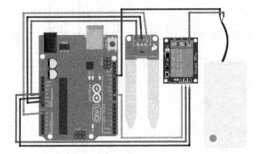

Connect the **soil moisture sensor** to **analog pin A0** on the Arduino.

The **water pump** (or LED for simulation) is controlled by a **relay module** connected to **digital pin 9** on the Arduino.

Code

```
int moistureLevel = 0;
int threshold = 300;  // Moisture threshold
void setup() {
  pinMode(9, OUTPUT);  // Set pin 9 for relay control
  Serial.begin(9600);  // Start serial communication
}
void loop() {
  moistureLevel = analogRead(A0);  // Read the moisture sensor value
  if (moistureLevel < threshold) {
    digitalWrite(9, HIGH);  // Turn on water pump
    Serial.println("Watering ON");
  } else {
    digitalWrite(9, LOW);   // Turn off water pump
    Serial.println("Watering OFF");
  }

  delay(1000);  // Delay for 1 second before the next reading
}
```

Code Walkthrough

- **Reading Moisture Level**: The **analog value** from the soil moisture sensor is read using `analogRead(A0)`. This value represents the current moisture level in the soil.
- **Threshold Check**:
  - If the **moisture level** is **below the threshold** (300 in this example), the system activates the **water pump** by sending a **HIGH signal** to **digital pin 9**, which controls the relay.
  - If the moisture level is **above the threshold**, the system turns off the water pump by sending a **LOW signal** to the relay, stopping the watering process.

Serial Monitor: The system prints whether the **watering** is ON or OFF to the **Serial Monitor** for easy debugging and monitoring:
`Serial.println("Watering ON");`

- **Delay**: A **1-second delay** is added at the end of each loop to give the system time to stabilize before reading the next moisture level.

Challenge
Add a **moisture sensor** to automate water control. If the soil is too dry, the system should automatically turn on the water pump, and turn it off when the soil is wet enough.

6.4 Project 4: Traffic Light Control with `switch...case` and Loops

This project simulates a **traffic light control system** using **switch...case statements** and **loops**. The system cycles between **red**, **yellow**, and **green lights**, with each light staying on for a specific duration, mimicking a real traffic light's operation. The project demonstrates how to use control structures in combination with loops to continuously manage the state of the traffic light.

Components List:

- **Arduino**
- **Red, yellow, and green LEDs**
- **Resistors**
- **Jumper wires**

Circuit Diagram

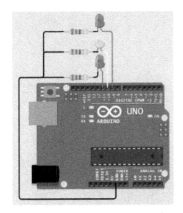

- Connect the **red LED** to **digital pin 9**.
- Connect the **yellow LED** to **digital pin 10**.
- Connect the **green LED** to **digital pin 11**.
- Each LED should have a **current-limiting resistor** connected to **ground (GND)**.

Code

```
int state = 0;

void setup() {
  pinMode(9, OUTPUT);   // Red LED
  pinMode(10, OUTPUT);   // Yellow LED
  pinMode(11, OUTPUT);   // Green LED
}

void loop() {
  switch (state) {
    case 0:  // Red light
      digitalWrite(9, HIGH);    // Turn on Red LED
      digitalWrite(10, LOW);    // Turn off Yellow LED
      digitalWrite(11, LOW);    // Turn off Green LED
      delay(5000);  // Red light stays on for 5 seconds
      state = 1;  // Move to the next state (green light)
      break;

    case 1:  // Green light
      digitalWrite(9, LOW);     // Turn off Red LED
      digitalWrite(10, LOW);    // Turn off Yellow LED
      digitalWrite(11, HIGH);   // Turn on Green LED
      delay(5000);  // Green light stays on for 5 seconds
      state = 2;  // Move to the next state (yellow light)
      break;

    case 2:  // Yellow light
```

```
        digitalWrite(9, LOW);     // Turn off Red LED
        digitalWrite(10, HIGH);   // Turn on Yellow LED
        digitalWrite(11, LOW);    // Turn off Green LED
        delay(2000);  // Yellow light stays on for 2 seconds
        state = 0;  // Reset back to the red light state
        break;
    }
}
```

Code Walkthrough

- **State Management**: The variable state is used to track the current phase of the traffic light (red, green, or yellow). Based on the current state, the appropriate LEDs are turned on or off, mimicking the traffic light's phases.
- **switch...case Statement**: The **switch...case** statement is used to control which **LED** is active:
    - **Case 0**: The **red LED** is turned on for 5 seconds (delay (5000)) while the yellow and green LEDs are turned off. After this, the state changes to **1**, moving to the green light.
    - **Case 1**: The **green LED** is turned on for 5 seconds (delay (5000)), then the state is updated to **2**, moving to the yellow light.
    - **Case 2**: The **yellow LED** is turned on for 2 seconds (delay (2000)), after which the state is set back to **0**, returning to the red light.
- **Loop**: The entire sequence repeats indefinitely due to the loop () function, ensuring the traffic lights cycle through red, green, and yellow continuously.

Challenge
Modify the traffic light system to include **pedestrian control** with a button. When the button is pressed, the traffic light should change to red, allowing pedestrians to cross.

7. Common Troubleshooting and Debugging Tips

7.1 Common Errors with Control Structures and How to Fix Them

What are common errors?
Common errors with control structures include **misplaced curly braces**, **incorrect conditions**, and **missing break statements** in switch cases. Logic errors, like accidentally using = (assignment) instead of == (comparison), are also frequent. These issues can lead to unexpected program behavior.

Why they happen?
These errors usually occur due to **syntax mistakes** or **logical misunderstandings** of how control structures work. For instance, forgetting to update a loop counter or misplacing an else block can cause the program to execute incorrectly.

How to fix them
Carefully check **curly braces** and **indentation** to ensure code blocks are correctly defined. Use **comments** to track logic flow. For switch statements, always include **break statements** to avoid unintended fall-through. Debugging tools or **print statements** can help identify where the logic goes wrong.

7.2 Preventing Infinite Loops in Arduino Code

What are infinite loops?
An **infinite loop** occurs when the **condition** for terminating a loop is never met, causing the loop to run indefinitely. This can cause the program to freeze or malfunction, as the Arduino continuously executes the loop without stopping.

Why are they problematic?
Infinite loops **consume processing power**, preventing other tasks from running, which can cause system failures. In Arduino, this may lead to non-responsive sensors or devices, draining batteries or halting the entire system.

How to prevent infinite loops
To avoid infinite loops, ensure that **loop conditions** eventually

become false. Regularly update loop counters or variables used in conditions. Add **timeout logic** or break conditions to force loop termination after a set number of iterations. Debugging with **serial prints** can help track the loop's behavior in real time.

8. Conclusion and Next Steps

8.1 Recap of Key Control Structures

What have we learned?
In this chapter, we explored **control structures** like `if`, `else`, `switch`, and loops (`for`, `while`, `do...while`) that direct the **flow of execution** in Arduino programs. We examined how these structures make decisions and repeat tasks, allowing for dynamic program behavior. We also looked at real-life applications, such as controlling LEDs, fans, and traffic lights, to understand how these structures work in practical scenarios.

Why are they important?
Mastering control structures is essential for creating **efficient**, **flexible**, and **responsive** programs. They allow developers to automate decisions, handle multiple conditions, and manage repetitive tasks effectively, making them fundamental for building more complex systems.

Chapter 6: Maths and Trigonometry Functions

Chapter 6 introduces the mathematical and trigonometric functions available in Arduino programming. These functions are crucial for performing complex calculations often needed in robotics, sensor data processing, and motion control. Functions such as **abs**() for calculating absolute values, **constrain**() for limiting values within a range, **map**() for scaling values, and trigonometric functions like **sin**(), **cos**(), and **tan**() are covered. Understanding these functions allows users to handle calculations easily, create precise movement patterns, and manage sensor data more efficiently in their projects.

Syntax Table: Arduino Math and Trigonometry Functions

Topic Name	Syntax	Simple Example
Absolute Value Calculation	abs(x)	int result = abs(-10); // Result: 10
Limiting Values	constrain(x, low, high)	int result = constrain(150, 0, 100); // Result: 100
Re-mapping Values	map(x, in_min, in_max, out_min, out_max)	int result = map(512, 0, 1023, 0, 255); // Result: 128
Maximum of Two Values	max(x, y)	int result = max(5, 10); // Result: 10
Minimum of Two Values	min(x, y)	int result = min(5, 10); // Result: 5
Raising to a Power	pow(base, exponent)	double result = pow(2, 3); // Result: 8
Squaring a Value	sq(x)	int result = sq(4); // Result: 16
Calculating Square Root	sqrt(x)	float result = sqrt(25); // Result: 5
Calculating Cosine	cos(angle)	float result = cos(PI / 3); // Result: 0.5
Calculating Sine	sin(angle)	float result = sin(PI / 2); // Result: 1

Calculating Tangent	`tan(angle)`	`float result = tan(PI / 4); // Result: 1`

1. Introduction to Math and Trigonometry Functions in Arduino

1.1 What are Math and Trigonometry Functions in Arduino?

What are Math and Trigonometry Functions?
Arduino provides built-in functions for performing mathematical operations. These include functions like `abs()` for absolute value, `pow()` for exponentiation, and trigonometric functions such as `sin()`, `cos()`, and `tan()`. These functions make it easy to handle calculations that are often necessary in robotics, sensor data processing, and motion control. With these functions, users can compute precise values to help control actuators, sensors, or other Arduino-driven devices.

Why are they important?
Math and trigonometry functions are essential for interpreting sensor data, performing calculations in real-time, and creating precise movement patterns. For example, when reading sensors or controlling motors, mathematical operations such as scaling values, limiting inputs, or using trigonometric functions to calculate angles are crucial for getting accurate results. Without these functions, performing complex calculations in Arduino projects would be tedious and error-prone.

1.2 Key Concepts and Terms (Glossary)

What is abs()?
The `abs()` function returns the absolute value of a number, which removes any negative sign. It's useful for working with sensor data that might return negative values.

Why is it important?
It helps avoid negative values when only positive values are needed, such as when measuring distances or time intervals.

What is constrain()?
constrain() limits a value to stay within a given range, ensuring it does not exceed the defined minimum and maximum values.

Why is it important?
It prevents sensor or motor values from going out of bounds, which could damage the system or cause inaccurate results.

What is map()?
map() re-maps a value from one range to another. This is often used to adjust sensor readings or motor outputs.

Why is it important?
It allows you to convert values from one scale to another, which is critical when dealing with different sensor ranges.

Include max(), min(), pow(), sq(), sqrt(), cos(), sin(), and tan().

1.3 Overview of Core Math and Trigonometry Functions

What are Core Math and Trigonometry Functions?
Core math functions in Arduino include abs() for calculating absolute values, constrain() for limiting values within a range, map() for re-scaling values, and trigonometric functions such as sin(), cos(), and tan() for calculating angles. These functions simplify working with complex mathematical concepts in projects, especially when dealing with robotics, sensor integration, and real-time signal processing. Using these built-in functions allows for efficient code and easy implementation of mathematical operations.

Why are they important?
These functions are critical for many practical applications. For example, map() can be used to adjust a potentiometer's input to match motor speed. Trigonometric functions like cos() or sin() are essential in creating precise movements in robotic arms or

calculating angles in geometric applications. Using these functions helps avoid complex manual calculations and allows for quicker development in Arduino projects.

Quiz: Test Your Understanding of Math and Trigonometry Functions

- **What does the abs () function do?**
  A. It returns the absolute value of a number, ensuring it's always positive. (Multiple Choice)
- **Define the purpose of map () in Arduino.**
  A. It remaps a number from one range to another. (Short Answer)
- **How do you calculate the cosine of an angle using cos ()?**
  A. Use cos (angle) where the angle is in radians. (Fill in the Blank)

---

2. Basic Math Functions

2.1 The abs () Function: Absolute Value Calculation

What is abs ()?
The abs () function returns the absolute value of a given number, removing any negative sign. It's commonly used when working with sensors that might output negative readings, such as accelerometers, or when calculating differences between two points.

Why is it important?
It ensures that values remain positive when negative numbers would cause errors, such as when calculating distances or time intervals. It's particularly useful for avoiding mathematical errors in applications where only positive values make sense.

Syntax:

```
abs(x)
```

Where x is the number whose absolute value will be returned.

Syntax Explanation
The input to the abs () function is any number, either positive or negative. The function returns the value without the sign, making it always positive.

Usage
Use abs () in projects where sensor values may fluctuate between positive and negative, but only positive values are required, like in motion tracking.

Code Example

```
int sensorValue = -50;
int absoluteValue = abs(sensorValue);
Serial.println(absoluteValue);  // Outputs 50
```

Notes
This function works for both integers and floating-point numbers. It's widely used in mathematical calculations, especially when you need non-negative results.

Warnings
Be mindful when using abs () with signed numbers; if the sign carries meaning (such as direction), removing it might lead to incorrect calculations.

Troubleshooting Tips
If you're seeing unexpected results, check if you've applied abs () to a number that should retain its negative value, like directional values in a movement-based project.

2.2 The constrain() Function: Limiting Values

What is `constrain()`?

The `constrain()` function limits a value to fall between a minimum and a maximum range. It's helpful for ensuring sensor values or outputs don't exceed safe or expected limits, such as keeping a motor's speed within a defined range.

Why is it important?

It ensures that values like sensor readings or motor speeds remain within safe operational limits. For example, if sensor data exceeds the expected range, `constrain()` prevents the value from causing unexpected behavior or damage to components.

Syntax:

```
constrain(x, low, high)
```

Where x is the value to limit, and `low` and `high` set the boundaries.

Syntax Explanation

The function accepts three arguments: the value x, and the `low` and `high` limits. It ensures that x stays within this range by returning `low` if it's smaller, or `high` if it's larger.

Usage

Use `constrain()` to keep sensor data, motor speeds, or other outputs within predefined limits, ensuring they don't exceed or fall below a safe range.

Code Example

```
int sensorValue = analogRead(A0);
int constrainedValue = constrain(sensorValue, 0, 1023);
Serial.println(constrainedValue);
```

Notes

This function is essential in safety-critical systems where values must remain within certain boundaries to avoid errors or malfunctions.

Warnings
Ensure that the values for low and high are logical for your system, as improper ranges can lead to issues.

Troubleshooting Tips
If you notice unexpected values, double-check that the ranges for constrain() are correctly set. Also, ensure that your sensor or input data is being read accurately.

2.3 The map () Function: Re-mapping Values

What is map ()?
The map () function re-maps a number from one range to another. For example, it can convert a value from a potentiometer reading between 0 and 1023 to a value between 0 and 255 for LED brightness control. This function is essential when you need to scale data from one range of values to another.

Why is it important?
It's useful when sensor readings or input values need to be adjusted to fit the required output range. For instance, when adjusting motor speed based on sensor input or scaling a temperature reading to control a fan.

Syntax:

```
map(x, in_min, in_max, out_min, out_max)
```

Where x is the input value to map, and the other parameters define the input and output ranges.

Syntax Explanation
map () takes the input value x and maps it from the in_min to in_max range into the out_min to out_max range. This re-scaling ensures that input values are transformed to fit within a specific range for the output.

Usage
Use map () to scale sensor data, such as converting analog input readings from a sensor into a different range for controlling an actuator, motor, or display.

Code Example

```
int sensorValue = analogRead(A0);
int mappedValue = map(sensorValue, 0, 1023, 0, 255);
analogWrite(9, mappedValue);  // Control LED brightness
```

Notes
The map() function is useful in projects where sensor inputs or user inputs like potentiometers need to control outputs like motors or LEDs in a different range.

Warnings
Ensure that the input range matches the expected sensor values, or the output may be inaccurate.

Troubleshooting Tips
If the output isn't behaving as expected, check that the ranges for in_min, in_max, out_min, and out_max are correct and that the sensor readings are within the expected range.

2.4 The max() Function: Ensuring a Minimum Value

What is max()?
The max() function returns the larger of two values. It's often used in cases where you need to ensure a minimum threshold for a value, such as when you want a motor speed or sensor reading to not fall below a certain value.

Why is it important?
It's essential when working with sensor data or controlling actuators, ensuring values don't go below a set minimum that could cause the system to malfunction. For example, ensuring that a fan speed or temperature reading remains within safe limits.

Syntax:

```
max(x, y)
```

Where x and y are the two values, and the function returns the greater of the two.

Syntax Explanation
The function takes two input values, x and y, and compares them. It returns the larger of the two values, ensuring that the output never drops below the threshold.

Usage
Use max () to ensure sensor data or calculated values never drop below a required minimum, ensuring reliable performance in your projects.

Code Example

```
int value1 = 100;
int value2 = 50;
int maxValue = max(value1, value2);   // Returns 100
Serial.println(maxValue);
```

Notes
max () is particularly useful in robotics and sensor data processing where maintaining a minimum threshold ensures reliable performance.

Warnings
Ensure that the comparison values (x and y) are correctly defined, as the result may not behave as expected if the inputs are out of range.

Troubleshooting Tips
If the max () function isn't returning the expected value, check the inputs for accuracy and verify that both values are correctly passed into the function.

2.5 The min() Function: Limiting Values to a Maximum

What is min()?
The min() function returns the smaller of two values. It's commonly used when you need to ensure that a value stays below a certain maximum. For example, when controlling the speed of a motor or processing sensor data, you might want to ensure that values don't exceed a certain safe limit.

Why is it important?
It helps keep values within safe operating limits. Whether you're working with sensor inputs or controlling devices, ensuring that values don't exceed a defined maximum is crucial for safe and reliable performance.

Syntax:

```
min(x, y)
```

Where x and y are the two values to compare, and the smaller value is returned.

Syntax Explanation
The function takes two input values, x and y, and returns the smaller of the two. This ensures that the output never exceeds the specified maximum.

Usage
Use min() to limit sensor data, actuator outputs, or other values to a safe maximum, ensuring system stability and avoiding potential damage to components.

Code Example

```
int value1 = 200;
int value2 = 150;
int minValue = min(value1, value2);   // Returns 150
Serial.println(minValue);
```

Notes
This function is useful for keeping values within safe ranges, especially when working with sensitive devices like motors or sensors.

Warnings
Ensure the values being compared are relevant to the system's limits; improper values could lead to unexpected behavior.

Troubleshooting Tips
If min() isn't producing the expected output, check that the input values are correct and verify that the smaller value is within the system's expected limits.

Quiz: Check Your Understanding of Basic Math Functions

- **What does the constrain() function do?**
  A. It limits a value to fall between a specified minimum and maximum. (Multiple Choice)
- **How do you limit a sensor reading using min()?**
  A. By setting a maximum value that the sensor reading cannot exceed using the min() function. (Fill in the Blank)

---

3. Advanced Math and Trigonometry Functions

3.1 The pow() Function: Raising to a Power

What is pow()?
The pow() function raises a number (the base) to the power of an exponent. This function is useful in many applications where exponential calculations are needed, such as calculating the power consumption of devices, generating curves, or creating exponential growth or decay models.

Why is it important?
pow() is essential for calculations involving exponential values, which are common in physics, engineering, and mathematics. For

example, it is useful when calculating the area of circles or modeling exponential growth in robotics applications.

Syntax:

```
pow(base, exponent)
```

The base is the number to be raised, and the exponent determines the power.

Syntax Explanation

The pow () function raises the base to the power of the exponent. For example, pow (2, 3) returns 8, because 2 raised to the power of 3 equals 8.

Usage

Use pow () in projects where you need to calculate exponential growth or other operations that involve raising numbers to a specific power, like voltage calculations or curve plotting.

Code Example

```
double result = pow(2, 3);  // Result will be 8
Serial.println(result);
```

Notes

This function works with both integers and floating-point numbers, making it versatile for different types of calculations.

Warnings

Ensure the exponent is appropriate for the application, as very high powers can lead to extremely large numbers that exceed the limits of your data type.

Troubleshooting Tips

If results seem incorrect, check the base and exponent values. Ensure you're using the correct data types, as integers and floating-point values may produce different results.

3.2 The sq() Function: Squaring a Value

What is sq()?
The sq() function squares a number, or multiplies it by itself. This is often used in calculations involving areas, distances, or energy, where the squared value is needed.

Why is it important?
Squaring is common in mathematical formulas, especially in geometry and physics. For example, squaring is used when calculating distances between two points or when determining the kinetic energy of an object.

Syntax:

```
sq(x)
```

Where x is the number to be squared.

Syntax Explanation
The sq() function takes a number x and returns the result of multiplying x by itself. For example, sq(4) returns 16.

Usage
Use sq() in projects that require square calculations, such as calculating areas, distances, or other squared values in engineering or physics-based projects.

Code Example

```
int result = sq(4);  // Result will be 16
Serial.println(result);
```

Notes
The sq() function is useful in any situation where you need to square a number, particularly in scientific or mathematical calculations.

Warnings
Make sure you understand when squaring is appropriate; incorrectly squaring values could lead to faulty results.

Troubleshooting Tips
If your results are incorrect, ensure that you're squaring the right values and that your input data is correct.

3.3 The sqrt() Function: Calculating Square Roots

What is sqrt()?
The sqrt() function returns the square root of a number. This function is essential for geometric calculations, such as finding the length of the sides of triangles or calculating distances between two points in 2D or 3D space.

Why is it important?
Calculating square roots is essential in geometry, trigonometry, and physics. It's used in applications like distance measurement, vector calculations, and real-world applications such as computing object movement paths in robotic projects.

Syntax:

```
sqrt(x)
```

Where x is the number to find the square root of.

Syntax Explanation
The sqrt() function calculates the square root of a number. For example, sqrt(16) returns 4 because the square root of 16 is 4. This function is used for values that require calculating geometric proportions or distance.

Usage
Use sqrt() to compute distances, find the magnitude of vectors, or for any calculations that involve square root operations, such as calculating the diagonal of a rectangle.

Code Example

```
float result = sqrt(25);   // Result will be 5
Serial.println(result);
```

Notes
The sqrt () function works with both integers and floating-point numbers, providing flexibility in mathematical calculations.

Warnings
Ensure the value passed to sqrt () is non-negative; otherwise, the result will be undefined for real numbers.

Troubleshooting Tips
If incorrect results occur, check that the value passed into sqrt () is non-negative. Negative values do not have real square roots.

3.4 The cos () Function: Calculating Cosine of an Angle

What is cos () ?
The cos () function returns the cosine of an angle in radians. Cosine is used in trigonometry to find the ratio of the adjacent side to the hypotenuse of a right triangle. This function is critical in geometric and signal processing calculations, such as controlling robot arms or creating waveforms.

Why is it important?
Cosine calculations are crucial in robotics, geometry, and wave signal processing. For instance, cos () can calculate angles when positioning robotic arms or adjusting signals in audio processing. It is also used in navigation and physics simulations.

Syntax:

```
cos(angle)
```

Where angle is the angle in radians.

Syntax Explanation
The cos () function calculates the cosine of an angle measured in radians. For example, cos (PI) returns -1, as the cosine of 180 degrees is -1. This function is widely used in projects involving geometric calculations.

Usage
Use cos () for angle calculations in robotics, wave generation, or to calculate horizontal components of motion in physics-based projects.

Code Example

```
float result = cos(PI/3);  // Result will be 0.5
Serial.println(result);
```

Notes
Remember, angles must be in radians. Convert degrees to radians if needed using radians () or by multiplying degrees by PI/180.

Warnings
Using degrees instead of radians will lead to incorrect results, so ensure the angle is properly converted.

Troubleshooting Tips
If you get wrong results, double-check that the angle is in radians. Use radians (degree) to convert from degrees to radians if necessary.

3.5 The sin () Function: Calculating Sine of an Angle

What is sin ()?
The sin () function returns the sine of an angle measured in radians. In trigonometry, sine refers to the ratio of the length of the opposite side of a right triangle to the hypotenuse. This function is useful for generating waveforms or calculating movement along circular paths.

Why is it important?
Sine functions are widely used in physics, engineering, and robotics

to model waves or periodic motion. For example, sine waves are important in generating sound, controlling motor movements, or modeling natural vibrations and oscillations in systems.

Syntax:

```
sin(angle)
```

Where `angle` is the angle in radians.

Syntax Explanation
The `sin()` function takes an angle in radians and returns its sine. For example, `sin(PI/2)` returns 1 because the sine of 90 degrees (or PI/2 radians) is 1. This function is key in many engineering and mathematical applications.

Usage
Use `sin()` to calculate sine waves in signal processing, robotic arm movements, or any physics-based motion modeling where periodic movement is needed.

Code Example

```
float result = sin(PI/2);  // Result will be 1
Serial.println(result);
```

Notes
Remember to convert degrees to radians when necessary using the formula `radians = degrees * (PI/180)`.

Warnings
Incorrect results may arise if the angle is in degrees instead of radians. Make sure angles are properly converted.

Troubleshooting Tips
If the sine values seem off, verify that the angles are in radians and not degrees. Use `radians()` to handle conversions.

3.6 The tan() Function: Calculating Tangent of an Angle

What is tan()?
The tan() function calculates the tangent of an angle in radians. Tangent is the ratio of the opposite side to the adjacent side in a right triangle. This function is essential for calculating angles in slopes, motion paths, and complex geometrical applications.

Why is it important?
Tangent is used in physics, geometry, and navigation for calculating angles of movement or slopes. In robotics, tan() can help determine the angle of inclination for robot movement, while in graphics, it can be used to calculate perspective projections.

Syntax:

```
tan(angle)
```

Where angle is in radians.

Syntax Explanation
The tan() function computes the tangent of an angle given in radians. For example, tan(PI/4) returns 1 because the tangent of 45 degrees is 1.

Usage
Use tan() in projects requiring angular calculations, slope detection, or calculating the angle of motion in navigation, physics, or geometric modeling.

Code Example

```
float result = tan(PI/4);   // Result will be 1
Serial.println(result);
```

Notes
Ensure the angle is in radians, not degrees. Tangent can also help calculate angles in triangle geometry and physics models.

Warnings

Using degrees instead of radians can lead to wrong results. Always verify the angle format before using tan ().

Troubleshooting Tips

If the output seems wrong, check whether the input angle is in radians. Convert degrees to radians using radians () if needed.

Quiz: Advanced Math and Trigonometry Functionality Check

- **How do you calculate the square root using sqrt ()?**
  A. By using sqrt (x) to return the square root of a number. (Multiple Choice)
- **What does the pow () function do?**
  A. It raises a base number to a specific power (exponent). (Short Answer)

---

4. Practical Projects for Mastering Math and Trigonometry Functions

4.1 **Project 1: Using pow () for Exponential LED Brightness Control**

we explore how to control the brightness of an **LED** using an **exponential curve** rather than a linear one, making the LED brightness more responsive to changes in a **potentiometer's** position. The **pow()** function is used to achieve this exponential control. This makes the brightness more sensitive to changes at lower potentiometer values, providing a smoother and more intuitive experience.

Components List:

- **Arduino**
- **LED**
- **Potentiometer**
- **Resistor** (for current limiting)
- **Wires**

- **Breadboard**

Circuit Diagram: The **potentiometer** is used as an **analog input** to control the **LED brightness**. The **LED** is connected to a **PWM-capable pin** on the Arduino, allowing for brightness control through **analogWrite()**.

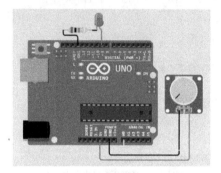

Circuit Connection:

1. Connect the **middle pin** of the potentiometer to an **analog pin** (e.g., A0) on the Arduino.
2. The **two outer pins** of the potentiometer should be connected to **5V** and **GND**.
3. Connect the **LED** (with a current-limiting **resistor**) to a **PWM-capable pin** (e.g., pin 9) of the Arduino.
4. Wire the circuit according to the above description to allow control of LED brightness using the **analogRead()** values from the potentiometer.

Code:

```
int potPin = A0;        // Pin for potentiometer
int ledPin = 9;         // PWM pin for LED
int potValue;
int brightness;
void setup() {
  pinMode(ledPin, OUTPUT);
}

void loop() {
  potValue = analogRead(potPin);                        // Read
potentiometer value (0-1023)
  brightness = pow(potValue / 1023.0, 1.5) * 255;   // Exponential
brightness control
  analogWrite(ledPin, brightness);                      // Write the
brightness to the LED
```

```
   delay(10);                                      // Short delay to
smooth operation
}
```

Code Walkthrough:

1. **Read the Potentiometer Value:** The **analogRead()** function reads the value from the potentiometer (range 0-1023).
2. **Exponential Control Using pow():** The potentiometer value is normalized by dividing by 1023, then raised to the power of **1.5** using **pow()** to create an exponential curve.
3. **Scale to PWM Range:** The result is multiplied by 255 to fit the **PWM** range (0-255), which controls the LED brightness.
4. **Write the Brightness:** The **analogWrite()** function outputs the brightness to the **LED** on a **PWM pin**.

This results in a **non-linear** increase in LED brightness, which feels smoother as the potentiometer is turned.

Challenge: Add a Button for Brightness Control You can modify the project to switch between **linear** and **exponential brightness control** using a **button**. When the button is pressed, the program will toggle between the two modes.

4.2 **Project 2: Calculating Distance Between Two Points using** sqrt()

Calculating Distance Between Two Points using sqrt() focuses on calculating the **distance** between two points in a 2D plane using sensor readings. This is useful for determining distances between objects, and the **Pythagorean theorem** is used to calculate the distance from two sensor values (like an **ultrasonic sensor** and an **accelerometer**).

Components List:

- **Arduino**
- **Ultrasonic sensor** (for distance measurement)
- **Accelerometer** (for x and y axis measurements)
- **Breadboard**
- **Wires**

Circuit Diagram: The **ultrasonic sensor** is used to measure the distance between two objects, and the **accelerometer** provides additional measurements, such as the position of the sensor in a 2D plane.

Circuit Connection:

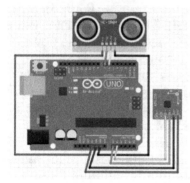

- **Ultrasonic sensor**: Connect the **trigger** pin to a digital pin on the Arduino (e.g., pin 7) and the **echo** pin to another digital pin (e.g., pin 6). The **VCC** and **GND** are connected to 5V and ground on the Arduino.
- **Accelerometer**: Connect the **x-axis** to A0 and the **y-axis** to A1 on the Arduino. The **VCC** and **GND** are connected to the Arduino's 5V and ground.

Code:

```
// Define pins for the ultrasonic sensor
const int trigPin = 7;
const int echoPin = 6;

void setup() {
  Serial.begin(9600);
  pinMode(trigPin, OUTPUT);
  pinMode(echoPin, INPUT);
}

void loop() {
  // Measure distance with ultrasonic sensor
  long duration;
  digitalWrite(trigPin, LOW);
  delayMicroseconds(2);
  digitalWrite(trigPin, HIGH);
  delayMicroseconds(10);
  digitalWrite(trigPin, LOW);

  duration = pulseIn(echoPin, HIGH);
```

```
  float distanceX = (duration * 0.034) / 2; // Distance in cm (for x-
axis)

  // Read accelerometer values for y-axis
  float distanceY = analogRead(A1) * (5.0 / 1023.0); // Analog to
actual value scaling

  // Calculate the distance between two points using the Pythagorean
theorem
  float distance = sqrt(sq(distanceX) + sq(distanceY));

  // Print the calculated distance
  Serial.print("Distance: ");
  Serial.println(distance);

  delay(1000);  // Add delay between measurements
}
```

Code Walkthrough:

1. **Ultrasonic Sensor Measurement**:
   o The **trigger pin** sends a pulse, and the **echo pin** receives the time it takes for the pulse to bounce back. The time is converted into a **distance** (in cm) for the **x-axis**.
2. **Analog Read for Accelerometer**:
   o The **y-axis** distance is obtained from the accelerometer by reading the analog pin and converting the value to a real-world distance using a scaling factor.
3. **Distance Calculation**:
   o The **Pythagorean theorem** is applied: $distance = sqrt(x^2 + y^2)$ to calculate the **distance** between two points based on the x and y distances.
4. **Serial Output**:
   o The calculated distance is displayed on the **Serial Monitor** for verification.

Challenge: Display the Distance on an OLED/LCD Display To make the project more user-friendly, you can add an **OLED** or **LCD** screen to display the calculated distance.

4.3 **Project 3: Creating a Sine Wave for Servo Motor Movement using** $\sin()$

Creating a Sine Wave for Servo Motor Movement using $\sin()$ demonstrates how to achieve smooth, wave-like movements for a **servo motor** by utilising the $\sin()$ function. Instead of linear or abrupt motions, the servo will move in a smooth, **sinusoidal** pattern.

Components List:

- **Arduino**
- **Servo motor**
- **Potentiometer**
- **Breadboard**
- **Wires**

Circuit Diagram: The **servo motor** is controlled by the Arduino through a **PWM pin**, and the **potentiometer** is connected to an analog input to influence the amplitude of the sine wave.

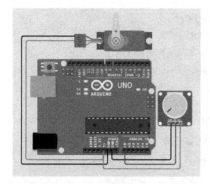

Circuit Connection:

- **Servo motor**: Connect the **signal pin** of the servo to a **PWM pin** (e.g., pin 9) on the Arduino, the **VCC** to 5V, and the **GND** to ground.
- **Potentiometer**: Connect one side to **5V**, the other side to **GND**, and the **wiper (middle pin)** to **A0** on the Arduino. This will be used to adjust the amplitude of the sine wave.

Code:

```
#include <Servo.h>

Servo servo;          // Create a servo object
int potPin = A0;      // Potentiometer pin
int potValue;         // Variable to store the potentiometer value
int angle;            // Servo angle

void setup() {
  servo.attach(9);       // Attach the servo to pin 9
  Serial.begin(9600);    // Begin serial communication for debugging
}

void loop() {
  // Read the potentiometer value
  potValue = analogRead(potPin);

  // Map the potentiometer value to an angle range and generate sine
wave motion
  angle = 90 + 30 * sin(potValue * 0.017);   // Adjust the 0.017 factor
to change wave speed

  // Write the angle to the servo
  servo.write(angle);

  // Print the angle for debugging
  Serial.println(angle);

  // Delay for smooth movement
  delay(15);
}
```

Code Walkthrough:

1. **Servo Setup**: The **Servo library** is included, and the servo is attached to pin 9. The **potentiometer** is connected to pin **A0**.
2. **Read Potentiometer**: The **analogRead()** function reads the potentiometer value, which is mapped to create **wave-like motion**.
3. **Generate Sine Wave**: The formula $angle = 90 + 30 * sin(potValue * 0.017)$ uses the $sin()$ function to generate a smooth oscillation around 90 degrees, with an amplitude of 30 degrees. The value 0.017 is a scaling factor to adjust the speed of the wave.
4. **Control Servo**: The calculated **angle** is sent to the servo motor, making it move in a **smooth, sinusoidal motion**.

5. **Serial Monitor**: The servo angle is printed to the **Serial Monitor** for debugging purposes.

This setup allows for **fluid, natural movement** of the servo motor, controlled by the potentiometer. The potentiometer affects the **amplitude** of the sine wave, adjusting how far the servo swings back and forth.

- **Challenge: Adjust the Wave Frequency with Potentiometer**
  Add another potentiometer to control the frequency of the sine wave, allowing for smoother or faster servo movements.

4.4 Project 4: Mapping Temperature Readings using map () for Fan Speed Control

Mapping Temperature Readings using map () for Fan Speed Control demonstrates how to use sensor data to control the speed of a fan. By using the **map ()** function, the temperature readings from a sensor are scaled to adjust the fan's speed proportionally to changes in temperature, making it a useful project for climate control.

Components List:

- **Arduino**
- **Temperature sensor** (e.g., LM35 or DHT11)
- **Fan**
- **Transistor** (e.g., NPN type like 2N2222)
- **Resistor** (for base of the transistor, typically 1kΩ)
- **Breadboard**
- **Wires**

Circuit Diagram: The **temperature sensor** measures the environment's temperature, and the fan's speed is controlled through the **PWM pin** of the Arduino using a **transistor** as a switch to control the power supplied to the fan.

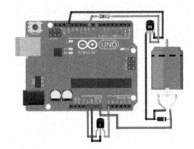

Circuit Connection:

1. **Temperature sensor**:
   - Connect the **VCC** and **GND** of the temperature sensor to 5V and ground on the Arduino.
   - Connect the **output pin** of the sensor to an analog pin (e.g., **A0**) on the Arduino.
2. **Fan control**:
   - Connect the **collector** of the **NPN transistor** to one lead of the **fan**.
   - The other fan lead goes to **5V**.
   - Connect the **emitter** of the transistor to **ground**.
   - The **base** of the transistor is connected to a **PWM pin** (e.g., **pin 9**) on the Arduino via a **1kΩ resistor**.

This setup allows the **PWM signal** from the Arduino to control the fan's speed based on the temperature.

Code:

```
int tempPin = A0;        // Temperature sensor pin
int fanPin = 9;          // PWM pin to control the fan

void setup() {
  pinMode(fanPin, OUTPUT);
  Serial.begin(9600);    // Start serial communication for monitoring
}

void loop() {
  // Read temperature sensor value
  int tempValue = analogRead(tempPin);

  // Map the temperature sensor reading to a fan speed (0-255 for PWM)
  int fanSpeed = map(tempValue, 0, 1023, 0, 255);

  // Output the mapped fan speed to the fan
  analogWrite(fanPin, fanSpeed);
```

```
  // Print temperature and fan speed to the Serial Monitor for
debugging
  Serial.print("Temperature Sensor Value: ");
  Serial.println(tempValue);
  Serial.print("Fan Speed: ");
  Serial.println(fanSpeed);

  delay(500);  // Small delay to stabilize readings
}
```

Code Walkthrough:

- **Reading Temperature**: The **analogRead()** function reads the temperature sensor's output from **A0** (range: 0-1023).
- **Mapping to Fan Speed**: The map () function is used to scale the sensor value (0-1023) to a **PWM** output range (0-255), which corresponds to the fan's speed.
- **Controlling the Fan**: The **analogWrite()** function sends the **PWM signal** to the **fanPin**, controlling the speed of the fan based on the temperature.
- **Serial Output**: Temperature readings and fan speed are printed to the **Serial Monitor** for debugging and observation.

Challenge: Add LED Indicators for Temperature Thresholds
Add LEDs that light up when the temperature reaches specific thresholds, providing a visual indication of environmental changes.

---

5. Common Troubleshooting and Debugging Tips

5.1 **Common Errors and How to Fix Them**

- **What are common errors?**
  Common errors include incorrect data types, using degrees instead of radians in trigonometric functions, and providing out-of-range values for functions like map () or constrain (). These mistakes can lead to inaccurate results or unexpected behavior.
- **Why do they happen?**
  These errors occur due to misunderstanding of function inputs, such as confusing radians and degrees, or using values that exceed the function's expected input range. Proper input validation can prevent these errors.

- **Use of Serial Monitor for debugging**
  The **Serial Monitor** is a valuable tool for debugging. Print sensor values, intermediate calculations, or function outputs to identify where things go wrong. This helps in tracing the source of incorrect behavior in mathematical calculations.

5.2 Optimizing Code for Performance and Accuracy

- **What is code optimization?**
  Code optimization involves improving your program's performance by reducing memory usage and speeding up execution. In Arduino projects, this ensures that calculations are done efficiently and that the system responds quickly to real-time inputs.
- **Why is it important?**
  Optimized code ensures that your Arduino project runs smoothly, without delays or missed inputs. This is especially important in time-sensitive applications, like controlling motors or processing sensor data at high speeds.
- **Tips for performance and accuracy**
  - **Use the right data types**: Use float or int as needed to balance accuracy and speed.
  - **Minimize delays**: Avoid unnecessary delay() calls, and use non-blocking code like millis() to keep the program responsive.
  - **Reduce unnecessary calculations**: Perform calculations only when needed, and store results if possible.

6. Conclusion and Next Steps
6.1 Recap of Key Math and Trigonometry Functions

- **What have we learned?**
  Throughout this chapter, you've explored key math and trigonometry functions in Arduino, such as abs(), pow(), sqrt(), and the trigonometric functions sin(), cos(), and tan(). These functions allow you to handle complex mathematical operations efficiently. You've also seen how these functions are applied in practical projects, from controlling LED brightness with exponential functions to calculating distances and controlling motors with smooth sine

waves. Mastering these functions is essential for building advanced Arduino projects.

Chapter 7: Comparison and Boolean Operators

This chapter explores comparison and Boolean operators that are crucial for making decisions in Arduino projects. Comparison operators such as ==, !=, >, <, >=, and <= are used to compare values, while Boolean operators (&&, ||, !) are used to combine multiple conditions for complex logical decisions. These operators help Arduino programs react to sensor readings, user inputs, or other dynamic data, enabling dynamic control of devices and real-time decision-making.

Syntax Table for Comparison and Boolean Operators

Topic Name	Syntax	Simple Example
Equal To	if (a == b)	if (temperature == 25)
Not Equal To	if (a != b)	if (level != 500)
Greater Than	if (a > b)	if (speed > 100)
Less Than	if (a < b)	if (light < 200)
Greater or Equal To	if (a >= b)	if (score >= 80)
Less or Equal To	if (a <= b)	if (pressure <= 30)
Logical AND	if (a && b)	if (temp > 20 && humidity > 50)
Logical NOT	if (!a)	if (!buttonPressed)

Combining AND & Equal	if (a == b && c == d)	if (sensor1 == 500 && sensor2 == 600)

1. Introduction to Comparison and Boolean Operators

1.1 What are Comparison and Boolean Operators?

What are Comparison and Boolean Operators?
Comparison operators like ==, >, <=, and others, are used in Arduino programs to **compare values**. For instance, == checks if two values are **equal**, and > checks if one value is **greater** than another. **Boolean operators**, such as && (AND), || (OR), and ! (NOT), allow programs to evaluate **multiple conditions** together. For example, && requires that **both conditions** are true, while || only requires **one** condition to be true. These operators play a key role in **decision-making** and **controlling devices** in Arduino projects.

Why are they important?
These operators enable **dynamic control** in Arduino projects. By comparing sensor readings or inputs, you can control devices or trigger actions when specific conditions are met. For instance, you can turn on a fan when the **temperature exceeds 30°C** or stop a motor if an **obstacle** is detected. This kind of **conditional logic** allows programs to react to their environment, making projects more **interactive** and **responsive**. Without comparison and Boolean operators, it would be difficult to implement **real-time decision-making**.

1.2 Key Concepts and Terms (Glossary)

What is a Comparison Operator?
A **comparison operator** compares two values and returns **true** or **false**. Examples include == (equal), > (greater than), and != (not equal). They are used in **if statements** and loops to make decisions.

What is a Boolean Operator?
A **Boolean operator** combines or modifies **logical conditions**. Examples include && (AND), || (OR), and ! (NOT). These operators help evaluate **multiple conditions** together, making your program respond to more complex inputs.

Common Operators and Their Roles:

- **== (Equal To)**
  Checks if **two values** are exactly **equal**. For example, if (x == 5) returns true only if **x is 5**. This operator is crucial for comparing variables in decision-making.
- **!= (Not Equal To)**
  Checks if **two values are different**. For instance, if (x != 10) returns true if **x is not equal to 10**. It's useful when you want to **exclude** a specific value.
- **&& (Logical AND)**
  Returns **true** only if **both conditions** are true. For example, if (a > 5 && b < 10) is true only if **a is greater than 5** and **b is less than 10**.
- **|| (Logical OR)**
  Returns **true** if **either condition** is true. For example, if (a == 5 || b == 10) will be true if **either** a equals 5 **or** b equals 10.

1.3 Overview of Core Comparison and Boolean Operators

What are Core Operators?
Core comparison operators like ==, !=, >, <, >=, and <= are essential for **evaluating relationships** between values. They allow programs to check whether a value is **equal**, **greater**, or **less than** another. Boolean operators like && and || further enable combining multiple **conditions**. For instance, you could check if a **sensor value** exceeds a threshold and if a button is pressed at the same time. These operators work together to allow **complex decision-making** in your program.

Why are they important?
These operators are essential for making programs **intelligent** and
dynamic. Without them, your program would always behave the
same way, without considering the current state of its environment.
By using comparison operators, your program can **react** to real-time
inputs from **sensors** or **user interactions**. Boolean operators let
you handle multiple conditions at once, such as turning on a light
only when the **room is dark** and **motion is detected**. This allows
Arduino projects to function with more **flexibility** and **control**.

**Quiz: Test Your Understanding of Comparison and Boolean
Operators**

1. **What is the role of the == operator?**
   - A) To assign values
   - B) To compare if two values are equal
   - C) To subtract values
   - **Answer: B**
2. **How does the && operator function in a conditional
   statement?**
   The && operator returns **true** only if **both conditions** are
   true.
3. **Which operator would you use to check if two values are
   not equal?**
   You would use the != operator to check if two values are not
   equal.

2. Core Comparison Operators

2.1 The == (Equal To) Operator

What is ==?
The == operator in Arduino is used to check if **two values are equal**.
When two values or variables are compared using ==, the result is
true if they are the same, and **false** if they are not. This is often
used in **conditional statements** to check whether a specific
condition is met. For example, checking if a **sensor reading** equals
a certain threshold.

Why is it important?

The == operator is important for **making decisions** in Arduino programs. It allows you to perform actions only when **two values match**, such as turning on a light when a **button is pressed** or triggering an alarm when a **temperature exceeds a limit**. Without it, comparing values in conditions would be difficult.

Syntax

The basic syntax of the == operator is:

```
if (a == b) {
  // Do something
}
```

This checks whether **a** and **b** are equal.

Syntax Explanation

In this syntax, the condition a == b checks if the values of **a** and **b** are **equal**. If they are, the **code block** inside the curly braces is executed. This operator is used in **if statements** to make decisions based on the comparison.

Usage

The == operator is used when you need to **compare two values** and perform an action if they match. For example, you can compare a **sensor reading** with a pre-defined value to trigger a response, such as turning on an LED.

Code Example

Here's an example comparing two sensor values:

```
int sensor1 = analogRead(A0);
int sensor2 = analogRead(A1);

if (sensor1 == sensor2) {
  digitalWrite(LED_BUILTIN, HIGH);  // Turn on LED if sensors are equal
}
```

This code checks if **sensor1** and **sensor2** have the same reading. If they are equal, the **LED** turns on.

Notes

Always use == to **compare** values, and remember that using just = assigns a value, which is not the same as comparing.

Warnings

Be careful not to confuse the == operator with the = operator, which is used for **assignment**. Using = instead of == will lead to unexpected behavior.

Troubleshooting Tips

If your condition using == isn't working as expected, check:

- Are you using == instead of =?
- Are the two values you're comparing really equal? Use Serial.print() to print their values and see.
  This can help you debug issues in your comparison logic.

2.2 The != (Not Equal To) Operator

What is !=?

The != operator checks whether **two values are not equal**. If the values are different, it returns **true**, and if they are the same, it returns **false**. This operator is helpful when you need to perform an action **only when two values don't match**. For example, checking if a sensor reading **differs** from a target value.

Why is it important?

The != operator is essential when you want to trigger an action when **two values don't match**. For example, you might want to turn off a fan when the **temperature is not within a specific range**. This is crucial in programs where avoiding certain conditions is important.

Syntax

The basic syntax of the != operator is:

```
if (a != b) {
   // Do something
}
```

This checks if **a** and **b** are **not equal**.

Syntax Explanation
In this syntax, the condition a != b checks if the values of **a** and **b** are **different**. If they are not equal, the **code block** inside the curly braces is executed. It is used in **if statements** to take actions when values don't match.

Usage
The != operator is commonly used when you want to **check for differences** between two values. For example, if a sensor's reading is **not equal** to a certain threshold, you can trigger an action, such as turning off a device.

Code Example
Here's an example of comparing a sensor reading to a threshold:

```
int sensorValue = analogRead(A0);
int threshold = 500;

if (sensorValue != threshold) {
  digitalWrite(LED_BUILTIN, LOW);  // Turn off LED if not equal to
threshold
}
```

This code checks if the **sensor value** is not equal to **500**. If it's different, the **LED** turns off.

Notes
The != operator is commonly used to ensure an action is triggered when values do **not match**. This is important when excluding specific conditions in your logic.

Warnings
Make sure you're using != when checking for **inequality**. Using == instead will only check for equality, which might not achieve your goal.

Troubleshooting Tips
If the != condition isn't working:

- Ensure that the values you're comparing are **different** as expected. Use **Serial.print()** to check the values.
- Check if you accidentally used == instead of !=. Printing the values helps you verify the cause.

2.3 The > (Greater Than) Operator

What is >?
The > operator checks if the value on the **left** side is **greater than** the value on the **right**. If the left value is greater, it returns **true**; otherwise, it returns **false**. This operator is typically used when comparing **numerical values**, such as checking if a sensor reading exceeds a specific threshold.

Why is it important?
The > operator is important when you want to compare values and take action only when a **value is larger** than another. For example, if the **temperature reading** is higher than a set point, the program can turn on a cooling device.

Syntax
The basic syntax of the > operator is:

```
if (a > b) {
  // Do something
}
```

This checks if **a** is greater than **b**.
Syntax Explanation
In this syntax, a > b compares two **values**. If a is **greater** than b, the **code block** inside the curly braces is executed. This is useful for **decision-making** based on sensor readings or other numerical inputs.
Usage
The > operator is often used when checking if a **sensor value** exceeds a specific threshold. For example, you can use this operator to turn on a fan if the **temperature** exceeds a certain level.

Code Example
Here's an example comparing sensor values:

```
int temperature = analogRead(A0);

if (temperature > 30) {
  digitalWrite(LED_BUILTIN, HIGH);   // Turn on LED if temperature
exceeds 30
```

```
}
```

This code turns on an LED if the **temperature** is greater than **30**.

Troubleshooting Tips
If the > condition doesn't seem to work:

- Check that you're comparing **numerical values**.
- Print the **sensor reading** to confirm the value is actually greater.
  Using **Serial.print()** helps you debug this issue.

2.4 The < (Less Than) Operator

What is <?
The < operator checks if the value on the **left** side is **less than** the value on the **right**. If the left value is smaller, it returns **true**; otherwise, it returns **false**. This operator is often used when comparing **sensor readings** or other values that need to be below a certain threshold.

Why is it important?
The < operator is essential when you need to check if a **value falls below** a certain point. For example, in a temperature control system, you may want to turn on a heater when the temperature is below a set threshold.

Syntax
The basic syntax of the < operator is:

```
if (a < b) {
  // Do something
}
```

This checks if **a** is less than **b**.

Syntax Explanation
In this syntax, a < b compares **two values**. If **a** is **less** than **b**, the code inside the curly braces is executed. This operator is widely

used in Arduino projects to **control devices** based on **sensor thresholds**.

Usage
The $<$ operator is commonly used in Arduino projects for **threshold-based actions**. For example, it can be used to turn on a heater when the **temperature** is below a certain value.

Code Example
Here's an example comparing a sensor reading to a threshold:

```
int lightLevel = analogRead(A0);

if (lightLevel < 500) {
  digitalWrite(LED_BUILTIN, HIGH);   // Turn on LED if light level is
low
}
```

This code turns on the **LED** if the **light level** is below **500**.

Troubleshooting Tips
If your $<$ condition isn't working, verify that:

- You're comparing the **correct values**.
- The **sensor reading** is indeed lower than the threshold. Use **Serial.print()** to display values for troubleshooting.

Quiz: Check Your Understanding of Comparison Operators

1. **What does the != operator do?**
   - A) Checks if values are equal
   - B) Checks if values are not equal
   - C) Assigns a value
   - **Answer: B**
2. **How does the == operator validate equality?**
   The == operator checks if **two values are the same**.

FAQ: Common Questions about Comparison Operators

1. **What's the difference between == and = in Arduino?**
   == compares two values, while = is used for **assigning** values.
2. **Can I compare different data types using comparison operators?**
   Yes, but it's important to be aware that comparing **different data types** (like int and float) can sometimes give **unexpected results**.

3. Core Boolean Operators

3.1 The && (Logical AND) Operator

What is &&?
The && operator, also known as **Logical AND**, is used to check if **both conditions** in a statement are true. If **both** conditions are met, the statement returns **true** and executes the corresponding code. If **either** condition is false, the statement returns **false** and the code is skipped. For example, you can use && to check if two sensors meet certain conditions before taking an action.

Why is it important?
The && operator is essential when you need **multiple conditions** to be true for an action to occur. It ensures that an action is only triggered when **both conditions** are met, making your program **more precise**. For example, you could ensure a fan only turns on if **both the temperature and humidity** exceed set values.

Syntax
The basic syntax of the && operator is:

```
if (a > b && c == d) {
  // Do something
}
```

This checks if **both conditions** are true.

Syntax Explanation
In this syntax, a > b && c == d checks if **two conditions** are true at the same time. If both conditions are met, the **code inside** the curly braces is executed. This operator is commonly used to ensure that **multiple criteria** are satisfied before triggering an action.

Usage
The && operator is useful when you want to check if **two conditions** are true simultaneously. For example, if **two sensors** both detect a certain condition, you might want to activate a device. This ensures the system reacts only when **both conditions** are met.

Code Example
Here's an example using && to check two sensor conditions:

```
int temp = analogRead(A0);
int humidity = analogRead(A1);

if (temp > 30 && humidity > 70) {
  digitalWrite(LED_BUILTIN, HIGH);   // Turn on LED if both conditions
are true
}
```

This code turns on the LED only if both the **temperature** is above 30 and **humidity** is above 70.

Troubleshooting Tips
If the && condition isn't working:

- Check that **both conditions** are true.
- Use Serial.print() to print the values of both conditions and verify if they meet the criteria.
  This helps you identify why the code block is not executing.

3.2 The || (Logical OR) Operator

What is ||?
The || operator, also called **Logical OR**, checks if **at least one** of the conditions is true. If either condition is true, the statement returns **true** and the code runs. If **both conditions** are false, the statement returns **false**. This operator is useful when you want an action to occur if **any one of several conditions** is met, such as triggering a response when one of multiple sensors detects a change.

Why is it important?
The || operator is important when you want an action to happen if **any one** of multiple conditions is true. It allows flexibility by ensuring that the system reacts even if only **one condition** is satisfied. For example, turning on an alarm when **either** temperature or humidity exceeds a certain value.

Syntax
The basic syntax of the || operator is:

```
if (a == b || c == d) {
  // Do something
}
```

This checks if **either condition** is true.

Syntax Explanation
In this syntax, a == b || c == d checks if **either condition** is true. If one or both conditions are true, the **code block** inside the curly braces is executed. This operator is commonly used to create programs that can react to **multiple possible inputs**.

Usage
The || operator is useful when you want a program to react if **any one** of multiple conditions is true. For example, turning on a light when **either** a **motion sensor** detects movement or a **light sensor** reads darkness.

Code Example
Here's an example of using || to trigger an action based on two sensors:

```
int motion = digitalRead(2);
int light = analogRead(A0);

if (motion == HIGH || light < 200) {
  digitalWrite(LED_BUILTIN, HIGH);   // Turn on LED if motion detected
or light is low
}
```

This code turns on the LED if **motion** is detected or if the **light level**
is below 200.

Troubleshooting Tips
If the || condition isn't working:

- Ensure that **at least one condition** is true.
- Use Serial.print() to check the values of the conditions
  and confirm that at least one meets the criteria.

3.3 The ! (Logical NOT) Operator

What is !?
The ! operator, also known as **Logical NOT**, is used to **negate a
condition**. If the condition is true, ! makes it **false**, and if the
condition is false, ! makes it **true**. This operator is useful when you
want to **reverse** a condition, such as checking if something **is not**
happening, like when a sensor is **not triggered**.

Why is it important?
The ! operator is important for situations where you want to check if
something **is not true**. For example, you might use it to check if a
button **is not pressed** or if a sensor **is not activated**. It's often used
for making sure conditions are **opposite** of the usual logic.

Syntax
The basic syntax of the ! operator is:

```
if (!a) {
  // Do something
}
```

This checks if **a** is **not true**.

Syntax Explanation
In this syntax, !a checks whether the condition **a** is **false**. If **a** is false, the **code block** inside the curly braces will execute. This is helpful when you want to ensure that an action is triggered when a condition is **not met**.

Usage
The ! operator is useful when you want to check if something **is not happening**. For example, turning on a light when a button **is not pressed**, or turning off a motor when a sensor **is not activated**.

Code Example
Here's an example of using ! to check if a button is not pressed:

```
int button = digitalRead(2);

if (!button) {
  digitalWrite(LED_BUILTIN, HIGH);  // Turn on LED if button is not
pressed
}
```

This code turns on the LED when the **button is not pressed**.

Troubleshooting Tips
If the ! condition isn't working:

- Check if the condition you're negating is actually **false** when you expect it to be.
- Use Serial.print() to check the value of the condition before applying !.

Quiz: Test Your Boolean Operator Knowledge

1. **How does the && operator function in multiple conditions?**
   The && operator returns **true** only if **both conditions** are true.
2. **When should you use the ! operator in a condition?**
   Use the ! operator when you want to check if something **is not true**.

4. Combining Comparison and Boolean Operators

4.1 Using == and && Together

What are == and &&?
The == operator checks if **two values are equal**, while the && operator ensures that **two or more conditions** are true at the same time. Combining them allows you to check if multiple conditions are true, and if the conditions match a specific value. This combination is useful when you want to ensure that **all criteria** are met before triggering an action.

Why is it important?
Combining == and && is important for **precise control** in Arduino projects. For example, you may want to check if a **button is pressed** and a **sensor reading** equals a certain value at the same time. This ensures the program only responds when **both conditions** are satisfied.

Syntax
The basic syntax for combining == and && is:

```
if (a == b && c == d) {
  // Do something
}
```

This checks if **both comparisons** are true.

Syntax Explanation
In this syntax, a == b && c == d checks if **two conditions** are true: both a == b and c == d. If both conditions are met, the **code block**

inside the curly braces will execute. This ensures that multiple conditions must be true simultaneously before triggering an action.

Usage
Use this combination when you need **two or more equalities** to be true before taking an action. For example, you can check if **two sensors** have reached specific values before turning on a device or activating an alert.

Code Example
Here's an example using == and && together to check two sensor conditions:

```
int sensor1 = analogRead(A0);
int sensor2 = analogRead(A1);

if (sensor1 == 500 && sensor2 == 600) {
  digitalWrite(LED_BUILTIN, HIGH);  // Turn on LED if both sensor
values match
}
```

This code turns on the LED if **sensor1** equals **500** and **sensor2** equals **600**.

Troubleshooting Tips
If the combined condition using == and && isn't working:

- Use Serial.print() to verify the values of the **sensors** and check if both conditions are met.
- Ensure that **both conditions** are actually true for the code to execute.

4.2 Using != and || Together

What are != and ||?
The != operator checks if **two values are not equal**, while the ||
operator checks if **at least one** condition is true. When combined,
you can check if **either one or both conditions are true** and if **one
value is not equal** to another. This is useful when you want to take
action when at least one condition is true, but you also want to
ensure that certain values **don't match**.

Why is it important?
The combination of != and || is useful when you want to trigger an
action based on **multiple possible conditions**, but also ensure that
a value is **not equal** to something. For instance, you can use it to
check if **either of two sensor readings** differ from a specific value.

Syntax
The basic syntax for combining != and || is:

```
if (a != b || c != d) {
    // Do something
}
```

This checks if **either comparison is not true**.

Syntax Explanation
In this syntax, a != b || c != d checks if **either of the conditions**
is true: a != b or c != d. If at least one of these conditions is true,
the **code block** inside the curly braces will execute. This ensures
flexibility when checking multiple possible conditions.

Usage
Use this combination when you want to take action if **either of two
values is not equal** to something. For example, if **either of two
sensor readings** is outside the expected range, you can trigger a
warning or alert.

Code Example
Here's an example using != and || together:

```
int temp = analogRead(A0);
int humidity = analogRead(A1);
```

```
if (temp != 30 || humidity != 70) {
  digitalWrite(LED_BUILTIN, HIGH);   // Turn on LED if either condition
is not met
}
```

This code turns on the LED if **temperature** is not 30 or **humidity** is
not 70.

Troubleshooting Tips
If the combined condition using != and || isn't working:

- Check if **either condition** is false. Use Serial.print() to
  verify the sensor values.
- Make sure that you're expecting one or both conditions to be
  unequal.

Quiz: Mastering Complex Conditions

1. **How can == and && be combined to check multiple
   conditions?**
   They can be combined to ensure **both conditions** are true
   at the same time before an action is triggered.
2. **What does != || mean when used in a conditional
   statement?**
   It means that the condition will be true if **either** of the values
   is not equal to the specified condition.

5. Practical Projects for Mastering Comparison and Boolean Operators

5.1 Project 1: Smart Temperature and Humidity Control System

This project focuses on building a smart temperature and humidity control system using an Arduino microcontroller and a DHT11 or DHT22 sensor. The system is designed to read temperature and humidity levels from the environment and automatically control a fan and heater based on the data received. By utilizing conditional logic and comparison operators (==, >, <, &&, ||), the system decides whether to turn the fan or heater on or off, ensuring optimal environmental conditions.

Why is it important?

The importance of this project lies in its practical application of conditional logic and Boolean operators to control devices in real-time. It illustrates how environmental conditions can be regulated automatically, which is a fundamental concept in smart home systems or automated HVAC systems (heating, ventilation, and air conditioning). The project helps in understanding how smart systems can dynamically respond to changes in temperature and humidity, making it essential for energy efficiency and comfort in residential or industrial setups.

Components List

- **Arduino**: Microcontroller for processing sensor data and controlling devices.
- **DHT11/DHT22 (temperature and humidity sensor)**: Sensor used to measure environmental temperature and humidity.
- **Relay module**: Acts as a switch to control the fan and heater based on sensor inputs.
- **Fan**: Cools the environment when temperature or humidity exceeds thresholds.
- **Heater (optional)**: Warms the environment when temperature or humidity drops below thresholds.

- **Wires**: Connect all components to the Arduino.

Circuit Diagram

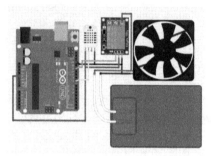

- **DHT11/DHT22 sensor**:
  - VCC to 5V
  - GND to ground
  - Data pin to digital pin 2 of Arduino
- **Relay module**: Connects to the fan and heater, with control signals coming from Arduino's digital output pins to switch devices on and off.

Circuit Connection

1. **DHT Sensor**: Connect the DHT sensor to the Arduino for temperature and humidity measurement.
2. **Relay Module**: The relay module controls the fan and heater based on the sensor readings. Depending on the environmental thresholds, the relay switches on the appropriate device (fan or heater) via the digital pins of the Arduino.
3. **Fan and Heater**: Connect the fan to digital pin 8 and the heater (optional) to digital pin 9. The relay activates the devices based on temperature and humidity conditions.

Code

```
#include <DHT.h>
#define DHTPIN 2
#define DHTTYPE DHT11

DHT dht(DHTPIN, DHTTYPE);

void setup() {
  pinMode(8, OUTPUT);   // Fan
  pinMode(9, OUTPUT);   // Heater
  dht.begin();
}

void loop() {
  float temp = dht.readTemperature();
  float humidity = dht.readHumidity();

  // Check if the readings are valid
  if (isnan(temp) || isnan(humidity)) {
    Serial.println("Failed to read from DHT sensor!");
    return;
  }

  // Logic for controlling the fan and heater
  if (temp > 25 && humidity > 60) {
    digitalWrite(8, HIGH);   // Turn on fan
    digitalWrite(9, LOW);    // Turn off heater
  } else if (temp < 18 || humidity < 40) {
    digitalWrite(9, HIGH);   // Turn on heater
    digitalWrite(8, LOW);    // Turn off fan
  } else {
    // Normal conditions, turn both off
    digitalWrite(8, LOW);    // Turn off fan
    digitalWrite(9, LOW);    // Turn off heater
  }

  delay(2000);   // Wait for 2 seconds before reading again
}
```

Code Walkthrough

1. **DHT Sensor Initialization**: The DHT object is created to read temperature and humidity from the sensor connected to pin 2 of the Arduino.
2. **Setup Function**: Pin modes are defined for the fan (pin 8) and heater (pin 9). The DHT sensor is initialized using dht.begin().
3. **Loop Function**:

- The system continuously reads temperature and humidity values using dht.readTemperature() and dht.readHumidity().
- **Validation**: If readings are invalid (isnan()), an error message is printed, and the loop skips to the next iteration.
- **Comparison Logic**:
  - If temperature is above 25°C **and** humidity is above 60%, the fan turns on, and the heater turns off.
  - If temperature is below 18°C **or** humidity is below 40%, the heater turns on, and the fan turns off.
  - If temperature and humidity are within the normal range ($18°C \leq$ temp $\leq 25°C$ and $40\% \leq$ humidity $\leq 60\%$), both the fan and heater remain off.
4. **Delay**: The system waits for 2 seconds before repeating the process to prevent excessive readings.

Challenge:
Add an **LCD display** to show the current **temperature**, **humidity**, and whether the **fan** or **heater** is active. This will provide real-time feedback for users.

5.2 Project 2: Home Security System with Multiple Sensors and Alarms

This project creates a **home security system** using multiple **sensors** like a **PIR motion sensor** and a **door switch**. When **motion is detected** or a **door is opened**, the system triggers an **alarm** using a **buzzer** and **LEDs**. The system relies on **comparison** and **Boolean operators** to evaluate sensor inputs and activate the alarm based on different conditions.

Why is it important?
This project demonstrates how to build a **security system** that responds to multiple **potential threats**. By using **comparison** and

Boolean operators like ==, !=, &&, ||, you can create a system that handles multiple sensor inputs and makes more **complex decisions**. This approach is essential for creating smart, automated **security responses**.

Components List:

- **Arduino**
- **PIR motion sensor**
- **Door switch**
- **Buzzer**
- **LEDs**
- Resistors
- Wires

Circuit Diagram

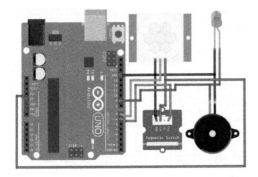

- **PIR sensor** connected to a **digital input pin** (e.g., pin 7).
- **Door switch** connected to another **input pin** (e.g., pin 6).
- **Buzzer** and **LEDs** connected to **output pins** for alarms.

Circuit Connection

- The **PIR sensor** detects **motion**, while the **door switch** detects if the **door is opened**.
- The **buzzer** and **LEDs** provide **audible** and **visual alerts**.
- If **motion is detected** or the **door is opened**, the **alarm is activated**.

Code

```
int motionPin = 7;
int doorPin = 6;
int alarmPin = 9;

void setup() {
  pinMode(motionPin, INPUT);
  pinMode(doorPin, INPUT);
  pinMode(alarmPin, OUTPUT);
}

void loop() {
  int motionDetected = digitalRead(motionPin);
  int doorOpened = digitalRead(doorPin);

  if (motionDetected == HIGH || doorOpened == HIGH) {
    digitalWrite(alarmPin, HIGH);  // Turn on alarm
  } else {
    digitalWrite(alarmPin, LOW);   // Turn off alarm
  }
}
```

Code Walkthrough

- The code reads inputs from the **PIR motion sensor** and **door switch**.
- Using the **|| (OR) operator**, it checks if **either condition** (motion detected or door opened) is **true**.
- If either is **true**, the **alarm is triggered** by turning on the **buzzer**.
- If both conditions are **false**, the **alarm is turned off**.

Challenge:
Add a **keypad** to allow users to enter a code to disable the alarm. This requires using char comparisons to check if the entered code matches a preset code.

5.3 Project 3: Automated Garden Watering System with Multiple Conditions

This project involves creating an **automated garden watering system** that uses a **soil moisture sensor** and a **real-time clock (RTC)** to decide when to water the garden. The system uses **comparison** and **Boolean operators** to ensure that watering occurs only when the soil is **dry** and during specific **times of the day**.

Why is it important?
This project combines **sensor-based automation** and **time-based control** to ensure efficient water usage. It demonstrates how to use **comparison operators** to water the garden **only when necessary**, preventing **water waste**. The system uses **Boolean logic** to check multiple conditions, such as soil moisture and time, ensuring the garden is watered optimally.

Components List:

- **Arduino**
- **Soil moisture sensor**
- **RTC module**
- **Relay module**
- **Water pump**
- Wires

Circuit Diagram

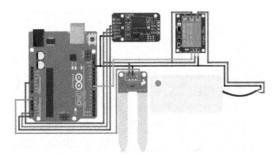

- The **soil moisture sensor** is connected to an **analog pin** (e.g., A0).

- The **RTC module** connects via **I2C pins** (SDA and SCL).
- The **relay module** controls the **water pump**.

Circuit Connection

- The **soil moisture sensor** measures the **moisture level** of the soil.
- The **RTC module** keeps track of the **current time**.
- The **relay** activates the **water pump** when the set conditions for moisture and time are met.

Code

```cpp
#include <Wire.h>
#include <RTClib.h>

RTC_DS3231 rtc;

void setup() {
  Serial.begin(9600); // Optional for debugging
  pinMode(A0, INPUT);  // Soil moisture sensor
  pinMode(8, OUTPUT);  // Water pump relay

  if (!rtc.begin()) {
    Serial.println("Couldn't find RTC");
    while (1);  // Stop the program if the RTC module isn't found
  }

  if (rtc.lostPower()) {
    Serial.println("RTC lost power, setting time!");
    rtc.adjust(DateTime(F(__DATE__), F(__TIME__)));  // Set time to
when the sketch was compiled
  }
}

void loop() {
  int moistureLevel = analogRead(A0);  // Read soil moisture level
  DateTime now = rtc.now();  // Get current time from RTC

  // Debugging information (optional)
  Serial.print("Moisture Level: ");
  Serial.println(moistureLevel);
  Serial.print("Current Hour: ");
  Serial.println(now.hour());

  // If soil is dry and it's between 6 AM and 8 AM
  if (moistureLevel < 400 && now.hour() >= 6 && now.hour() <= 8) {
    digitalWrite(8, HIGH);  // Turn on water pump
  } else {
    digitalWrite(8, LOW);   // Turn off water pump
  }

  delay(5000);  // Check conditions every 5 seconds
}
```

Code Walkthrough

- **Soil moisture sensor** measures the moisture level and sends an analog value to the Arduino.
- The **RTC module** provides the current time, allowing the system to check if it is within the watering period.
- **Comparison operators** are used to check two conditions:
    1. If the **moisture level** is below a certain threshold (400, indicating dry soil).
    2. If the **current time** is between **6 AM and 8 AM**.
- If both conditions are true, the **water pump is activated**. If either condition is false, the pump remains off.

Challenge:

Add a **rain sensor** to prevent the system from watering the garden during rainfall. This would require adding another condition to the logic to check if rain is detected.

5.4 Project 4: Traffic Light System with Emergency Vehicle Detection

---

This project creates a **traffic light system** that gives **priority to emergency vehicles** using an **ultrasonic sensor**. When an **emergency vehicle** is detected within a certain distance, the system overrides the regular traffic light sequence, giving priority to the emergency vehicle. The system uses **comparison** and **Boolean operators** to manage both normal traffic flow and emergency overrides.

Why is it important?
This project simulates a **real-world traffic management system** that prioritizes **emergency vehicles**, ensuring they can move through intersections without delays. It shows how **conditional logic** can be used to **override normal operations** during critical conditions, demonstrating how **comparison** and **Boolean operators** allow for efficient decision-making in time-sensitive scenarios.

Components List:

- **Arduino**
- **Ultrasonic sensor**
- **RGB LEDs** (for traffic light simulation)
- **Resistors**
- **Wires**

Circuit Diagram

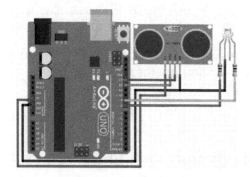

- The **ultrasonic sensor** detects the distance of approaching vehicles and is connected to **digital pins** for distance measurement.
- **RGB LEDs** simulate the traffic lights, with each color (red, yellow, green) connected to separate **output pins**.

Circuit Connection

- The **ultrasonic sensor** is connected to the Arduino and measures the distance to approaching vehicles.
- **RGB LEDs** are connected to digital pins to control the red and green lights for the traffic light system.
- The system switches between normal traffic light operation and **emergency vehicle detection mode** based on the distance measured by the ultrasonic sensor.

Code

```
#include <Ultrasonic.h>
Ultrasonic ultrasonic(12, 13);   // Trigger pin = 12, Echo pin = 13

void setup() {
  pinMode(8, OUTPUT);   // Red light
  pinMode(9, OUTPUT);   // Green light
  Serial.begin(9600);   // Optional: Start the Serial monitor for
debugging
}

void loop() {
  int distance = ultrasonic.read();   // Read distance from ultrasonic
sensor

  // Debugging: Print the distance to the Serial Monitor
  Serial.print("Distance: ");
  Serial.println(distance);

  // Control lights based on distance
  if (distance < 50) {
    digitalWrite(8, HIGH);   // Turn on red light for emergency vehicle
    digitalWrite(9, LOW);    // Turn off green light
  } else {
    digitalWrite(9, HIGH);   // Normal green light
    digitalWrite(8, LOW);    // Turn off red light
  }

  delay(200);   // Small delay to stabilize the sensor reading and avoid
flickering
}
```

Code Walkthrough

- The **ultrasonic sensor** measures the **distance** of an approaching vehicle.
- If a vehicle is detected within **50 cm**, the system turns on the **red light**, stopping normal traffic to allow the emergency vehicle to pass.
- If no emergency vehicle is detected, the **green light** remains on, simulating **normal traffic flow**.
- The code uses **comparison operators** to check the distance and **Boolean logic** to control the **traffic light** system based on the sensor's reading.

Chapter 8. Random Numbers in Arduino

Chapter 8 explores the concept of random number generation in Arduino programming. Random numbers are generated using the `random()` function, which produces pseudo-random numbers that seem unpredictable but follow a sequence based on an initial condition called the seed. This chapter also covers the `randomSeed()` function, which allows control over the sequence by setting the starting point, adding true variability to random number generation. Random numbers are vital for creating unpredictability in projects like games, simulations, or testing systems with fluctuating data, making the outcomes more dynamic and realistic.

Syntax Table: Arduino Random Number Functions

Topic Name	Syntax	Simple Example
Generating Random Numbers	`random(min, max)`	`int randomValue = random(0, 10); // Result: 0-9`
Initializing Random Number Generator	`randomSeed(value)`	`randomSeed(analogRead(A0));`

1. Introduction to Random Numbers in Arduino

1.1 What are Random Numbers in Arduino?

What are Random Numbers?

In Arduino, random numbers are generated using the `random()` function. These numbers are *pseudo-random*, meaning they follow a sequence that seems random but is actually predetermined based on the initial conditions, called the seed. The random number generator in Arduino is useful for creating unpredictability in projects, such as in games, simulations, or even controlling LED patterns. This randomness can be used to add variability to outputs or to test systems under different conditions.

Why are they important?
Random numbers play a key role in various applications. In simulations, they add unpredictability, making the outcomes more realistic. In games, random numbers decide events or actions, making the game more exciting. Additionally, random numbers can help test systems with fluctuating data, simulating real-world sensor behavior. Without random numbers, many projects would have predictable and repetitive results, reducing the effectiveness of simulations and interactivity.

1.2 **Key Concepts and Terms (Glossary)**

What is random()?
The random() function generates pseudo-random numbers. These numbers seem random but follow a pattern based on the seed.

Why is it important?
It is used to introduce unpredictability into programs, such as games or sensor testing, by generating different outputs each time.

What is randomSeed()?
The randomSeed() function sets the starting point (seed) for random number generation, ensuring varied sequences of random numbers.

Why is it important?
Without seeding, random() will generate the same sequence every time the program runs, reducing variability and realism.

1.3 **Overview of Core Random Number Functions**

What are Core Random Number Functions?
The two core functions are random() and randomSeed(). random() generates pseudo-random numbers in a specified range, adding variability to outputs. randomSeed() sets the initial value for the random number generator, ensuring different results each time the program is run. Together, they allow you to control randomness and ensure that your project behaves unpredictably in useful ways.

Why are they important?

These functions are crucial for introducing variability in games, simulations, and testing systems that require random inputs. For example, in a game, random numbers can be used to determine when an obstacle appears or how fast it moves. In simulations, they are useful for modeling real-world unpredictability, such as random sensor readings. They are also helpful in testing how systems react to different random inputs.

Quiz: Test Your Understanding of Random Numbers

- **What is the purpose of random()?**
  A. To generate a random number between two specified limits. (Multiple Choice)
- **How does randomSeed() work?**
  A. It initializes the random number generator, ensuring different results each time the program is run. (Short Answer)
- **How do you generate a random number between 0 and 9 using random()?**
  A. By using random(0, 10). (Fill in the Blank)

---

2. Basic Random Number Functions

2.1 The random() Function: Generating Random Numbers

What is random()?

The random() function generates pseudo-random numbers within a specified range. It can take two parameters, a minimum and a maximum value, and it returns a number between these values. If you only provide one value, it generates a number between 0 and that value.

Why is it important?

random() is crucial for adding variability to programs, making them more dynamic. For example, it can randomize the position of game objects, control LED patterns, or simulate fluctuating sensor readings.

Syntax:

```
random(min, max)
```

Where `min` is the lower limit and `max` is the upper limit.

Syntax Explanation
The `random()` function returns a number between `min` and `max` − 1. If only one argument is provided, it generates a number from 0 to that value.

Usage
Use `random()` in projects where outputs need to vary, such as randomly turning on and off LEDs or determining the outcome in a game.

Code Example

```
int randomValue = random(0, 10);   // Generates a random number between
0 and 9
Serial.println(randomValue);
```

Notes
Remember that the maximum value is exclusive, so `random(0, 10)` generates numbers from 0 to 9, not 10.

Warnings
If you do not set a seed with `randomSeed()`, the sequence of random numbers will repeat every time the program runs.

Troubleshooting Tips
If you see the same numbers repeatedly, try using `randomSeed()` with a dynamic value, such as an analog sensor reading, to initialize the generator.

2.2 The randomSeed() Function: Initializing Random Number Generator

What is randomSeed()?
The randomSeed() function sets the starting point for the pseudo-random number generator. By giving it a unique seed, you ensure that the sequence of numbers generated by random() will be different each time the program runs.

Why is it important?
Without randomSeed(), the random numbers generated by random() will follow the same sequence every time you restart the Arduino. By using randomSeed(), you can add true variability to your projects.

Syntax:

```
randomSeed(value)
```

Where value is the seed that initializes the random number generator.

Syntax Explanation
The randomSeed() function takes a single parameter that initializes the random number generator. This seed can be a fixed number or a value from an analog input, such as noise on an unused pin.

Usage
Use randomSeed() to ensure that random sequences vary between program runs, making your project behave more dynamically.

Code Example

```
int seed = analogRead(A0);  // Read from an unused analog pin for randomness
randomSeed(seed);
```

Notes
Using an analog pin that is not connected to anything as the seed value introduces true randomness into the number generator.

Warnings
Using the same seed will result in the same sequence of numbers every time. Ensure you use dynamic values for true randomness.

Troubleshooting Tips
If the random numbers seem too predictable, make sure the seed value comes from a source with enough variability, such as analog noise.

Quiz: Check Your Understanding of Basic Random Number Functions

- **How does random() generate different numbers?**
  A. It uses a seed to start a pseudo-random sequence. (Multiple Choice)
- **What does randomSeed() do?**
  A. It initializes the random number generator with a seed value to ensure different sequences. (Fill in the Blank)

---

3. Advanced Random Number Applications

3.1 Generating Random Numbers for Dynamic LED Behavior

What is this application about?
In this project, you will use random numbers to control the on/off state of LEDs. The randomness ensures that the pattern of LEDs changes each time the program runs, making the output unpredictable.

Why is it important?
Adding randomness makes the output more engaging and interactive. It simulates natural behavior, where things are rarely repetitive or predictable.

Components List

- Arduino
- LEDs

- o Resistors
- o Wires
- o Breadboard

Circuit Diagram

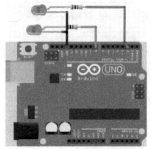

Show how the LEDs are connected to the Arduino for random control.

Circuit Connection
Each LED is connected to a digital pin through a resistor. Connect the ground wire to the common ground.

Code

```
void setup() {
  // Set pins 2 to 7 as output
  for (int i = 2; i < 8; i++) {
    pinMode(i, OUTPUT);
  }
}

void loop() {
  int ledPin = random(2, 8);      // Randomly select an LED pin
  int brightness = random(0, 256); // Randomly select a brightness
value (0-255)

  analogWrite(ledPin, brightness); // Set the brightness of the
selected LED
  delay(500);                      // Wait for 500ms
  digitalWrite(ledPin, LOW);       // Turn off the LED
  delay(500);                      // Wait for 500ms before selecting
another
}
```

Code Walkthrough
This code randomly selects one of the LED pins (2 to 7) and turns it on. The randomness ensures that different LEDs light up each time.

Challenge: Control Brightness Randomly
Modify the project to control LED brightness using analogWrite()
and random values between 0 and 255.

3.2 Using random() in Games or Simulations

What is this application about?
This project uses random() to create variability in a simple game. For
example, you can create a game where LEDs light up randomly, and
the player must press a button to turn them off.

Why is it important?
Randomness makes games more exciting, as it introduces
unpredictability. It also allows simulations to mimic real-life behavior,
where outcomes are not always the same.

Components List

- Arduino
- Push Button
- LEDs
- Buzzer
- Wires

- Breadboard

Circuit Diagram

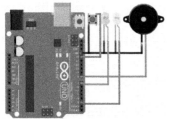

Provide the wiring for random LED control in a game setup.

Circuit Connection
The LEDs are connected to digital pins, and the push button is wired
to an input pin. The buzzer is connected for sound output.

Code

```
int buttonPin = 7;    // Pin where the button is connected
int buzzerPin = 8;    // Pin where the buzzer is connected

void setup() {
  // Set LED pins as output
  for (int i = 2; i < 7; i++) {
    pinMode(i, OUTPUT);
  }

  pinMode(buttonPin, INPUT_PULLUP);  // Set button pin as input with
internal pull-up
  pinMode(buzzerPin, OUTPUT);         // Set buzzer pin as output
}

void loop() {
  int randomLED = random(2, 7);  // Randomly select an LED pin (2 to 6)
  digitalWrite(randomLED, HIGH); // Light up the randomly selected LED

  delay(1000);  // Keep the LED on for 1 second

  if (digitalRead(buttonPin) == LOW) {  // Check if the button is
pressed
    digitalWrite(randomLED, LOW);       // Turn off the LED
    tone(buzzerPin, 1000, 200);         // Play a tone on the buzzer
for 200ms
  } else {
    digitalWrite(randomLED, LOW);       // Turn off the LED if no
button press
  }

  delay(500);  // Small delay before selecting the next random LED
}
```

Code Walkthrough
The program randomly selects an LED to light up. If the player presses the button, the LED turns off. This randomness adds excitement to the game.

Challenge: Add More Random Events
Add more random events, such as different sound patterns using a buzzer or varying the time the LEDs stay on.

---

4. Practical Projects for Mastering Random Numbers

4.1 **Project 1: Creating Random LED Blink Patterns**

Creating Random LED Blink Patterns is about using random number generation to create a dynamic and unpredictable blinking pattern for multiple **LEDs**. Each **LED** will randomly turn on and off, with random time intervals, resulting in a visually interesting effect.

Why is it important?
This project is a great demonstration of how **random numbers** can be used in programming to create non-repetitive, engaging patterns. It has practical applications in **lighting installations**, **interactive art**, or **decorative projects**, where predictable blinking patterns might be boring or repetitive.

Components List:

- **Arduino**
- **LEDs** (at least 5 for a more interesting pattern)
- **Resistors** (220Ω for each LED)
- **Wires**
- **Breadboard**

Circuit Diagram:

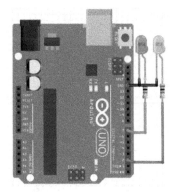

The diagram should show several **LEDs** connected to **digital pins** on the Arduino, each with a **resistor** in series to limit current. All **grounds** should be connected to the Arduino's **GND** pin.

Circuit Connection:
1. Connect the **positive leg** (anode) of each **LED** to a different **digital pin** on the Arduino (e.g., pins 2-6).

2. Connect a **220Ω resistor** in series with each LED.
3. Connect the **negative leg** (cathode) of each LED to **GND**.
4. Connect the **Arduino** to your **computer** via a USB cable for power and programming.

Code:

```
// Define LED pins
int ledPins[] = {2, 3, 4, 5, 6};  // Array to hold LED pin numbers
int numLeds = 5;  // Number of LEDs

void setup() {
  // Set all pins to OUTPUT
  for (int i = 0; i < numLeds; i++) {
    pinMode(ledPins[i], OUTPUT);
  }
}

void loop() {
  // Randomly choose an LED and turn it on
  int ledPin = ledPins[random(0, numLeds)];
  digitalWrite(ledPin, HIGH);

  // Wait for a random duration between 100 and 1000 milliseconds
  delay(random(100, 1000));

  // Turn off the LED
  digitalWrite(ledPin, LOW);

  // Optional: Small delay to create a visual break between blinks
  delay(random(100, 500));
}
```

Code Walkthrough:

1. **LED Pin Array**: The **ledPins[]** array holds the pin numbers for all the LEDs connected to the Arduino. This makes it easy to randomly select one for blinking.
2. **Random LED Selection**: The random() function selects a random index from the **ledPins[]** array, choosing an LED to turn on.
3. **Random Delay**: A random delay time is generated (between 100 and 1000 milliseconds) to keep the LED on for a random duration, making the blink patterns unpredictable.
4. **Turning Off the LED**: After the delay, the selected LED is turned off using digitalWrite(ledPin, LOW).
5. **Looping**: The process repeats, ensuring the LEDs blink in **random patterns** with random timings.

Challenge: Vary Blink Duration Randomly
Modify the project to randomize both the blink duration and the time between blinks, creating more dynamic patterns.

4.2 **Project 2: Random Sensor Data Simulation**

Random Sensor Data Simulation involves generating random values to simulate **sensor data**. This allows for the testing of systems that rely on sensor input without needing actual environmental changes. It's particularly useful for debugging and optimizing systems such as **environmental monitoring** or **feedback systems**.

Why is it important?
Simulating sensor data with random values helps developers test and observe how their systems will respond to different input conditions, saving time and allowing testing without needing the physical environment or actual sensors to change.

Components List:

- **Arduino**
- **Sensor** (or a **potentiometer** to simulate sensor readings)
- **Wires**
- **Breadboard**

Circuit Diagram:

The circuit diagram should show a **sensor** or **potentiometer** connected to an analog input on the Arduino. The sensor will simulate fluctuating readings for testing purposes.

Circuit Connection:

1. Connect one pin of the **potentiometer** to **5V** and the other to **GND**.
2. Connect the middle pin (wiper) of the potentiometer to **A0** (analog input pin) on the Arduino.
3. If you're using an actual sensor, connect it similarly, with the **output** going to an **analog input pin** (A0 in this case).

Code:

```
void setup() {
  Serial.begin(9600);   // Start serial communication for debugging
}

void loop() {
  // Simulate random sensor reading between 0 and 1023 (analog input range)
  int sensorValue = random(0, 1023);

  // Print the simulated sensor value to the Serial Monitor
  Serial.println(sensorValue);

  delay(500);  // Wait 500ms before generating the next random value
}
```

Code Walkthrough:

- **Serial Communication**: The code begins with Serial.begin(9600) to initialize communication with the **Serial Monitor** for displaying simulated sensor values.
- **Simulated Sensor Reading**: The random(0, 1023) function generates a **random number** in the range of 0 to 1023, simulating the range of an **analog sensor** in Arduino.
- **Serial Output**: The Serial.println(sensorValue) command sends the simulated sensor value to the **Serial Monitor**, allowing you to see the simulated readings.
- **Delay**: The delay(500) adds a half-second pause between each simulated reading to prevent the values from changing too quickly.

Challenge: Display Data on OLED/LCD
Add functionality to display the random sensor data on an OLED or LCD screen for visual feedback.

5. Common Troubleshooting and Debugging Tips

5.1 Common Errors and How to Fix Them

What are common errors?
Common errors include using the same seed value repeatedly, resulting in predictable sequences, or misunderstanding the range of the random() function. These mistakes can make the randomness less effective.

Why do they happen?
These errors usually happen when users don't initialize the random number generator properly or when they expect inclusive ranges from the random() function.

Use of Serial Monitor for debugging
Use the **Serial Monitor** to print out random values during development. This will help you verify that the numbers are actually varying as expected.

5.2 Optimizing Random Number Generation for Performance

What is code optimization for random numbers?
Optimizing random number generation means ensuring that the numbers are generated efficiently without unnecessary delays or overuse of the random() function.

Why is it important?
In games or simulations, too many calls to random() in a short time can slow down performance. Optimized code ensures smooth and efficient operation.

Tips for performance and accuracy
Use randomSeed() to ensure true randomness and minimize repeated calls to random() unless necessary. Try to structure your code to avoid unnecessary randomness.

6. Conclusion and Next Steps

6.1 Recap of Key Random Number Functions

- **What have we learned?**
  In this chapter, we explored key random number functions in
  Arduino, including random() and randomSeed(). These
  functions are essential for adding unpredictability and
  variability to your projects, such as in games, simulations,
  and testing sensor-based systems. Understanding how to
  use and optimize these functions is important for developing
  dynamic and interactive Arduino projects.

Chapter 9: Interrupts in Arduino

Interrupts are a critical feature in Arduino programming that enable
the microcontroller to handle high-priority events immediately by
pausing the current task and executing an Interrupt Service Routine
(ISR). They are vital for real-time applications, allowing the Arduino
to respond instantly to external or internal events without constantly
checking for their status (polling). In this chapter, you will learn how
interrupts function, how to use the attachInterrupt() and
detachInterrupt() functions, and best practices like debouncing
and edge detection modes.

Syntax Table

Topic Name	Syntax	Simple Example
attachInterrupt()	attachInterrupt(digitalPinToInterrupt(pin), ISR, mode);	attachInterrupt(digitalPinToInterrupt(2), buttonPress, RISING);
detachInterrupt()	detachInterrupt(digitalPinToInterrupt(pin));	detachInterrupt(digitalPinToInterrupt(2));
Interrupt Service Routine (ISR)	void ISR_Function() { /* code */ }	void buttonPress() { counter++; }

Edge Detection Modes	`attachInterrupt(digitalPinToInterrupt(pin), ISR, mode);`	`attachInterrupt(digitalPinToInterrupt(2), toggleLED, FALLING);`
Polling	`while (condition) { /* code */ }`	`while (digitalRead(buttonPin) == LOW) { /* wait */ }`
Debouncing with Interrupts	`if ((millis() - lastDebounceTime) > debounceDelay) { /* code */ }`	`if ((millis() - lastDebounceTime) > debounceDelay) { buttonPressed = !buttonPressed; }`

1. Introduction to Interrupts in Arduino

What are Interrupts?
Interrupts are signals that inform the **Arduino microcontroller** to pause its current tasks and handle a higher-priority event. They allow the program to respond quickly to external inputs without constantly checking their status. Interrupts can be **hardware-based**, triggered by external devices like buttons or sensors, or **software-based**, triggered by internal events like timers. When an interrupt occurs, the microcontroller stops executing its regular code and runs a special function called the **Interrupt Service Routine (ISR)** to handle the event.

Why are Interrupts Important?
Interrupts are crucial for **real-time event handling**. They allow the Arduino to **respond instantly** to critical inputs, like detecting motion or changes in sensor values, without needing to continuously monitor these signals. By using interrupts, the Arduino can **multitask efficiently**, performing other operations while still being ready to handle urgent events. This ensures that the system can act immediately when necessary, which is vital in applications like **safety systems**, **robotics**, and **sensor monitoring**.

Types of Interrupts
Interrupts come in two main types:

1. **External interrupts**: Triggered by external devices on specific pins.
2. **Pin change interrupts**: Triggered when the state of any pin changes. Both types enable quick responses to changes in hardware, making them useful for handling real-time inputs.

Real-Life Application
A **motion detection system** uses interrupts to trigger an alarm when a sensor detects movement. The Arduino immediately pauses its current task to sound the alarm, ensuring timely action.

---

2. attachInterrupt() Function: Attaching Interrupts to Pins

What is attachInterrupt()?
The `attachInterrupt()` function links an external interrupt to a specific **pin** and tells the Arduino how to respond to changes on that pin. It's used to **trigger a function** (ISR) when an external event occurs, such as a button press or sensor activation.

Syntax

```
attachInterrupt(digitalPinToInterrupt(pin), ISR, mode);
```

Syntax Explanation

- **pin**: The pin number that will trigger the interrupt (e.g., 2 or 3).
- **ISR**: The name of the function (Interrupt Service Routine) to call when the interrupt occurs.
- **mode**: Defines the event that triggers the interrupt (RISING, FALLING, CHANGE, LOW). This function assigns the interrupt to respond to specific changes in the pin's state.

Usage
Use `attachInterrupt()` when you need to respond to external events like **button presses** or **sensor inputs**. It allows the Arduino to pause other tasks and focus on handling critical inputs immediately.

Code Example

```
void setup() {
  pinMode(2, INPUT);
  attachInterrupt(digitalPinToInterrupt(2), buttonPress, RISING);
}

void buttonPress() {
  // Code to execute on button press
}
```

This example triggers the buttonPress () function whenever the
button connected to **pin 2** is pressed.

Notes
The **ISR function** should be short and efficient, as the Arduino will
not perform other tasks while the ISR is running.

Warnings
Always use the **volatile** keyword for variables shared between the
main program and the ISR. This ensures proper handling of
changes in memory.

Troubleshooting Tips
If the interrupt doesn't trigger, ensure you've used the correct **pin
number** and **mode**. Make sure the ISR is properly defined and that
no **delays** or **complex operations** are performed inside it.

---

3. detachInterrupt() Function: Detaching Interrupts

What is detachInterrupt()?
The **detachInterrupt** () function disables an interrupt from a specific
pin. It's used when you want to **stop responding** to external events
or free up the microcontroller for other tasks without being
interrupted.

Syntax

```
detachInterrupt(digitalPinToInterrupt(pin));
```

Syntax Explanation
The **pin** parameter specifies the pin connected to the interrupt.
When detachInterrupt () is called, the Arduino stops monitoring

changes on that pin, preventing the ISR from being triggered. This is useful when you want to **temporarily or permanently disable** an interrupt.

Usage
Use detachInterrupt() to **disable** an interrupt when it's no longer needed, such as when an event has been handled or after a specific condition is met.

Code Example

```
detachInterrupt(digitalPinToInterrupt(2));
```

This example disables the interrupt on **pin 2**, stopping the Arduino from calling the associated ISR when the pin's state changes.

Notes
Use detachInterrupt() when you want to **conserve resources** or prevent interrupts from interfering with other tasks.

Warnings
Ensure that **important tasks** in the ISR are completed before detaching the interrupt, as the ISR will no longer run after detachment.

Troubleshooting Tips
If the ISR continues running after calling detachInterrupt(), ensure that you've correctly specified the **pin number**. Check that the **interrupt mode** isn't still being triggered elsewhere.

---

4. Interrupt Service Routine (ISR) in Arduino

What is an Interrupt Service Routine (ISR)?
An **ISR (Interrupt Service Routine)** is a **special function** that runs when an interrupt occurs. Its role is to handle **urgent tasks** like

reading sensor data or processing input events. The ISR must be **quick and efficient** to avoid delaying other tasks on the Arduino.

Syntax

```
void ISR_Function() {
    // Code to execute during the interrupt
}
```

Syntax Explanation
An ISR is defined as a **void function** with no parameters and no return value. It runs automatically when an interrupt is triggered, executing the code inside the function. It should be kept as short and **efficient** as possible.

Usage
Use ISRs for **time-sensitive tasks**, such as **reading sensor data** or **triggering alarms**. It allows the Arduino to handle **critical events** immediately without delays.

Code Example

```
volatile int counter = 0;

void incrementCounter() {
    counter++;
}
```

In this example, the ISR function incrementCounter() increments the **counter variable** every time an interrupt occurs.

Notes
Avoid using **delays** or **complex calculations** inside the ISR, as this can cause the Arduino to become unresponsive.

Warnings
Using functions like delay() or Serial.print() inside an ISR is **dangerous** because they rely on interrupts, which are temporarily disabled when an ISR is running.

Troubleshooting Tips
If the ISR isn't performing correctly, ensure it's **short and simple**. Check that no forbidden functions like delay() are being used inside

the ISR. Verify that **volatile** is used for variables shared with the main program.

---

5. Polling vs Interrupts

What is Polling?
Polling is a technique where the Arduino **continuously checks** the status of an input pin to detect changes. It involves reading the pin state repeatedly in a loop. Although simple, polling is **inefficient** because the Arduino wastes time and processing power checking the pin, even when no change occurs.

Why Use Interrupts Instead?
Interrupts are more **efficient** than polling because they allow the Arduino to respond to changes **immediately** without constantly monitoring the pin. While polling uses processing resources even when nothing happens, interrupts save resources by only acting when an event occurs.

Code Example

```
while (digitalRead(buttonPin) == LOW) {
  // Do nothing, just waiting for the button press
}
```

This is an example of **polling**, where the Arduino waits in a loop until the button is pressed. In contrast, interrupts handle the event immediately without waiting.

Notes
Use **polling** for simple, non-critical tasks, but rely on **interrupts** for time-sensitive or urgent events.

Warnings
Avoid using polling for **high-priority tasks**, as it can lead to delayed responses and wasted resources.

6. Debouncing and Interrupts

What is Debouncing?
Debouncing is the process of ensuring that a mechanical switch,

like a button, sends a clean signal when pressed or released. Without debouncing, pressing a button can produce **multiple rapid signals**, causing the Arduino to register **multiple interrupts** instead of just one. Debouncing cleans up these signals so only one event is registered.

Why is it Important with Interrupts?
When using interrupts with buttons or other mechanical switches, **debouncing** prevents the Arduino from **misinterpreting multiple presses** from a single button press. Without debouncing, the button might trigger multiple interrupts in quick succession, leading to **unintended behaviors**. Proper debouncing ensures the system reacts **only once** to each button press.

Code Example

```
volatile bool buttonPressed = false;
unsigned long lastDebounceTime = 0;
const unsigned long debounceDelay = 50;

void ISR_button() {
  if ((millis() - lastDebounceTime) > debounceDelay) {
    buttonPressed = !buttonPressed;
    lastDebounceTime = millis();
  }
}
```

This example uses a **debounce delay** to prevent the ISR from triggering multiple times due to signal noise from a button press.

Notes
Debouncing can be done in **software** (by adding delays in code) or **hardware** (using capacitors and resistors).

Warnings
If interrupts trigger too frequently, check if **debouncing** is necessary. Failure to debounce may result in multiple unintended responses from a single event.

Troubleshooting Tips
If your button press results in multiple actions, check your **debounce timing**. Increase the debounce delay if needed and make sure to store the **last press time** correctly.

7. Edge Detection Modes in Interrupts

What are Edge Detection Modes?
Edge detection in interrupts allows the Arduino to trigger an event when the signal on a pin changes state. The key modes are:

- **RISING**: Trigger on a transition from LOW to HIGH.
- **FALLING**: Trigger on a transition from HIGH to LOW.
- **CHANGE**: Trigger on any change (HIGH to LOW or LOW to HIGH).
- **LOW**: Trigger continuously while the signal remains LOW.

Syntax

```
attachInterrupt(digitalPinToInterrupt(pin), ISR, mode);
```

Syntax Explanation
The **mode** defines which type of **edge** will trigger the interrupt. RISING detects when the signal changes from LOW to HIGH, FALLING detects the reverse, and CHANGE detects both. Use **LOW** when the interrupt needs to respond to a continuous LOW signal rather than a transition.

Code Example

```
attachInterrupt(digitalPinToInterrupt(2), toggleLED, RISING);
```

This code triggers the toggleLED function whenever the signal on **pin 2** changes from LOW to HIGH, effectively detecting a rising edge.

Notes
Choose the appropriate **edge detection mode** depending on your application's needs, whether you need to respond to **signal transitions** or continuous states.

Warnings
Using the wrong **edge detection mode** can lead to missed or false triggers. Ensure the mode matches your event's expected signal behavior.

Practical Exercise
Set up an Arduino project where an **LED toggles** on a rising edge and resets to off on a falling edge. This will help you understand **edge detection** in practice.

---

8. Common Mistakes and Best Practices with Interrupts

Common Mistakes

- **Using delay() in ISRs**: Delays block the entire program, making it unresponsive.
- **Using Serial prints**: Serial communication uses interrupts, which can cause the system to hang inside an ISR.
- **Not using volatile**: Variables shared between the main program and ISRs need the **volatile** keyword to ensure they are correctly handled by the compiler.
- **Long ISRs**: Interrupts should be quick; long ISRs can cause delays in handling other tasks.

Best Practices

- **Keep ISRs short**: Only handle critical, time-sensitive tasks inside the ISR. Use flags or simple variables to signal the main loop.
- **Avoid delays and complex operations**: Use the **minimum necessary code** in the ISR to avoid freezing the system.
- **Use volatile for shared variables**: Always declare variables shared between the ISR and the main program as volatile to ensure correct handling.
- **Debounce input**: When using interrupts with mechanical switches, add **debouncing** to avoid multiple triggers.

FAQ on Interrupts

- **Why isn't my interrupt working?** Check the **pin number** and **edge detection mode**. Make sure the ISR is properly defined and doesn't contain any **forbidden functions** like delay().
- **Can I use multiple interrupts?** Yes, but ensure that each ISR is short and doesn't interfere with others.

9. Practical Project: Motion Detection using Interrupts

What is this project about?
This project demonstrates how to use a **PIR motion sensor** with interrupts to detect motion and trigger an **LED**. When the PIR sensor detects movement, an interrupt is triggered, causing the Arduino to immediately light up the LED. This is a simple but effective example of using interrupts to handle real-time events like motion detection.

Components List

- Arduino
- PIR motion sensor
- LED
- Resistors
- Jumper wires
- Breadboard

Circuit Diagram

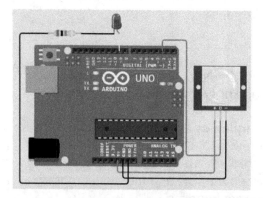

- Connect the **PIR sensor** output to **digital pin 2** of the Arduino.
- The **LED** is connected to **digital pin 9** with a resistor in series to limit the current.
- Connect power (5V) and ground to the sensor and the LED.

Code Example

```
volatile bool motionDetected = false;

void setup() {
  pinMode(2, INPUT);  // PIR sensor pin
```

```
  pinMode(9, OUTPUT);   // LED pin
  attachInterrupt(digitalPinToInterrupt(2), motionISR, RISING);   //
Trigger on motion
  Serial.begin(9600);
}

void motionISR() {
  motionDetected = true;
}
void loop() {
  if (motionDetected) {
    digitalWrite(9, HIGH);   // Turn on LED
    Serial.println("Motion Detected!");
    delay(2000);   // Keep the LED on for 2 seconds
    digitalWrite(9, LOW);   // Turn off LED
    motionDetected = false;   // Reset the flag
  }
}
```

This code triggers an interrupt when the **PIR sensor** detects motion.
The interrupt calls the motionISR() function, setting the
motionDetected flag to **true**. The loop then turns on the LED for 2
seconds and prints a message to the **Serial Monitor**.

Challenge
Extend this project by adding a **buzzer** that sounds when motion is
detected. Modify the code to include the buzzer, ensuring the
system can handle multiple events simultaneously by using
additional interrupts or managing them within the main loop.

10. Quiz: Test Your Understanding of Interrupts

Sample Questions:

1. What is the purpose of an interrupt in Arduino?
   A) To run functions continuously
   B) To stop all code execution

C) To handle urgent tasks when certain conditions are met
Answer: C
2. Which function stops an interrupt?
Answer: detachInterrupt()
3. Can interrupts be used for analog pin inputs?
Answer: No

This quiz helps reinforce your understanding of the purpose and correct usage of interrupts in Arduino, covering key concepts like **event handling** and **interrupt functions**.

---

11. Conclusion and Next Steps

Recap of Key Points
In this chapter, we explored the fundamentals of **interrupts** in Arduino, including their importance in **real-time event handling**. You learned how to use the **attachInterrupt()** and **detachInterrupt()** functions to manage external interrupts, write efficient **Interrupt Service Routines (ISRs)**, and avoid common mistakes like using **delay()** inside ISRs. We also covered practical applications, such as the **motion detection** project, demonstrating the power of interrupts in real-world scenarios.

Next Steps
To advance your knowledge, explore more complex applications like using **timers** and **software interrupts** in Arduino. These concepts will further enhance your ability to build **responsive** and **efficient** systems. Resources like **Arduino's documentation** and books like "Programming Arduino: Getting Started with Sketches" provide excellent opportunities for further learning.

Chapter 10: Advanced Input/Output Functions

Chapter 10 explores advanced input/output (I/O) functions in Arduino programming, providing more complex control capabilities than basic I/O functions. These functions, such as **noTone()**, **pulseIn()**, **pulseInLong()**, **shiftIn()**, and **shiftOut()**, enable specialized tasks like stopping sound output, measuring pulse widths, and serially reading or sending data bit by bit. They are crucial for projects that require precise timing, expanded input/output capabilities, or sophisticated control over devices. Mastering these functions enhances your ability to handle advanced hardware and manage complex operations effectively.

Syntax Table: Advanced Arduino I/O Functions

Topic Name	Syntax	Simple Example
Stop Sound Output	`noTone(pin)`	`noTone(8); // Stop sound on pin 8`
Measure Pulse Width	`pulseIn(pin, value)`	`long duration = pulseIn(7, HIGH);`
Measure Long Pulse Width	`pulseInLong(pin, value)`	`unsigned long duration = pulseInLong(5, HIGH);`
Read Data Bit by Bit	`shiftIn(dataPin, clockPin, bitOrder)`	`byte data = shiftIn(7, 8, MSBFIRST);`
Send Data Bit by Bit	`shiftOut(dataPin, clockPin, bitOrder, value)`	`shiftOut(11, 12, MSBFIRST, 0xFF);`

1. Introduction to Advanced I/O Operations

1.1 What are Advanced I/O Functions?

What are Advanced I/O Functions?
Advanced I/O functions allow more complex input and output control in Arduino projects. Functions like `noTone()`, `pulseIn()`, `pulseInLong()`, `shiftIn()`, and `shiftOut()` enable specialized tasks such as stopping sound output, measuring pulse widths, and reading or sending data bit by bit. These functions provide greater

flexibility and control over your hardware, making them essential for advanced projects that require precise timing, signal measurement, or handling multiple input/output signals with limited pins.

Why are they important?
Advanced I/O functions are crucial for complex projects where basic digital and analog functions are not sufficient. For example, pulseIn() allows accurate timing measurements, which are necessary for ultrasonic distance sensors, while shiftIn() and shiftOut() enable communication with multiple devices using only a few pins. These functions enhance the control and capabilities of your Arduino, allowing you to handle more sophisticated tasks like motor control, sensor data processing, and signal generation.

1.2 **Key Concepts and Terms (Glossary)**

What is noTone()?
The noTone() function stops any sound output that was started with tone(). It's useful in projects where you need to control sound duration, like alarms or musical projects.

Why is it important?
It is important to stop sound output cleanly to avoid continuous noise in projects such as alarm systems or sound notifications.

What is pulseIn()?
pulseIn() measures the duration of a pulse on a specific pin, either HIGH or LOW. It returns the pulse width in microseconds.

Why is it important?
It is essential for tasks like reading sensor data from devices such as ultrasonic distance sensors that rely on pulse measurement.

What is pulseInLong()?
pulseInLong() functions similarly to pulseIn(), but it measures longer pulses with greater precision.

Why is it important?
This function is useful when accurate long-pulse timing is required, especially in applications where millisecond-level accuracy is needed.

What is shiftIn()?

shiftIn() reads data one bit at a time from a shift register or other serial device. It allows you to expand input capabilities using fewer pins.

Why is it important?

It's essential for reading data from multiple inputs, especially when you want to conserve I/O pins.

What is shiftOut()?

shiftOut() sends data one bit at a time to a shift register, useful for controlling multiple outputs like LEDs or displays.

Why is it important?

It's important for expanding output capabilities in projects that require controlling many outputs with minimal pins.

1.3 Overview of Core Advanced I/O Functions

What are Core Advanced I/O Functions?

Core advanced I/O functions include noTone(), pulseIn(), pulseInLong(), shiftIn(), and shiftOut(). Each of these functions adds specialized capabilities to your projects. noTone() stops sound output, while pulseIn() and pulseInLong() measure pulse durations in microseconds and longer durations, respectively. shiftIn() reads data serially from devices like shift registers, and shiftOut() sends data serially to output devices. Together, these functions provide essential tools for handling complex I/O tasks in Arduino projects.

Why are they important?

These functions are crucial for building sophisticated projects that require precise control over time, signals, and data. For example, pulseIn() enables ultrasonic distance measurement, while shiftIn() and shiftOut() allow you to control multiple devices using fewer pins, which is valuable in space-constrained or I/O-limited designs. By mastering these functions, you can handle more complex I/O tasks, enhance the performance of your projects, and improve the overall efficiency of your designs.

Quiz: Test Your Understanding of Advanced I/O Functions

- **What does the noTone () function do?**
  A. It stops sound output that was started by the tone ()
  function. (Multiple Choice)
- **How is pulseIn () used in Arduino?**
  A. It measures the duration of a pulse on a specific pin,
  typically used in sensors like ultrasonic sensors. (Short
  Answer)

---

2. Basic Advanced I/O Functions

2.1 The noTone() Function: Stopping Sound Output

What is noTone()?
The noTone() function is used to stop sound output from a buzzer or speaker that was previously started using the tone() function. It stops the sound by halting the square wave signal generated by tone(). This is useful in projects where you need to control sound generation, such as alarm systems, musical projects, or notification systems.

Why is it important?
noTone() is important because it allows you to stop sound output at the correct time, preventing continuous noise. In alarm or notification systems, sound control is crucial for ensuring the proper timing and sequence of sounds.

Syntax

```
noTone(pin)
```

Where pin is the number of the pin that is currently generating sound.

Syntax Explanation
In the noTone() function, the parameter pin specifies the pin on which sound was generated by the tone() function. Calling noTone() will stop the sound on that pin.

Usage
You can use noTone() in projects to stop a buzzer or speaker when a certain condition is met, such as stopping an alarm after the reset button is pressed.

Code Example

```
void loop() {
  tone(8, 1000);  // Start sound on pin 8
  delay(5000);    // Sound plays for 5 seconds
  noTone(8);      // Stop sound after 5 seconds
}
```

Notes
The noTone () function only works on pins that are capable of generating sound using tone (). It stops the square wave signal on the specified pin.

Warnings
Ensure that the correct pin is specified when calling noTone (), as an incorrect pin may result in no effect on the sound output.

Troubleshooting Tips
If noTone () doesn't stop the sound as expected, double-check that the pin number matches the one used with tone (). Also, verify that the hardware, such as the speaker or buzzer, is connected properly.

2.2 The pulseIn () Function: Measuring Pulse Widths

What is pulseIn ()?
The pulseIn () function measures the length of a pulse (HIGH or LOW) on a specified pin in **microseconds**. This function is commonly used for reading data from sensors like ultrasonic distance sensors, which send out pulses and expect return pulses after bouncing off an object. By timing how long the pulse stays HIGH or LOW, you can calculate things like distance or signal timing.

Why is it important?
It is essential for applications that require precise timing, such as measuring the time it takes for a sound wave to travel to an object and back (as in ultrasonic sensors). The ability to accurately measure pulse width is crucial for reliable sensor data.

Syntax

```
pulseIn(pin, value)
```

Where pin is the input pin and value is either HIGH or LOW to specify which pulse to measure.

Syntax Explanation

The pulseIn() function measures the duration of a pulse on pin where value determines whether to measure the HIGH or LOW pulse. It returns the pulse width in microseconds, which can be used to compute distances or other time-based data.

Usage

Use pulseIn() when working with sensors that provide information via pulses, such as ultrasonic distance sensors. It measures the duration of these pulses to provide accurate readings of distances or timings.

Code Example

```
long duration;
duration = pulseIn(7, HIGH);   // Measure the HIGH pulse duration on pin
7
Serial.println(duration);      // Output pulse length in microseconds
```

Notes

pulseIn() returns the pulse length in microseconds. The maximum pulse duration it can measure is up to 3 minutes (18 million microseconds).

Warnings

If your sensor isn't providing accurate data, double-check the wiring and connections to ensure that pulses are being properly sent and received.

Troubleshooting Tips

If the pulseIn() function returns unexpected values, ensure the sensor is wired correctly and that the pin number in the function matches the one connected to the sensor. Also, verify the sensor's specifications to ensure it's compatible.

2.3 The pulseInLong() Function: Measuring Long Pulses

What is pulseInLong()?

pulseInLong() works similarly to pulseIn(), but it's used to measure longer-duration pulses with greater precision. Like pulseIn(), it measures the time a pin stays in either a HIGH or LOW state but is optimized for long pulses that require extended measurement. This function is particularly useful for applications where longer intervals need to be captured accurately.

Why is it important?

This function is essential for projects that require timing over extended periods with microsecond-level accuracy. It's used in applications such as data logging, communication protocols, or motor control where long pulse measurements are needed.

Syntax

```
pulseInLong(pin, value)
```

Where pin is the input pin and value is either HIGH or LOW, specifying which type of pulse to measure.

Syntax Explanation

In pulseInLong(), pin identifies the pin to be measured, while value specifies whether to measure the HIGH or LOW pulse. The function returns the duration of the pulse in microseconds, optimized for longer time periods.

Usage

Use pulseInLong() when precise measurement of long pulses is required, such as in motor control or data logging tasks that involve extended timing.

Code Example

```
unsigned long duration;
duration = pulseInLong(5, HIGH);   // Measure the HIGH pulse duration on
pin 5
Serial.println(duration);          // Output pulse length in
microseconds
```

Notes

pulseInLong() is ideal for measuring long pulses when pulseIn() does not provide enough resolution or accuracy.

Warnings
Ensure that the hardware being used is capable of sending long pulses; otherwise, results may be inaccurate.

Troubleshooting Tips
If inaccurate measurements occur, confirm that the pulseInLong() function is being used with a sensor that can produce long-duration pulses. Also, check connections and pin assignments.

2.4 The shiftIn() Function: Reading Data Bit by Bit

What is shiftIn()?
The shiftIn() function reads data **one bit at a time** from a serial device such as a shift register. This allows for expanding the input capabilities of the Arduino when the number of available pins is limited. The function reads a byte of data in a bitwise fashion, controlled by a clock signal provided by the user.

Why is it important?
It's crucial for projects that need to read data from multiple input sources using minimal pins. shiftIn() allows you to interface with devices like shift registers, which can store and provide multiple input signals to the Arduino.

Syntax

```
shiftIn(dataPin, clockPin, bitOrder)
```

Where dataPin is the pin reading data, clockPin is the clock signal, and bitOrder specifies the bit order (MSBFIRST or LSBFIRST).

Syntax Explanation
In shiftIn(), the dataPin receives the serial data, while clockPin provides the timing signal for reading each bit. bitOrder determines whether the most significant bit (MSB) or least significant bit (LSB) is read first.

Usage

Use `shiftIn()` when you need to read serial data from devices like shift registers or other serial input devices that send one bit at a time.

Code Example

```
byte data = shiftIn(7, 8, MSBFIRST);  // Read a byte from dataPin 7
using clockPin 8
Serial.println(data);                 // Output the received byte
```

Notes

This function is useful for reading multiple inputs, especially when you need to save on pin usage. You can read 8 bits (1 byte) of data using only 2 Arduino pins.

Warnings

Make sure the clock signal is consistent and accurate, or data may not be read correctly. Incorrect `bitOrder` settings may also result in incorrect data.

Troubleshooting Tips

If data isn't being read correctly, check the clock timing and ensure that the correct pin is assigned for the data input. Also, verify the `bitOrder` matches the device's configuration.

2.5 The `shiftOut()` Function: Sending Data Bit by Bit

What is `shiftOut()`?

The `shiftOut()` function sends data one bit at a time from the Arduino to an external device, such as a shift register or serial-controlled output device. This function is useful for expanding output capabilities, such as controlling multiple LEDs or displays using fewer pins.

Why is it important?

`shiftOut()` is essential for projects that require controlling multiple output devices with minimal pins. By shifting out data, you can control multiple devices like 7-segment displays, LEDs, or other devices that require serial data input.

Syntax

```
shiftOut(dataPin, clockPin, bitOrder, value)
```

Where dataPin sends data, clockPin provides the timing signal, bitOrder specifies the order, and value is the byte of data to be sent.

Syntax Explanation
shiftOut() sends one byte of data bit by bit from the dataPin, with the timing controlled by clockPin. bitOrder determines whether to send the most significant bit (MSB) or least significant bit (LSB) first, and value is the data to send.

Usage
Use shiftOut() to send data serially to devices like shift registers. This is commonly used for controlling outputs such as LEDs or displays in projects where you need to conserve pins.

Code Example

```
shiftOut(11, 12, MSBFIRST, 0xFF);   // Send a byte of data to turn on
all LEDs
```

Notes
This function helps control multiple outputs, reducing the number of pins required to control devices like LEDs or 7-segment displays.

Warnings
Ensure that the clock signal is consistent to prevent timing issues. Incorrect data values or bit order can result in incorrect output.

Troubleshooting Tips
If output devices don't behave as expected, double-check the wiring, clock signal, and bitOrder settings. Ensure the value being shifted out matches the intended result.

Quiz: Check Your Understanding of Basic Advanced I/O Functions

- **What is the purpose of the** `pulseIn()` **function?**
  A. It measures the duration of a pulse on a specified pin in microseconds. (Multiple Choice)
- **What does the** `shiftIn()` **function do?**
  A. It reads data one bit at a time from a serial input device, such as a shift register. (Short Answer)

4. Practical Projects for Mastering Advanced I/O Functions

4.1 Project 1: Using `pulseIn()` with an Ultrasonic Sensor

Project Overview:

This project demonstrates how to use an **HC-SR04 Ultrasonic Sensor** with an Arduino to measure distances. The sensor sends out a pulse of ultrasonic sound and measures the time it takes for the echo to return. Using this time, the Arduino calculates the distance to an object. The project uses the `pulseIn()` function to measure the pulse duration and convert it to a distance.

Components List:

1. Arduino (e.g., Uno, Nano)
2. Ultrasonic Sensor (HC-SR04)
3. Resistors (as needed for signal conditioning)
4. Wires
5. Breadboard

Circuit Diagram:

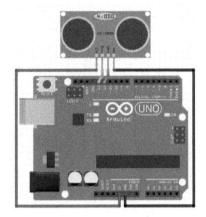

- **Ultrasonic Sensor (HC-SR04)**:
  - VCC pin connects to **5V** on the Arduino.
  - GND pin connects to **GND** on the Arduino.
  - **Trig** pin connects to **digital pin 9** on the Arduino (for sending the pulse).
  - **Echo** pin connects to **digital pin 10** on the Arduino (for receiving the pulse).

Circuit Diagram Analysis:

- The **Trig pin** of the ultrasonic sensor is connected to an output pin of the Arduino and is used to trigger the sensor by sending a short pulse.
- The **Echo pin** is connected to an input pin and listens for the returning pulse. The Arduino measures the time it takes for the pulse to travel to the object and back using the pulseIn() function.
- The time measured by the pulseIn() function is proportional to the distance of the object.

Code:

```
const int trigPin = 9;      // Trigger pin for the ultrasonic sensor
const int echoPin = 10;     // Echo pin for the ultrasonic sensor
long duration;              // Variable to store the time it takes for
the pulse to return
int distance;               // Variable to store the calculated distance

void setup() {
  pinMode(trigPin, OUTPUT);  // Set trigger pin as an output
  pinMode(echoPin, INPUT);   // Set echo pin as an input
  Serial.begin(9600);        // Begin serial communication for output
}

void loop() {
  // Clear the trigger pin by setting it LOW
  digitalWrite(trigPin, LOW);
  delayMicroseconds(2);

  // Send a 10-microsecond pulse to trigger the sensor
  digitalWrite(trigPin, HIGH);
  delayMicroseconds(10);
  digitalWrite(trigPin, LOW);

  // Measure the time it takes for the pulse to return
  duration = pulseIn(echoPin, HIGH);

  // Calculate the distance (in cm)
  distance = duration * 0.034 / 2;

  // Output the distance to the Serial Monitor
  Serial.println(distance);

  // Wait for a second before the next measurement
  delay(1000);
}
```

Code Walkthrough:

1. **Global Variables**:
   - **trigPin**: Pin 9 is used to send the trigger pulse to the sensor.
   - **echoPin**: Pin 10 is used to read the returning pulse from the sensor.
   - **duration**: Stores the time (in microseconds) between sending the pulse and receiving the echo.

Circuit Diagram:

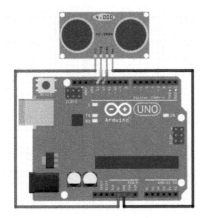

- **Ultrasonic Sensor (HC-SR04)**:
    - VCC pin connects to **5V** on the Arduino.
    - GND pin connects to **GND** on the Arduino.
    - **Trig** pin connects to **digital pin 9** on the Arduino (for sending the pulse).
    - **Echo** pin connects to **digital pin 10** on the Arduino (for receiving the pulse).

Circuit Diagram Analysis:

- The **Trig pin** of the ultrasonic sensor is connected to an output pin of the Arduino and is used to trigger the sensor by sending a short pulse.
- The **Echo pin** is connected to an input pin and listens for the returning pulse. The Arduino measures the time it takes for the pulse to travel to the object and back using the pulseIn() function.
- The time measured by the pulseIn() function is proportional to the distance of the object.

Code:

```
const int trigPin = 9;      // Trigger pin for the ultrasonic sensor
const int echoPin = 10;     // Echo pin for the ultrasonic sensor
long duration;              // Variable to store the time it takes for
the pulse to return
int distance;               // Variable to store the calculated distance

void setup() {
  pinMode(trigPin, OUTPUT);  // Set trigger pin as an output
  pinMode(echoPin, INPUT);   // Set echo pin as an input
  Serial.begin(9600);        // Begin serial communication for output
}

void loop() {
  // Clear the trigger pin by setting it LOW
  digitalWrite(trigPin, LOW);
  delayMicroseconds(2);

  // Send a 10-microsecond pulse to trigger the sensor
  digitalWrite(trigPin, HIGH);
  delayMicroseconds(10);
  digitalWrite(trigPin, LOW);

  // Measure the time it takes for the pulse to return
  duration = pulseIn(echoPin, HIGH);

  // Calculate the distance (in cm)
  distance = duration * 0.034 / 2;

  // Output the distance to the Serial Monitor
  Serial.println(distance);

  // Wait for a second before the next measurement
  delay(1000);
}
```

Code Walkthrough:

1. **Global Variables**:
   - **trigPin**: Pin 9 is used to send the trigger pulse to the sensor.
   - **echoPin**: Pin 10 is used to read the returning pulse from the sensor.
   - **duration**: Stores the time (in microseconds) between sending the pulse and receiving the echo.

- o **distance**: Stores the calculated distance based on the duration of the pulse.
2. **setup ()**:
   - o **pinMode(trigPin, OUTPUT)** configures the trigger pin as an output to send the pulse.
   - o **pinMode(echoPin, INPUT)** configures the echo pin as an input to receive the pulse.
   - o **Serial.begin(9600)** initializes the serial communication to display the calculated distance.
3. **loop ()**:
   - o The code sends a 10-microsecond pulse to the **trigPin** to initiate the distance measurement.
   - o The **pulseIn(echoPin, HIGH)** function measures the time (in microseconds) that the echo pin remains HIGH, which corresponds to the time taken for the ultrasonic wave to bounce off an object and return.
   - o The duration is then converted to a **distance** in centimeters using the formula: Distance (in cm)=Duration×0.0342\text{Distance (in cm)} = \frac{\text{Duration} \times 0.034}{2}Distance (in cm)=2Duration×0.034
   - o The calculated distance is printed to the Serial Monitor.
   - o The loop delays for 1 second before repeating the measurement.

Challenge: Display Distance on OLED
Modify the project to display the calculated distance on an **OLED** display for a more practical, real-world application.

4.2 **Project 2: Controlling an 8-Segment Display using** shiftOut ()

In this project, we will control an **8-segment display** using the **shiftOut()** function, which sends data from the **Arduino** to a **shift register (74HC595)**. The shift register reduces the number of pins required on the Arduino to control the display by using **serial communication**.

Components List:

- **Arduino**
- **8-segment display**
- **Shift register (74HC595)**
- **Resistors** (220Ω to limit current)
- **Wires**
- **Breadboard**

Circuit Diagram:

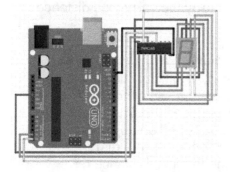

The **shift register** receives data from the Arduino using **three control pins**:

- **Data pin** (e.g., D11) connects to the **shift register's data input**
- **Clock pin** (e.g., D12) connects to the **clock input**
- **Latch pin** (e.g., D8) connects to the **latch control**
  The display's **segments** connect to the **shift register's outputs (Q0-Q7)**. **Resistors** are placed between the **display's segments** and the **register's outputs** to prevent overcurrent.

Circuit Connection:

- The **shift register** takes **serial data** from the Arduino and controls the display's segments in **parallel**.
- The **shiftOut()** function is used to send a **byte** from the Arduino to the register. Each **bit** in the byte corresponds to a **segment** on the display.

Code:

```
int latchPin = 8;    // ST_CP
```

```
int clockPin = 12;    // SH_CP
int dataPin = 11;     // DS

void setup() {
  pinMode(latchPin, OUTPUT);
  pinMode(clockPin, OUTPUT);
  pinMode(dataPin, OUTPUT);
}

void loop() {
  // Send data to display '0'
  digitalWrite(latchPin, LOW);
  shiftOut(dataPin, clockPin, MSBFIRST, 0x3F);  // 0x3F corresponds to
'0'
  digitalWrite(latchPin, HIGH);
  delay(1000);
}
```

Code Walkthrough:

- **Pin Definitions:** latchPin, clockPin, and dataPin are connected to the **shift register**.
- In the **setup()** function, the pins are set to **output mode**.
- In the **loop()**, **latchPin** is set **LOW** to prepare for data. The **shiftOut()** function sends the byte 0x3F to the **shift register**, lighting up the display to show the number **0**. After the byte is sent, **latchPin** is set **HIGH** to lock the data, and there is a **1-second delay** before repeating.

Each **byte** corresponds to a different **digit** to be displayed. For example:

- **0x3F = 0**
- **0x06 = 1**
- **0x5B = 2**

Your Challenge:
Modify the code to display numbers **0-9** sequentially, pausing for **1 second** between each number.

- **Challenge: Add Multiple Shift Registers**
  Expand the project to control multiple 8-segment displays using two or more shift registers in series, allowing you to display multi-digit numbers.

4.3 Project 3: Reading Data from Multiple Shift Registers with shiftIn()

Reading Data from Multiple Shift Registers with **shiftIn()** involves using the **74HC165** shift registers to read multiple inputs (like switches or sensors) using minimal Arduino pins. This project expands the ability of the Arduino to handle a large number of inputs by chaining multiple shift registers together in **series**.

Components List:

- **Arduino**
- **Multiple shift registers (74HC165)**
- **LEDs** or **switches**
- **Resistors** (to limit current)
- **Wires**
- **Breadboard**

Circuit Diagram:

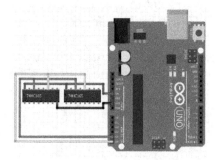

- Connect the **data pin** from each shift register to a single pin on the **Arduino** (e.g., pin D11).
- Connect the **clock pin** of all shift registers to another Arduino pin (e.g., pin D12).
- The **shift/load** pin of each shift register is connected together and controlled by an Arduino pin (e.g., pin D8).
- **Outputs** from each shift register correspond to **8 inputs**, and shift registers can be **daisy-chained** by connecting the **serial out (Q7)** of one register to the **serial in** of the next.

Circuit Connection:

- **Data pin** from each shift register is connected to a single pin on the Arduino.

- The **clock signal** is shared by all shift registers, allowing synchronized data reads.
- This setup enables the Arduino to read data from **multiple shift registers in series** using only three pins (data, clock, and latch/load).

Code:

```
int latchPin = 8;      // Connected to shift/load pin of 74HC165
int clockPin = 12;     // Connected to clock pin
int dataPin = 11;      // Connected to data pin

void setup() {
  pinMode(latchPin, OUTPUT);
  pinMode(clockPin, OUTPUT);
  pinMode(dataPin, INPUT);      // Set the data pin as an input
  Serial.begin(9600);           // Initialize serial communication
}

void loop() {
  // Load parallel data into the shift registers
  digitalWrite(latchPin, LOW);    // Pulse the latch pin to load data
  digitalWrite(latchPin, HIGH);

  // Read data from the first shift register
  byte inputs1 = shiftIn(dataPin, clockPin, MSBFIRST);

  // Read data from the second shift register
  byte inputs2 = shiftIn(dataPin, clockPin, MSBFIRST);

  // Print the results to the serial monitor
  Serial.print("Shift Register 1: ");
  Serial.println(inputs1, BIN);  // Display in binary format
  Serial.print("Shift Register 2: ");
  Serial.println(inputs2, BIN);  // Display in binary format

  delay(1000);  // Add a delay between readings
}
```

Code Walkthrough:

- **Pin Definitions**:
  - latchPin controls when the shift registers load data.
  - clockPin provides the clock signal for reading data.
  - dataPin reads the serial data from the shift registers.
- **setup()**: Initializes the pins and sets up serial communication for monitoring input data.
- **loop()**:

- First, the **latch pin** is pulsed to load the data from the switches/inputs into the shift registers.
- Then, the **shiftIn()** function is used to read a **byte** of data from each shift register. Each byte represents the state of **8 inputs**.
- The input states are printed to the **Serial Monitor** in **binary format**, showing whether each input is HIGH or LOW.

- The code reads from **two shift registers** in this example, but it can be extended to handle more.

Challenge: Extend the Project to Control More LEDs:

- To handle **more than two shift registers**, you can add additional **shiftIn()** calls to read data from more registers.
- Each shift register adds **8 more inputs**, and you only need to chain the registers by connecting the **serial out** of one register to the **serial in** of the next. You can still control all registers using the same **three pins** (data, clock, and latch).

---

5. Common Troubleshooting and Debugging Tips

5.1 **Common Errors and How to Fix Them**

- **What are common errors?**
  Common errors when using advanced I/O functions include miswiring components, incorrect pin assignments, and incorrect syntax for functions like shiftIn() and pulseIn(). These mistakes can result in inaccurate data readings or incorrect behavior in the system.
- **Why do they happen?**
  These errors often occur due to overlooking hardware connections or misunderstanding how the functions work. Incorrect timing or clock signal issues can also cause the system to malfunction, especially with serial devices like shift registers.
- **Use of Serial Monitor for debugging**
  Using the **Serial Monitor** to print values from functions like pulseIn() or shiftIn() can help diagnose where the issue lies. By printing real-time data, you can see if the sensor or

input device is working correctly and adjust your code or wiring accordingly.

5.2 Optimizing Code for Performance and Accuracy

- **What is code optimization?**
  Code optimization is the process of making your program more efficient by reducing unnecessary code, speeding up execution, and ensuring the program runs smoothly. In Arduino projects, this can be crucial for time-sensitive applications where accurate timing and performance are necessary.
- **Why is it important?**
  Optimizing your code ensures that your Arduino project runs efficiently, especially in applications involving sensors, motors, or real-time data. Poorly optimized code can result in missed data or slow performance, particularly when handling multiple input/output devices.
- **Tips for performance and accuracy**
  - **Minimize delays**: Avoid using delay() in tasks that require quick responses. Instead, use non-blocking code like millis().
  - **Optimize sensor readings**: Only read sensor data when necessary, and reduce the number of times the program polls the sensors to improve performance.
  - **Efficient use of memory**: Reduce memory usage by using the appropriate data types (e.g., byte instead of int).

6. Conclusion and Next Steps

6.1 Recap of Key Advanced I/O Functions

In this chapter, you've learned about the key advanced I/O functions in Arduino: noTone(), pulseIn(), pulseInLong(), shiftIn(), and shiftOut(). Each of these functions adds powerful new capabilities to your projects, enabling you to stop sound output, measure pulse widths, and handle data input and output with fewer pins. Mastering these functions is essential for building more complex Arduino applications and expanding your project possibilities.

Chapter 11: Communication Protocols with Arduino

Communication protocols are essential for transmitting data between the Arduino and other devices like sensors, displays, and peripherals. The main communication protocols used with Arduino are I2C, SPI, and UART. Each protocol serves different purposes depending on the number of devices, speed, and distance required for communication. Understanding these protocols helps in building complex, efficient systems with multiple components communicating seamlessly.

Syntax Table

Topic Name	Syntax	Simple Example

I2C (Inter-Integrated Circuit)	`Wire.begin();`
	`Wire.requestFrom(address, bytes);`
	`Wire.endTransmission();`
		`Wire.requestFrom(0x48, 1);`

SPI (Serial Peripheral Interface)	`SPI.begin();`
	`SPI.transfer(data);`
	`SPI.end();`
		`byte response = SPI.transfer(0x42);`

UART (Universal Asynchronous Receiver-Transmitter)	`Serial.begin(baud_rate);`
	`Serial.print(data);`
	`Serial.read();`
		`Serial.println("Received: " + incomingData);`

1. Introduction to Communication Protocols in Arduino

What are Communication Protocols?
Communication protocols define how **data is transmitted** between devices. In Arduino, the main communication protocols include **I2C (Inter-Integrated Circuit)**, **SPI (Serial Peripheral Interface)**, and **UART (Universal Asynchronous Receiver-Transmitter)**. Each protocol allows the Arduino to communicate with other microcontrollers, sensors, and peripherals. **I2C** uses two wires to connect multiple devices on a shared bus, **SPI** provides fast communication between a master and multiple slave devices, and **UART** allows direct serial communication over two pins (TX, RX). These protocols enable **efficient data exchange** between components in complex projects.

Why Are Communication Protocols Important?
Communication protocols are essential because they allow devices like sensors, displays, and controllers to **share information** with the Arduino. Without these protocols, Arduino would have to rely on complex wiring and direct pin-to-pin communication, which isn't scalable. Protocols like **I2C** and **SPI** make it easier to connect multiple devices using fewer pins, while **UART** is crucial for debugging and sending data over longer distances. They simplify project development and ensure **smooth data exchange** between components.

Key Concepts (Glossary)

- **SDA (Serial Data Line)**: I2C data line for communication.
- **SCL (Serial Clock Line)**: I2C clock line to synchronize communication.
- **MOSI (Master Out Slave In)**: SPI data line for sending data from the master to the slave.
- **MISO (Master In Slave Out)**: SPI data line for receiving data from the slave to the master.
- **SCLK (Serial Clock)**: SPI clock signal generated by the master.
- **TX (Transmit)**: UART pin used to send data.
- **RX (Receive)**: UART pin used to receive data.
- **Baud Rate**: The speed of data transmission in bits per second (bps).

2. I2C Protocol: Communicating with Multiple Devices

What is I2C?

I2C (Inter-Integrated Circuit) is a communication protocol that allows multiple devices to connect to a microcontroller over just **two wires**: **SDA** (data) and **SCL** (clock). Each device on the bus has a unique **address**, and the **master device** (Arduino) communicates with them by sending or requesting data. I2C is commonly used for **sensors, displays**, and other peripherals that require simple, two-wire communication.

Why is I2C Important?

I2C is valued for its **simplicity** and the ability to connect **multiple devices** on the same bus. It reduces the number of pins needed for communication and is especially useful in projects with many sensors or components, making it a popular choice for embedded systems.

Syntax Explanation

- `Wire.begin()`: Initializes the I2C bus.
- `Wire.requestFrom(address, bytes)`: Requests data from a device at the given address.
- `Wire.endTransmission()`: Ends communication with the I2C device. These functions allow the Arduino to send and receive data from multiple I2C devices.

Usage

I2C allows efficient communication between multiple devices like sensors and displays, using only two wires. It's ideal for projects where you need to minimize wiring and connect **several peripherals**.

Code Example

```
#include <Wire.h>

void setup() {
  Wire.begin();  // Join I2C bus as master
  Serial.begin(9600);
}
void loop() {
  Wire.requestFrom(0x48, 1);  // Request 1 byte from device at address
0x48
  while (Wire.available()) {
    char c = Wire.read();  // Read byte
    Serial.println(c);
  }
  delay(500);
```

```
}
```

This example reads data from an I2C temperature sensor.

Notes
Remember to connect **pull-up resistors** to the SDA and SCL lines
for proper I2C communication.

Warnings
Ensure that each I2C device has a **unique address**. Address
conflicts can prevent proper communication.

Troubleshooting Tips
If your I2C device isn't responding, check for correct wiring, **device
addresses**, and proper use of **pull-up resistors**. Use the **I2C
scanner** sketch to identify active devices on the bus.

---

3. SPI Protocol: High-Speed Communication

What is SPI?
SPI (Serial Peripheral Interface) is a communication protocol
designed for **high-speed data transfer** between a **master** device
and **slave** devices. SPI uses four main lines: **MOSI, MISO, SCLK,**
and **SS** (Slave Select). It is faster than I2C and is commonly used in
applications like **SD cards, displays,** and **sensors** that need **rapid
data exchange**.

Why is SPI Important?
SPI is important for applications that require **high-speed data
transfer,** such as when working with **memory cards, graphic
displays,** or **sensors**. It provides **fast, reliable** communication over
short distances and can handle **large amounts of data** quickly.

Syntax Explanation

- `SPI.begin()`: Initializes the SPI bus.
- `SPI.transfer(data)`: Sends and receives data on the SPI
  bus.
- `SPI.end()`: Ends the SPI communication. These functions
  allow fast data transfer between the master and slave
  devices.

Usage

SPI is ideal for **speed-critical** projects, such as reading data from **SD cards** or controlling **displays**, where fast communication is essential.

Code Example

```
#include <SPI.h>

void setup() {
  SPI.begin();
  pinMode(10, OUTPUT);   // SS pin
  Serial.begin(9600);
}

void loop() {
  digitalWrite(10, LOW);   // Select the slave
  byte response = SPI.transfer(0x42);   // Send data and receive
response
  digitalWrite(10, HIGH);   // Deselect the slave
  Serial.println(response);
  delay(1000);
}
```

This example demonstrates communication with an SPI device.

Notes

Use **separate SS pins** for each slave device to prevent communication conflicts.

Warnings

Ensure the **clock speed** is set appropriately for each device.

Troubleshooting Tips

If SPI isn't working, check that **MOSI**, **MISO**, and **SCLK** are correctly wired, and the **clock speed** is compatible with the slave device.

4. UART Communication: Serial Data Transfer

What is UART?

UART (Universal Asynchronous Receiver-Transmitter) is a serial communication protocol used for direct data exchange between two devices using **TX (Transmit)** and **RX (Receive)** pins. Unlike I2C and SPI, UART is typically used for **one-to-one** communication.

It's the simplest method for serial data transfer and is often used for **debugging**, **sensor communication**, and connecting Arduino to devices like GPS modules or Bluetooth.

Why is UART Important?

UART is crucial because it allows **easy and reliable** communication between Arduino and external devices like computers, GPS modules, or serial peripherals. It is commonly used for **sending and receiving data** over long distances, such as between an Arduino and a PC for debugging or monitoring.

Syntax Explanation

- `Serial.begin(baud_rate)`: Initializes serial communication with the specified baud rate.
- `Serial.print(data)`: Sends data to the serial port.
- `Serial.read()`: Reads incoming data from the serial port. These functions enable easy data exchange between Arduino and other devices using UART.

Usage

UART is commonly used for **sending sensor data** to a computer or communicating between multiple Arduino boards in **simple projects**. It's essential for debugging because you can monitor real-time data using the **Serial Monitor**.

Code Example

```
void setup() {
  Serial.begin(9600);   // Start UART communication at 9600 baud
}

void loop() {
  if (Serial.available() > 0) {
    char incomingData = Serial.read();   // Read incoming data
    Serial.print("Received: ");
    Serial.println(incomingData);   // Send the received data back to
the serial monitor
  }
}
```

This example demonstrates basic UART communication, reading and echoing data.

Notes
Ensure that both devices use the **same baud rate** for successful communication.

Warnings
Mismatch in **baud rates** between devices will result in **incorrect or lost data** during transmission.

Troubleshooting Tips
If UART communication is unreliable, check for **correct wiring of TX and RX pins** and ensure that both devices are using the **same baud rate**. Also, make sure no other devices are interfering with the serial port.

---

5. Practical Project: Communication with Multiple Devices

Project Overview: Reading Data from Multiple Sensors Using I2C
In this project, we'll use the **I2C bus** to communicate with multiple sensors connected to a single Arduino. The Arduino will gather data from **a temperature sensor** and **a light sensor**, displaying the data on the Serial Monitor.

Why is This Project Important?
This project shows how to handle **multiple devices** efficiently using the I2C protocol. It's useful in large-scale projects like **weather stations** or **home automation systems**, where multiple sensors need to share data with a single Arduino.

Components List

- Arduino
- Temperature sensor (I2C-based, e.g., TMP102)
- Light sensor (I2C-based, e.g., BH1750)
- Jumper wires
- Breadboard

Circuit Diagram

- Connect **SDA** and **SCL** from the Arduino to both sensors.
- The **TMP102** and **BH1750** share the same **SDA** and **SCL** lines, with unique addresses.
- Power the sensors with **5V** and **GND**.

Code Example

```
#include <Wire.h>
#include <Adafruit_Sensor.h>   // Include I2C libraries for sensors
#include <Adafruit_BH1750.h>
#include <Adafruit_TMP102.h>

Adafruit_BH1750 lightSensor;
Adafruit_TMP102 tempSensor;

void setup() {
  Serial.begin(9600);  // Initialize serial communication
  Wire.begin();  // Start the I2C bus

  if (!lightSensor.begin()) {
    Serial.println("Light sensor not detected");
    while (1);
  }

  if (!tempSensor.begin()) {
    Serial.println("Temp sensor not detected");
    while (1);
  }
}

void loop() {
  float lightLevel = lightSensor.readLightLevel();
  float temperature = tempSensor.readTemperature();

  Serial.print("Light Level: ");
  Serial.print(lightLevel);
  Serial.print(" lx | Temperature: ");
  Serial.print(temperature);
  Serial.println(" °C");

  delay(1000);  // Wait 1 second before the next reading
}
```

This code reads data from a light sensor and a temperature sensor on the **I2C bus**, displaying it on the Serial Monitor.

Challenge
Enhance this project by adding an **SPI-based SD card module** to

log sensor data. Use **I2C** for the sensors and **SPI** for the SD card, allowing you to store readings in a text file for later analysis.

6. FAQ: Common Questions About Communication Protocols

- **Q: Can I use both SPI and I2C on the same Arduino project?**
  A: Yes, both protocols use different pins, but ensure there are no pin conflicts.
- **Q: Why is my I2C device not responding?**
  A: Check for correct wiring, device address, and the use of **pull-up resistors** on the **SDA** and **SCL** lines.
- **Q: How do I handle baud rate mismatches in UART communication?**
  A: Ensure the same baud rate is set on both devices using `Serial.begin(baud_rate)`.
- **Q: When should I use I2C instead of SPI?**
  A: Use I2C when connecting **multiple devices** with fewer wires. SPI is better for **high-speed** communication.
- **Q: What are the maximum speeds of I2C and SPI?**
  A: I2C typically runs up to **400 kHz**, while SPI can reach several **MHz**, depending on the devices.

7. Quiz: Test Your Understanding of Communication Protocols

Sample Questions:

1. **What is the key difference between I2C and SPI?**
   A) I2C uses two wires; SPI uses four.
2. **What is the correct syntax for beginning UART communication in Arduino?**
   A: `Serial.begin(baud_rate)`
3. **Which pins are used in I2C communication on Arduino?**
   A) SDA, SCL
4. **What happens if you don't set the correct baud rate for UART?**

A: Data transmission will fail, causing corrupted data or loss of communication.
5. **How many wires does SPI require?**
   A) Four

Chapter 12: Bitwise Operators

Introduction to Bitwise Operators: Bitwise operators manipulate data at the bit level, directly affecting individual bits rather than whole numbers. They are critical in low-level programming for optimizing memory usage and controlling hardware. Bitwise operators allow efficient data manipulation by working on smaller scales, which is essential in embedded systems, hardware control, and performance-critical applications.

Syntax Table

Topic Name	Syntax	Simple Example
Left Shift	`result = value << number_of_bits;`	`int result = 5 << 2; // result = 20`
Right Shift	`result = value >> number_of_bits;`	`int result = 20 >> 2; // result = 5`
Bitwise AND	`result = value1 & value2;`	`int result = 5 & 3; // result = 1`
Bitwise NOT	`result = ~value;`	`int result = ~5; // result = -6`
Bit Masking with AND	`masked_value = value & mask;`	`int masked_value = 0b10101100 & 0b00001111; // result = 0b1100`
Combining Shifts and AND	`result = (value << shift_amount) & mask;`	`int result = (0b1101 << 2) & 0b11110000; // result = 0b10100000`

1. Introduction to Bitwise Operators

1.1 What are Bitwise Operators?

What are Bitwise Operators?
Bitwise operators manipulate data at the **bit level**, affecting individual bits of numbers instead of whole numbers. These operators include << (left shift), >> (right shift), & (bitwise AND), | (bitwise OR), and ~ (bitwise NOT). They are used to **modify data directly** in memory. For example, & checks if both bits are 1, and | sets a bit if one or both bits are 1. Bitwise operators are essential for **low-level control** in programming.

Why are they important?
Bitwise operators are crucial in **low-level programming** because they allow you to directly **control hardware** and **manipulate data efficiently**. They are used in **embedded systems** and when working with **hardware registers** to set, clear, or toggle specific bits. Bitwise operations also **optimize memory usage** by allowing you to work on a smaller scale with bits instead of entire variables. This is essential for **performance-critical applications** like controlling sensors, actuators, and communication protocols.

1.2 Key Concepts and Terms (Glossary)

What is Bit Shifting (Left and Right Shift)?
Bit shifting moves bits in a number to the left (<<) or right (>>), effectively **multiplying** or **dividing** the number by powers of two. Left shift (<<) adds zeros on the right, while right shift (>>) drops bits.

What is Bit Masking?
Bit masking is the process of using **AND**, **OR**, or **XOR** operators with a **mask** (a binary pattern) to **extract** or **set specific bits** in a number, controlling which bits you want to keep or change.

What is the AND, OR, NOT operator?

- **AND (&)** compares two bits and returns 1 only if **both bits are 1**. It's used for bit masking and checking specific bits.
- **OR (|)** compares two bits and returns 1 if **either bit is 1**. It's used to **set bits** in a value.
- **NOT (~)** inverts every bit in a number, flipping 0 to 1 and 1 to 0. It's used to **invert bit patterns**.

1.3 Overview of Core Bitwise Operators

What are Core Bitwise Operators?
The core bitwise operators are << (left shift), >> (right shift), & (AND), | (OR), and ~ (NOT). These operators work directly on **binary data**, allowing you to **modify bits** of integers. **Left shift (<<)** multiplies a number by 2 for every shift, while **right shift (>>)** divides by 2. **AND (&)** is used to **clear bits**, **OR (|)** sets bits, and **NOT (~)** inverts bits. These are fundamental tools for efficient **bit manipulation** in embedded systems.

Why are they important?
Bitwise operators are vital for **low-level hardware control** because they allow you to work with specific **bits** in registers or memory locations. In **embedded systems**, memory and processing power are limited, so using bitwise operations helps **optimize resource usage**. These operators are also crucial when programming **microcontrollers**, **communication protocols**, and **sensor interfaces**, where you often need to **modify individual bits** to achieve precise control.

Quiz: Test Your Understanding of Bitwise Operators

1. **What does the << operator do?**
   - A) Shifts bits to the right
   - B) Shifts bits to the left

- C) Inverts bits
  - **Answer: B**
2. **How does the & operator function?**
   The & operator compares **two bits** and returns **1** only if **both bits are 1**.
3. **Which operator is used to invert bits?**
   The ~ **operator** is used to **invert** bits.

2. Core Bitwise Operators

2.1 The << (Left Shift) Operator

What is <<?
The << **(left shift)** operator shifts bits to the **left**, effectively **multiplying** the value by powers of two. Each left shift moves bits one position to the left, and a 0 is added to the right. For example, shifting 5 (00000101) two places to the left (5 << 2) results in 20 (00010100). This operation multiplies the original value by 2 for every shift.

Why is it important?
The << **operator** is an efficient way to **multiply** numbers by powers of two. It's widely used in **low-level programming** where resource efficiency is crucial, such as in **embedded systems** and **hardware control**. This operator saves processing time and memory compared to regular multiplication.

Syntax

```
result = value << number_of_bits;
```

This syntax shifts the bits of value to the left by number_of_bits.

Syntax Explanation
In this syntax, the **value** is shifted to the left by the specified **number_of_bits**, multiplying the value by 2 for each shift. The result is stored in the variable **result**.

Usage

Left shifts are used to **multiply** numbers by powers of two. For example, if you want to **double** a number, shifting the bits to the left by 1 achieves this quickly.

Code Example

```
int value = 5;
int result = value << 2;   // Left shift by 2, result is 20
Serial.println(result);    // Outputs 20
```

In this example, shifting 5 by 2 results in 20 since each shift multiplies the value by 2.

Notes

Remember that left shifting adds **zeros** on the right, so it can lead to **data overflow** if the shifted value exceeds the maximum allowed by the data type.

Warnings

Shifting too far can cause **data loss**, as bits shifted beyond the data type's size are **discarded**. Always ensure the number of shifts doesn't exceed the bit size of the data type (e.g., 16 bits for an int).

Troubleshooting Tips

If the result is unexpected, ensure that you're not shifting too far and check the **data type** size. Use Serial.print() to display values before and after shifting to verify the behavior.

2.2 The >> (Right Shift) Operator

What is >>?

The >> **(right shift)** operator shifts bits to the **right**, effectively **dividing** the value by powers of two. For each shift to the right, bits are moved one position, and a 0 (or the sign bit for signed integers) is added to the left. For example, shifting 20 (00010100) two places to the right (20 >> 2) results in 5 (00000101).

Why is it important?
The **>> operator** is an efficient way to **divide** numbers by powers of two. It's commonly used in **embedded systems** and **hardware control** where quick division is needed without the computational overhead of regular division.

Syntax

```
result = value >> number_of_bits;
```

This syntax shifts the bits of **value** to the right by **number_of_bits**.

Syntax Explanation
In this syntax, the **value** is shifted to the right by the specified **number_of_bits**, dividing the value by 2 for each shift. The result is stored in the variable **result**.

Usage
Right shifts are useful for **dividing** numbers by powers of two. For example, shifting right by 1 will **halve** the value quickly, which is useful in low-level programming.

Code Example

```
int value = 20;
int result = value >> 2;   // Right shift by 2, result is 5
Serial.println(result);    // Outputs 5
```

In this example, shifting 20 by 2 results in 5, as each right shift divides the value by 2.

Notes
Right shifts are **efficient for division**, but they discard the bits shifted off, potentially losing data. For signed integers, the **sign bit** is maintained.

Warnings
Shifting too far to the right can result in **data loss**, as bits are discarded. Always ensure that the number of shifts stays within the bounds of the data type's bit size.

Troubleshooting Tips
If the output is incorrect, verify that the value isn't being shifted too far to the right. Also, check if signed values behave as expected, as the **sign bit** may affect the results.

2.3 The & (Bitwise AND) Operator

What is &?
The **& (bitwise AND)** operator compares each bit of two values. If **both** bits are 1, the result is 1; otherwise, the result is 0. This operator is mainly used for **bit masking**, where you can **check specific bits** in a value. For example, 5 & 3 results in 1 because only the lowest bit is set in both values.

Why is it important?
The & operator is essential for **bit masking**, a technique used in **hardware control** and **low-level programming** to manipulate specific bits in a value. It allows you to **check or modify** individual bits in registers or memory.

Syntax

```
result = value1 & value2;
```

This syntax performs a bitwise AND on **value1** and **value2**.

Syntax Explanation
In this syntax, the **& operator** compares the bits of **value1** and **value2**. For each bit, the result is 1 if **both bits are 1**, and 0 otherwise. The result is stored in **result**.

Usage
Bitwise AND is often used for **masking** bits. For example, you can use it to **extract specific bits** from a byte or integer, such as checking whether certain flags are set.

Code Example

```
int value1 = 5;    // 00000101
int value2 = 3;    // 00000011
```

```
int result = value1 & value2;    // result is 1
Serial.println(result);          // Outputs 1
```

In this example, the **bitwise AND** operation results in 1, since only
the lowest bit is set in both numbers.

Notes
Bitwise AND is commonly used to **mask** bits or **check specific
flags** in hardware registers. This allows efficient control of individual
bits.

Troubleshooting Tips
If the AND operation doesn't give the expected result, check if the
bits you're comparing are correctly set. Use Serial.print() to
inspect both values in binary format.

2.4 The | (Bitwise OR) Operator

What is |?
The | **(bitwise OR)** operator compares each bit of two values and
sets the result to 1 if **either bit** is 1. This operator is used to **set
specific bits** in a value. For example, 5 | 3 results in 7 because
bits that are 1 in either value are set in the result.

Why is it important?
The **bitwise OR operator** is useful for **setting specific bits** in
hardware registers. By combining two values, you can **activate
certain flags** or options without affecting other bits. This is critical
for **low-level control** of devices and components.

Syntax

```
result = value1 | value2;
```

This syntax performs a bitwise OR on **value1** and **value2**.

Syntax Explanation
In this syntax, the | **operator** compares each bit of **value1** and
value2. If **either bit** is 1, the corresponding bit in the **result** is set to

1. This is often used to **activate multiple features** without altering the existing settings.

Usage
The OR operator is commonly used to **set multiple bits** at once. For example, in microcontrollers, it's used to turn on multiple outputs, or configure certain features by setting the appropriate bits.

Code Example

```
int value1 = 5;     // 00000101
int value2 = 3;     // 00000011
int result = value1 | value2;  // result is 7
Serial.println(result);       // Outputs 7
```

In this example, the **bitwise OR** results in 7, as all bits that are 1 in either number are set.

Notes
Bitwise OR is often used to **set multiple bits** in hardware registers without affecting the rest of the bits.

2.5 The ~ (Bitwise NOT) Operator

What is ~?
The ~ **(bitwise NOT)** operator **inverts all bits** of an integer. Every 1 becomes 0, and every 0 becomes 1. For example, applying ~ to the number 5 (00000101) results in −6, which is the **complement** of 5 in binary representation. This is often used for **negating values** in low-level programming.

Why is it important?
The ~ **operator** is useful for **complementing values**, especially when working with **binary numbers** or **flags** in hardware registers. It helps to **toggle** all bits, making it an essential tool in bit manipulation, such as in **checksum calculations** or memory manipulation.

Syntax

```
result = ~value;
```

This syntax inverts all the bits of **value** and stores the result in **result**.

Syntax Explanation
In this syntax, ~ flips each bit in the **value**. If the bit is 1, it becomes 0, and if it's 0, it becomes 1. The **inverted value** is then stored in the **result**. This is used when you need to **invert** all bits in a variable.

Usage
Bitwise NOT is often used to **toggle** bits, such as when creating the **complement** of a binary number. It's also useful for **managing flags** or working with negative values in **two's complement arithmetic**.

Code Example

```
int value = 5;      // 00000101
int result = ~value;  // result is -6 (11111010)
Serial.println(result);  // Outputs -6
```

In this example, the **bitwise NOT** inverts the bits of 5, resulting in −6 using **two's complement** representation.

Notes
The result of using **bitwise NOT** depends on the **size of the data type**, as it affects how the bits are inverted, especially for negative numbers.

Warnings
Be cautious when using **bitwise NOT** on **signed integers**, as it may produce **unexpected negative values** due to the inversion of the sign bit.

Quiz: Check Your Understanding of Bitwise Operators

---

1. **What is the difference between ≪ and ≫?**

- o A) $\ll$ shifts bits left, multiplying by powers of 2.
- o B) $\gg$ shifts bits right, dividing by powers of 2.
2. **How does the & operator work for masking?**
The & operator compares **two bits** and returns 1 only if **both bits are 1**. It's used to **mask bits** by isolating specific ones.

FAQ: Common Questions about Bitwise Operators

---

1. **What happens if you shift a bit too far with $\ll$ or $\gg$?**
Shifting bits too far causes **data loss**, as bits shifted beyond the size of the data type are **discarded**. Ensure that the number of shifts doesn't exceed the bit size (e.g., 16 bits for an int).
2. **How is bit masking used in hardware control?**
Bit masking allows you to **manipulate specific bits** in hardware registers. For example, you can **set, clear**, or **check individual bits** to control specific features in hardware components.

3. Combining Bitwise Operators

3.1 Using & and | for Bit Masking

What are & and | for Bit Masking?
The **& (AND)** and **| (OR)** operators are commonly used for **bit masking**, which allows you to **manipulate specific bits** in a value. The & operator is used to **clear bits** or **check if specific bits are set**, while the | operator is used to **set bits** without affecting others. For example, masking allows you to extract parts of a byte or modify bits in a controlled way.

Why is it important?
Bit masking is crucial in **embedded systems** and **hardware control**, where individual bits in registers need to be managed. Using & and |, you can selectively manipulate certain bits without

affecting the rest of the value, allowing for precise control over **hardware features** such as enabling or disabling specific functions.

Syntax

```
masked_value = value & mask;   // Clear bits
new_value = value | mask;      // Set bits
```

Syntax Explanation

In these examples, value & mask will **clear bits** where the mask has 0s, and value | mask will **set bits** where the mask has 1s. This allows you to either **preserve certain bits** or **modify them** according to the mask.

Usage

Bit masking is often used to **toggle, set, or clear specific bits** in a hardware register. For example, to enable a feature in a system by setting a flag or to read a specific part of a memory address by masking.

Code Example

```
int value = 0b10101100;
int mask = 0b00001111;
int result = value & mask;  // result = 00001100
Serial.println(result, BIN);  // Outputs: 1100 (binary)
```

In this example, the **mask** clears the higher bits of value, keeping only the last four bits.

Notes

Bit masking is a powerful tool for **manipulating bits efficiently** in **low-level programming**, enabling control over specific features or states in a system.

Warnings

Ensure that the **mask** is designed correctly, as using the wrong mask can result in clearing or setting **unintended bits**, potentially causing unexpected behavior in the system.

3.2 Using ˜ to Invert Bits for Complementary Values

What is ˜?
The ˜ **(bitwise NOT)** operator **inverts all bits** of a value, turning 1s into 0s and 0s into 1s. For example, applying ˜ to 5 (which is 00000101 in binary) results in −6 (11111010 in two's complement form). This operator is commonly used when creating **complementary values**, such as when you need the **opposite** of a bit pattern.

Why is it important?
The ˜ **operator** is important for creating **bitwise complements**, which are useful in **arithmetic operations**, **checksum calculations**, and **bit manipulation**. In systems that use **two's complement arithmetic**, the NOT operation helps in **negating values** and inverting bit patterns for specific purposes.

Syntax

```
result = ~value;
```

This syntax inverts the bits of **value** and stores the result in **result**.

Syntax Explanation
In this syntax, ˜ inverts every bit in the value. A **1** becomes **0**, and a **0** becomes **1**. The **inverted result** is often used to toggle bits or to produce **complementary values** in low-level systems.

Usage
The ˜ operator is commonly used for **bitwise negation** in **two's complement systems**, especially in **binary arithmetic** or **memory manipulation**. It's useful for creating **inverted patterns** or toggling states in hardware.

Code Example

```
int value = 5;      // 00000101
int result = ~value;  // result is -6 (11111010)
Serial.println(result);   // Outputs -6
```

In this example, **bitwise NOT** inverts the bits of 5, resulting in −6.

affecting the rest of the value, allowing for precise control over **hardware features** such as enabling or disabling specific functions.

Syntax

```
masked_value = value & mask;   // Clear bits
new_value = value | mask;      // Set bits
```

Syntax Explanation

In these examples, value & mask will **clear bits** where the mask has 0s, and value | mask will **set bits** where the mask has 1s. This allows you to either **preserve certain bits** or **modify them** according to the mask.

Usage

Bit masking is often used to **toggle, set, or clear specific bits** in a hardware register. For example, to enable a feature in a system by setting a flag or to read a specific part of a memory address by masking.

Code Example

```
int value = 0b10101100;
int mask = 0b00001111;
int result = value & mask;   // result = 00001100
Serial.println(result, BIN);   // Outputs: 1100 (binary)
```

In this example, the **mask** clears the higher bits of value, keeping only the last four bits.

Notes

Bit masking is a powerful tool for **manipulating bits efficiently** in **low-level programming**, enabling control over specific features or states in a system.

Warnings

Ensure that the **mask** is designed correctly, as using the wrong mask can result in clearing or setting **unintended bits**, potentially causing unexpected behavior in the system.

3.2 Using ~ to Invert Bits for Complementary Values

What is ~?
The ~ **(bitwise NOT)** operator **inverts all bits** of a value, turning 1s into 0s and 0s into 1s. For example, applying ~ to 5 (which is 00000101 in binary) results in −6 (11111010 in two's complement form). This operator is commonly used when creating **complementary values**, such as when you need the **opposite** of a bit pattern.

Why is it important?
The ~ **operator** is important for creating **bitwise complements**, which are useful in **arithmetic operations**, **checksum calculations**, and **bit manipulation**. In systems that use **two's complement arithmetic**, the NOT operation helps in **negating values** and inverting bit patterns for specific purposes.

Syntax

```
result = ~value;
```

This syntax inverts the bits of **value** and stores the result in **result**.

Syntax Explanation
In this syntax, ~ inverts every bit in the value. A **1** becomes **0**, and a **0** becomes **1**. The **inverted result** is often used to toggle bits or to produce **complementary values** in low-level systems.

Usage
The ~ operator is commonly used for **bitwise negation** in **two's complement systems**, especially in **binary arithmetic** or **memory manipulation**. It's useful for creating **inverted patterns** or toggling states in hardware.

Code Example

```
int value = 5;      // 00000101
int result = ~value;  // result is -6 (11111010)
Serial.println(result);  // Outputs -6
```

In this example, **bitwise NOT** inverts the bits of 5, resulting in −6.

Notes
The result of using **bitwise NOT** depends on the **data type** and how many bits are represented. Inverting too many bits can yield unexpected negative values.

Warnings
Be cautious when using ~ with signed integers, as it can result in **negative values** when you're not expecting them due to the nature of **two's complement**.

3.3 Advanced Bit Shifting Techniques

What are Advanced Bit Shifting Techniques?
Advanced **bit shifting** techniques combine **left (<<)** and **right (>>) shifts** with other bitwise operators to create **efficient manipulations** of data. For example, bit shifts can be used to create a **cyclic shift** (where bits shift out one side and back into the other), or combined with **masking** to isolate specific bits after shifting. These techniques are critical in **signal processing**, **cryptography**, and **embedded systems**.

Why are they important?
These advanced techniques help to **optimize performance** in systems where speed and **memory efficiency** are critical. Using bit shifts instead of standard arithmetic operations can make a program much faster, especially in **low-level programming** where hardware control and precise data handling are essential.

Syntax

```
result = (value << shift_amount) & mask;
```

This syntax shifts value left and then applies a **mask** to extract specific bits.

Syntax Explanation
Here, the **value** is shifted left by **shift_amount**, multiplying it by powers of two, and then the **mask** is applied using & to keep only

certain bits. This technique can combine **shifting** and **bit masking** for more precise data manipulation.

Usage
Advanced shifts are used in **signal processing**, where data must be **manipulated efficiently**. For example, **cyclic shifts** can be used to rotate bits, and shifting combined with masking allows for **efficient memory addressing** in systems like microcontrollers.

Code Example

```
int value = 0b11010010;
int result = (value << 2) & 0b11110000;  // Shift left by 2, then mask
Serial.println(result, BIN);  // Outputs: 10100000
```

This example shifts the bits of value to the left by 2 and then applies a mask to keep only the top four bits.

Notes
Combining shifts with **masking** provides a flexible way to control data at the **bit level**. It's commonly used in **hardware registers** where specific bits represent certain functions.

Warnings
Be aware of **overflow** when shifting too far, as bits shifted beyond the register size will be **discarded**. Always ensure your shifts are within the valid range for the data type.

Quiz: Mastering Bitwise Operator Combinations

1. **How does combining & and | allow for setting and clearing bits?**
   Combining these two operators allows you to **set specific bits** with | while **clearing other bits** with & in a controlled way.
2. **What does ~ do when applied to an integer in binary format?**
   The ~ operator **inverts all the bits** of the integer, turning 1s into 0s and 0s into 1s.

4. Practical Projects for Mastering Bitwise Operators

4.1 Project 1: Controlling Multiple LEDs with a Single Variable

This project involves controlling **multiple LEDs** using a **single variable** that holds the **binary state** of each LED. By using **bitwise operators**, specific LEDs can be turned **on** or **off** by setting or clearing the corresponding **bits** in the variable. Each bit in the variable represents an individual LED, meaning an **8-bit integer** can control up to **8 LEDs**.

Why is it important?
This project demonstrates how to efficiently manage multiple **outputs** (like LEDs) using just **one variable**. Instead of assigning separate variables to each LED, you can control several devices at once, conserving **memory** and **processing time**. This method is crucial for **embedded systems** where resources are limited.

Components List:

- **Arduino**
- **8 LEDs**
- **Resistors**
- **Breadboard**
- **Jumper wires**

Circuit Diagram

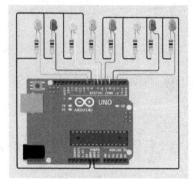

The **8 LEDs** are connected to the Arduino, each with its own
resistor. The **cathodes** of the LEDs are connected to **ground** via
resistors, while the **anodes** are connected to 8 **digital pins** (e.g.,
pins 2 through 9).

Circuit Connection
Each LED is controlled by a specific **bit** in the variable. For example,
bit 0 might represent **LED 1**, **bit 1** might represent **LED 2**, and so
on. By changing the **bits** in the variable, you can control which LEDs
are **on (1)** or **off (0)**.

Code

```
int ledState = 0b00000000;  // All LEDs off
int ledPins[8] = {2, 3, 4, 5, 6, 7, 8, 9};  // Pins for the LEDs

void setup() {
  for (int i = 0; i < 8; i++) {
    pinMode(ledPins[i], OUTPUT);
  }
}

void loop() {
  ledState |= (1 << 3);   // Turn on LED 4 (bit 3)
  ledState &= ~(1 << 5);  // Turn off LED 6 (bit 5)
  updateLEDs();
  delay(500);
}

void updateLEDs() {
  for (int i = 0; i < 8; i++) {
    digitalWrite(ledPins[i], (ledState >> i) & 1);  // Shift the bits
and update each LED
  }
}
```

Code Walkthrough

- The **ledState variable** holds the state of all 8 LEDs.
- The **| operator** is used to **set a bit** (turning an LED on), while the **& operator** combined with **~ (NOT)** clears a bit (turning an LED off).
- The **updateLEDs function** shifts the bits of the **ledState** variable and updates the **LEDs** accordingly by checking whether each bit is **1** or **0**.

Challenge:
Add **push buttons** to allow users to toggle individual LEDs. Use **bitwise XOR (^)** to toggle a specific bit in the **ledState** variable when a button is pressed, flipping the LED's current state.

Common Troubleshooting and Debugging Tips

5.1 Common Errors with Bitwise Operators and How to Fix Them

What are common errors?
Common errors with bitwise operators include **shifting too far** with << or >>, which can cause **data loss** or **overflow** when bits shift beyond the size of the data type. Another mistake is incorrectly using **AND (&)** and **OR (|)** operators, where users may set or clear the wrong bits, leading to unexpected outcomes. Misapplying **NOT** **(~)** on signed integers can also produce negative values unintentionally.

Why do they happen?
These errors often occur due to **misunderstanding operator precedence** or the **overflow behavior** of bitwise operations. Shifting too far left or right exceeds the number of bits the variable can hold, while incorrect application of AND/OR can lead to unexpected masking or setting of bits. Understanding how each operator affects bits is crucial for avoiding such mistakes.

Using the Serial Monitor for Debugging
The **Serial Monitor** is an excellent tool for **tracking errors** in bitwise operations. By printing the **binary representation** of variables using `Serial.print(variable, BIN)`, you can see how bits are being

manipulated in real time. This helps to catch **overflow**, incorrect shifts, or wrong masks and allows you to verify if the bits are being set or cleared correctly.

5.2 Optimizing Bitwise Operations for Performance

What is code optimization for bitwise operations?
Bitwise operations are much faster than arithmetic operations because they directly manipulate bits. By using them to perform tasks like **multiplication, division**, or **conditional checks**, you can optimize your code for **low-memory environments** and ensure your program runs efficiently on **microcontrollers** or **embedded systems**.

Why is it important?
Optimizing code with bitwise operators is crucial for **performance-critical applications**. Since bitwise operations are processed faster and use less memory, they're ideal for **real-time systems** where speed and resource usage are limited, such as in sensor management or device control in **Arduino projects**. Efficient bitwise operations make a significant difference in **battery-powered devices**.

Tips for Performance and Accuracy

- Use **bit shifts** ($\ll$, $\gg$) instead of multiplication or division when working with powers of two.
- Combine **bit masking** and shifting to **extract specific bits** from values efficiently.
- Avoid **shifting too far**, which can cause **data loss**; always ensure shifts are within the bit size of the data type.
- Use **bitwise operations** over loops to reduce processing time.

6. Conclusion and Next Steps

6.1 Recap of Key Bitwise Operators

What have we learned?
In this guide, we explored the fundamental **bitwise operators** such as **left shift (<<), right shift (>>), AND (&), OR (|),** and **NOT (~)**. These operators allow direct manipulation of bits, making them powerful tools for **low-level programming**. You've seen how they can be used for tasks like controlling multiple devices with a single variable, encoding and decoding data, and optimizing memory usage in **embedded systems**. Mastering these operators provides a solid foundation for working on more complex projects that require precise control over hardware.

Why is it important to master these operators?
Mastering bitwise operators is essential for creating **efficient, optimized code**, especially in **microcontroller programming** and **hardware control**. They enable **precise manipulation of data**, which is necessary for tasks like **bit masking, data encoding**, and **real-time processing** in systems with limited memory and processing power.

Chapter 13: Memory Management in Arduino

Memory in Arduino is divided into three main types: **SRAM, Flash,** and **EEPROM**. SRAM is used for storing variables and data during program execution but is volatile. Flash Memory stores the program code and is non-volatile, retaining data even after power loss. EEPROM is non-volatile memory for storing persistent data like settings or calibration values. Understanding how to manage these memory types is crucial for building efficient and reliable Arduino projects, especially given the limited memory resources available on most Arduino boards.

Syntax Table

Topic Name	Syntax	Simple Example
SRAM	`int value = 10;`	`int value = 10; // Stored in SRAM`
Flash Memory	`const int table[] PROGMEM = {1, 2, 3};`	`const char msg[] PROGMEM = "Hello";`
EEPROM	`EEPROM.write(address, value);` `EEPROM.read(address);`	`EEPROM.write(0, value);`
Reading from Flash	`pgm_read_byte_near(address);`	`pgm_read_byte_near(&table[0]);`

---

1. Introduction to Memory Management in Arduino

What is Memory in Arduino?
Memory in Arduino is divided into three main types: **SRAM, Flash,** and **EEPROM**. **SRAM (Static Random-Access Memory)** is used for **storing variables** and data during program execution. **Flash Memory** is where the **program code** is stored and retained even after power is off. **EEPROM** is a type of **non-volatile memory** used

for storing data that needs to **persist after power loss**, such as configuration settings. Each of these memory types has its own purpose, and understanding how to manage them effectively is crucial for optimizing Arduino projects.

Why is Memory Management Important?
Arduino boards have **limited memory resources**, and improper management can lead to **program crashes**, **data loss**, or **malfunctions**. Efficient memory management ensures that programs run **smoothly**, even in large or complex projects. Knowing when to use **SRAM, Flash,** or **EEPROM** allows you to optimize memory usage and ensure your Arduino functions effectively, avoiding common issues like **stack overflow** or running out of memory.

Key Concepts (Glossary)

- **Volatile Memory**: Memory that is lost when power is turned off, like **SRAM**.
- **Non-Volatile Memory**: Memory that retains data even after power is off, like **EEPROM** and **Flash Memory**.
- **Stack**: A section of **SRAM** used for **function calls** and **local variables**.
- **Heap**: A section of **SRAM** used for **dynamic memory allocation**.
- **Global Variables**: Variables stored in **SRAM** that are available throughout the program.
- **Local Variables**: Variables stored in **SRAM** and only accessible within a function.

2. Understanding Memory Types in Arduino

What is SRAM?
SRAM stands for **Static Random-Access Memory**. It is the memory where **variables** are stored during program execution. However, it is **volatile**, meaning that all data is lost when the Arduino is powered off. **SRAM** is limited, and inefficient use can lead to issues like **stack overflow**. Managing **SRAM** effectively is critical in memory-intensive projects.

What is Flash Memory?
Flash Memory is where the **program code** is stored. It is **non-**

volatile, meaning the data is retained even after the Arduino is turned off. Flash memory is used to store **constant data** and large datasets. It is ideal for storing data that doesn't change, such as **lookup tables** or **static configurations**.

What is EEPROM?
EEPROM (Electrically Erasable Programmable Read-Only Memory) is used for **non-volatile storage** of data. It retains its content even when the power is off. **EEPROM** is useful for storing **user settings** or **sensor calibration data** that must persist between power cycles. However, EEPROM has a **limited number of write cycles** (usually around 100,000).

Why are These Memory Types Important?
Each memory type has its role in Arduino projects. **SRAM** is for temporary data, **Flash** stores code and constants, and **EEPROM** preserves data across power cycles. Knowing which to use helps **optimize performance** and **prevent memory issues**.

Code Example

```
#include <EEPROM.h>
int value = 10;  // SRAM
const int lookupTable[5] PROGMEM = {1, 2, 3, 4, 5};  // Flash
EEPROM.write(0, value);  // EEPROM
```

This example demonstrates how to use **SRAM**, **Flash**, and **EEPROM**.

Practical Exercise
Create a program that stores a **sensor value** in **SRAM**, a **lookup table** in **Flash**, and **user settings** in **EEPROM**. Practice writing, reading, and optimizing memory usage.

---

3. Storing and Reading Data from EEPROM

What is EEPROM Storage?
EEPROM is a type of non-volatile memory in Arduino. It is used to store **data that needs to persist** even when the Arduino is powered off, such as user settings or sensor calibration values. EEPROM is essential for **saving important data** between resets or power cycles.

Why is EEPROM Useful?

EEPROM is useful when you need to **store data** that must survive **power loss**, like **user preferences, calibration settings**, or **sensor data**. It is commonly used in projects where long-term data storage is needed.

Syntax Explanation

- `EEPROM.write(address, value)`: Writes a value to the specified address in EEPROM.
- `EEPROM.read(address)`: Reads a value from the specified EEPROM address. These functions allow for easy data storage and retrieval in **non-volatile memory**.

Usage

Use EEPROM to store **critical data** like **counters, settings**, or **sensor readings** that need to be retained across restarts.

Code Example

```
#include <EEPROM.h>
int counter = EEPROM.read(0);  // Read the counter from EEPROM
void setup() {
  counter++;
  EEPROM.write(0, counter);  // Store the updated counter
  Serial.begin(9600);
  Serial.print("Counter: ");
  Serial.println(counter);
}
```

This code reads and writes a **counter value** to EEPROM.

Practical Exercise

Create a project where a **counter** is stored in **EEPROM**, and each time the Arduino restarts, the counter value is incremented and saved.

Troubleshooting Tips

If EEPROM isn't working, ensure that you are not exceeding the **write cycle limit**. Excessive writes can wear out EEPROM memory.

4. Flash Memory: Storing Data Efficiently

What is Flash Memory in Arduino?
Flash Memory stores the Arduino **program code** and **constant data**. It is **non-volatile**, so the data is retained even when the device is powered off. Flash is typically used for storing large constant data like **lookup tables** and **string constants**.

Why is Flash Memory Important?
Flash memory is crucial for **efficiently storing large datasets** that don't need to change during program execution. It helps free up **SRAM** for variable storage, improving the overall performance of the program.

Syntax Explanation

- **PROGMEM**: Used to store data in Flash memory instead of **SRAM**.
- **pgm_read_byte_near ()**: Reads data stored in Flash memory.

These commands help store **large constants** in Flash, leaving **SRAM** free for dynamic variables.

Code Example

```
const char message[] PROGMEM = "Hello from Flash memory!";

void setup() {
  Serial.begin(9600);
  Serial.println(F(message));   // Read and print from Flash
}
void loop() {}
```

This code stores a string in **Flash memory** and prints it from there.

Practical Exercise
Store a **large dataset** like a **lookup table** or string array in Flash memory using **PROGMEM**. Optimize the code to minimize **SRAM** usage.

Troubleshooting Tips
If you run out of **Flash memory**, consider **optimizing your code** by using **efficient libraries** or storing more data in **EEPROM**.

5. Optimizing SRAM Usage in Large Projects

What is SRAM Optimization?
SRAM optimization involves using techniques that reduce the amount of **SRAM** consumed by your program. Key methods include **variable scoping** (limiting the scope of variables), choosing the **right data types**, and storing constants in **Flash memory** using **PROGMEM**. By using these techniques, you can avoid **running out of memory** and ensure smoother program execution, especially in **large projects**.

Why is SRAM Optimization Important?
In large projects, **SRAM** can quickly become exhausted if not managed well, leading to **stack overflows**, **program crashes**, and **data corruption**. Optimizing **SRAM** usage ensures that your program runs smoothly and efficiently, especially on **memory-limited devices** like Arduino.

Syntax Explanation

- **PROGMEM**: Used to store constant data in **Flash** rather than **SRAM**.
- **Local Variables**: Declaring variables within a function to limit their scope to that function.
- **Smaller Data Types**: Using `byte`, `char`, or `int` where possible instead of larger data types like `long`.

These techniques help reduce the amount of **SRAM** required by your program.

Code Example

```
const char text[] PROGMEM = "Optimizing memory!";
void setup() {
  Serial.begin(9600);
  Serial.println(F(text));   // Read from Flash memory
}
```

This example stores a string in **Flash** instead of **SRAM**, freeing up more memory for variables.

Practical Exercise
Refactor a memory-heavy program by moving constants to **Flash** using **PROGMEM**. Limit the use of **global variables** and choose **smaller data types** where possible to reduce **SRAM usage**.

Troubleshooting Tips

Watch out for **memory fragmentation** and **stack overflow** issues when working with **dynamic memory allocation** or large programs. Use **local variables** and avoid **global arrays** when possible.

---

6. Practical Project: Using EEPROM for Non-Volatile Storage

Project Overview: Storing User Settings in EEPROM
In this project, you will store **user settings** like brightness or mode in **EEPROM**. These settings will persist after the device is powered off, allowing the user to maintain their preferences between sessions.

Why is This Project Important?
Storing settings in **EEPROM** is useful in projects where user preferences must be **saved across power cycles**. Examples include **appliances, lighting systems**, or any project where custom settings need to persist.

Components, Circuit Diagram, and Code Walkthrough Components:

- Arduino
- Potentiometer (for brightness control)
- LED
- Push button

Circuit Diagram:

- Connect the potentiometer to an **analog input pin** to adjust brightness.
- Connect the **LED** to a **digital output pin** to display brightness.
- Use the **push button** to save the current brightness setting to **EEPROM**.

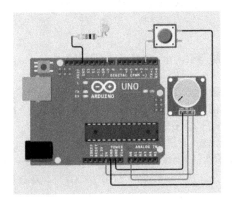

Code Walkthrough:

```
#include <EEPROM.h>
int brightness;
int potPin = A0;   // Potentiometer pin
int ledPin = 9;    // LED pin
int buttonPin = 2;  // Button pin
void setup() {
  pinMode(ledPin, OUTPUT);
  pinMode(buttonPin, INPUT_PULLUP);
  brightness = EEPROM.read(0);  // Read saved brightness from EEPROM
  analogWrite(ledPin, brightness);
}
void loop() {
  int potValue = analogRead(potPin);
  brightness = map(potValue, 0, 1023, 0, 255);
  analogWrite(ledPin, brightness);

  if (digitalRead(buttonPin) == LOW) {  // Button pressed
    EEPROM.write(0, brightness);  // Save brightness to EEPROM
    delay(500);  // Debounce delay
  }
}
```

This project uses a **potentiometer** to adjust the **LED brightness**, and the **push button** saves the brightness to **EEPROM**.

Challenge
Extend the project by storing multiple **user profiles** in **EEPROM**, each containing settings like brightness and mode. Use multiple **EEPROM addresses** to save different profiles and allow the user to switch between them.

7. FAQ: Common Questions About Memory Management

- **Q: How much SRAM, Flash, and EEPROM does an Arduino board have?**
  A: The Arduino **Uno** has **2 KB of SRAM**, **32 KB of Flash**, and **1 KB of EEPROM**. The **Mega** has **8 KB of SRAM**, **256 KB of Flash**, and **4 KB of EEPROM**.
- **Q: What happens when SRAM runs out?**
  A: Running out of **SRAM** can lead to **stack overflow, data corruption**, and program crashes. Your Arduino may stop working properly.
- **Q: How do I check how much memory my program is using?**
  A: Use the **F ()** **macro** for **constant strings** and check memory usage with **memory-checking tools** like the **freeMemory()** function.
- **Q: Can EEPROM wear out?**
  A: Yes, EEPROM has a **limited write cycle** (usually about **100,000** writes). Exceeding this limit may cause data corruption.
- **Q: Can I increase Arduino memory?**
  A: You can use **external EEPROM** or **memory-efficient libraries** to maximize available memory.

---

8. Quiz: Test Your Memory Management Knowledge
Sample Questions:

1. **What type of memory is used for variables in Arduino?**
   A) SRAM
2. **How do you store a constant value in Flash memory?**
   A: Using the `PROGMEM` keyword.
3. **What is the typical lifetime of EEPROM in terms of write cycles?**
   A) Approximately **100,000 write cycles**.
4. **Which memory type is lost when power is turned off?**
   A: SRAM.
5. **What is the correct syntax for writing a value to EEPROM?**
   A) `EEPROM.write(address, value)`
6. **How do you reduce SRAM usage in large projects?**
   A: Use **PROGMEM** for constants and smaller **data types**.

Chapter 14: Conversion Techniques,

Chapter 14 covers conversion techniques that are essential in Arduino programming to ensure different types of data are handled correctly. Conversions allow you to change one data type into another to make sure the data is compatible with various components and calculations in your project. This chapter introduces common conversion functions like byte (), char (), float(), int(), long(), unsigned int, and unsigned long, highlighting their usage, importance, and how they help in efficient data management and memory optimization in Arduino projects.

Syntax Table: Conversion Techniques in Arduino

Topic Name	Syntax	Simple Example
Converting to Byte	byte(variable)	byte sensorByte = byte(sensorValue);
Converting to Char	char(variable)	char character = char(65); // 'A'
Converting to Float	float(variable)	float voltage = float(sensorValue);
Converting to Int	int(variable)	int roundedValue = int(4.9); // 4
Converting to Long	long(variable)	long largeValue = long(50000);
Converting to Unsigned Int	(unsigned int)(variable)	unsigned int posValue = (unsigned int)(value);
Converting to Unsigned Long	(unsigned long)(variable)	unsigned long time = millis();

1. Introduction to Conversion Techniques

1.1 Why is Conversion Important in Arduino?

What is Conversion?
Conversion is the process of **changing one data type into another**. In Arduino programming, different sensors and devices work with different data types. For example, a temperature sensor may return a **floating-point number** (decimal), but you may need to convert it to an **integer** for other parts of the program, like controlling a display. Converting data types ensures that components can **communicate smoothly** and that data is handled in the right format for calculations, output, or transmission. Without proper conversion, the data could lead to errors or incorrect results.

Why is it important?
In Arduino projects, converting data types like **integers, floats, chars**, and **bytes** is crucial for **effective data handling**. For instance, sensor data might need to be converted from one type to another for precise calculations or to save memory. Conversions are also essential when communicating with other hardware, such as **displays, motors**, or **external devices**, to ensure that each component understands the data it receives. Proper conversions help avoid **memory issues** and **overflow errors**, which can cause programs to malfunction.

1.2 Overview of Common Conversion Functions

What are Common Conversion Functions?
Arduino provides several functions to convert between data types. Common ones include:

- byte (): Converts values to **byte** for small numbers (0-255).
- char (): Converts numbers to **characters** (ASCII).
- float (): Converts values to **floating-point numbers** for decimal precision.
- int (): Converts values to **integers** for whole numbers.
- long (): Converts values to **long integers** for larger numbers.

- (unsigned int), (unsigned long): Converts values to **unsigned integers**, which are always positive and allow a larger range for positive numbers. These functions ensure the correct data type is used for **storing**, **processing**, and **displaying** data.

Why are they important?
These conversion functions are essential for making Arduino programs run **efficiently**. For example, using byte() saves memory when working with small numbers, while float() is used when you need **precise decimal values**, such as in **sensor readings**. long() and (unsigned long) are vital for handling **large numbers**, especially when working with **timing functions** like millis(). Each conversion function has a specific use that helps you **optimize memory**, **improve performance**, and prevent errors caused by using the wrong data type.

Quiz: Test Your Understanding of Conversion Techniques

1. When would you use int() instead of float()? (Multiple Choice)
    - o A. When you need whole numbers and memory efficiency
    - o B. When you need decimal precision
    - o C. When working with characters
2. How can unsigned long be used in time tracking? (Short Answer)
    - o unsigned long can store large positive values, which is useful for tracking **time in milliseconds** using the millis() function. This prevents overflow in long-duration projects.

2. The byte() Function

The byte() function in Arduino converts values to the **byte data type**, which stores **whole numbers** from **0 to 255**. This is helpful when working with small numbers that don't need more space, like those in the int or long types. By using byte(), you can save memory and **optimize your program's efficiency**, especially when dealing with **multiple variables** or sensor data.

What is byte()?

The byte() function in Arduino converts a value to the **byte data type**, which stores numbers from **0 to 255**. It's useful when your program only needs to handle **small positive numbers**. For example, if you have a value that will always be between 0 and 255, converting it to a byte saves memory compared to using an int. This is especially important in **memory-constrained** projects, ensuring you use resources effectively.

Why is it Important?

The byte() function helps **optimize memory usage** by allowing you to store small values using **less space**. This is especially useful when working with many variables or when the program needs to run efficiently on Arduino's **limited memory**. By storing values as bytes, you can **prevent memory overuse**, which helps your projects run smoothly.

Syntax

The syntax for using the byte() function is:

```
byte(variable)
```

This converts the value of a variable to the **byte data type**, storing numbers from **0 to 255**.

Syntax Explanation

The byte() function takes a **value** or **variable** as its parameter and converts it to a **byte**. If the value is larger than **255**, it will be **truncated** to fit within the **byte's range** of **0 to 255**. This makes it perfect for **small positive numbers**, helping you manage memory efficiently.

Usage

You can use byte() to store **sensor values** or other small numbers. For example, if a light sensor provides values between **0 and 100**, you can store these as bytes to **save memory**. This is especially useful when handling **multiple sensors** in a project.

Code Example

Here's an example of how to use byte() to store a sensor reading:

```
int sensorValue = analogRead(A0);   // Read sensor value
byte sensorByte = byte(sensorValue);  // Convert sensor value to byte
Serial.println(sensorByte);  // Print the byte value
```

This code reads a sensor value, converts it to a **byte**, and then prints it to the **Serial Monitor**.

Notes

The byte() function is useful when working with **small positive numbers**. It helps **save memory**, which is important in projects where you need to optimize resources.

Warnings

Be cautious when converting values larger than **255**. If you try to store a number beyond this range using byte(), the value will be **truncated**, potentially causing **unexpected results** in your program.

Troubleshooting Tips

If your program behaves unexpectedly when using byte (), check if the values you're converting are **too large**. Numbers greater than **255** will be **truncated**. Also, make sure you are using byte () in cases where **small numbers** are sufficient. Always monitor variable values with the **Serial Monitor** to check for problems.

Quiz: Test Your Understanding of byte ()

1. **What is the range of values a byte can store?**
   - A) 0 to 255
   - B) -128 to 127
   - C) 0 to 1023
   - Answer: **A) 0 to 255**
2. **What happens if you convert a value larger than 255 using byte () ?**
   - The value will be **truncated** to fit within the range of **0 to 255**.

3. The char () Function

The char () function in Arduino converts values to the **char data type**, which stores **characters** using **ASCII values**. It is commonly used in **serial communication**, where characters are transmitted or received. By converting numeric values to characters, the char () function enables **display** or **communication** with external devices, such as computers.

What is char () ?

The char () function converts a value to the **char data type**, which represents characters using **ASCII values**. For example, the integer **65** corresponds to the character **'A'** in ASCII. This function is useful when you need to display or send characters in your project. It is often used when you need to work with **text characters** in **serial communication** or when handling characters on displays like LCDs.

Why is it Important?

The char () function is important because it allows you to convert **numeric data** into **characters**. This is essential for **serial communication**, where devices transmit or receive **characters** as part of text strings. Without converting data to the char type, communication or displaying **readable text** would not be possible.

Syntax

The basic syntax for the char () function is:

```
char(variable)
```

This converts the given **variable** into a **char**, which corresponds to a **character** based on its **ASCII value**.

Syntax Explanation

The char () function takes a **number** or **variable** and converts it to a **character** using the **ASCII table**. For example, the number **65** corresponds to the character **'A'**. This is useful for **serial communication** when transmitting **text characters** to devices.

Usage

You can use char () to convert **numeric values** into **characters** for **display** or **serial transmission**. For instance, converting an integer into a character allows it to be sent to the **Serial Monitor** or displayed on an LCD.

Code Example

Here's a basic example of using char () to convert an integer into a **character** for serial display:

```
int value = 65;  // ASCII value for 'A'
char character = char(value);  // Convert to character
Serial.println(character);  // Display character in Serial Monitor
```

This code converts the value **65** into the character **'A'** and sends it to the **Serial Monitor** for display.

Notes

The char () function is helpful when working with **ASCII characters** in **serial communication**. Make sure to use **valid ASCII values** to avoid unexpected behavior.

Warnings

Make sure that the values you convert to char are within the valid **ASCII range**. Converting numbers outside this range may result in **unintended characters** or errors in your program.

Troubleshooting Tips

If characters are not displaying correctly, ensure that you are using valid **ASCII values**. Check that the baud rate for **serial communication** is set correctly. Use Serial.print () to debug and track **converted characters**. This can help pinpoint **conversion issues**.

Quiz: Test Your Understanding of char ()

1. **What is the ASCII value of 'A'?**
   - A) 97
   - B) 65
   - C) 100
   - **Answer: B) 65**
2. **How is char () used in serial communication?**
   - char () converts **numeric values** to **characters** for transmission over the **Serial Monitor** or display devices.

4. The float () Function

What is float ()?
The float () function converts values to the **float data type**, which stores numbers with **decimal points**. It is ideal when precise values are required, such as in sensor readings or calculations involving **fractions**. Without float (), Arduino would only handle **whole numbers**, limiting accuracy. For example, using float (1. 234) allows your program to work with more precise values compared to using integers.

Why is it Important?
The float () function is necessary for projects requiring **decimal precision**, such as temperature readings, distance calculations, or other sensor data. Without using float (), you would lose **accuracy** when working with decimal numbers. This is important in projects where **small variations** in numbers matter.

Syntax
The syntax for the float () function is:

```
float(variable)
```

This converts the variable to a **floating-point number** for calculations involving **decimal precision**.

Syntax Explanation

The float() function converts a **numeric value** or **variable** to a **floating-point number**, meaning it can store numbers with **decimal points**. This is crucial when working with measurements that require **high precision**, such as temperature or distance.

Usage

Use float() to convert numbers for **precise calculations**, such as when reading data from sensors that provide **decimal values**. For instance, when working with temperature or distance sensors, float() ensures the **accuracy** of the data.

Code Example

Here is an example of using float() in an Arduino program:

```
int sensorValue = analogRead(A0);
float voltage = float(sensorValue) * (5.0 / 1023.0);
Serial.println(voltage);
```

This code reads a sensor value and converts it into a **floating-point number** for more accurate **voltage** calculations.

Notes

Use the float() function for calculations involving **decimal values**. This helps ensure the **accuracy** of data, especially when working with **sensors**.

Warnings

Be aware that **floating-point precision** is limited on Arduino. Extremely large or small decimal numbers may not be handled accurately, especially on **memory-constrained** devices.

Troubleshooting Tips

If your program gives incorrect results, check that the values are within Arduino's **precision limits** for floating-point numbers. Use Serial.print() to monitor the converted values and ensure the **float** conversion is correct.

Quiz: Test Your Understanding of float()

- **When should you use float() instead of int()?**
  - When you need to store **decimal values**.
- **How does Arduino handle floating-point precision?**
  - Arduino has **limited precision** for floating-point numbers.

5. The int() Function

What is int()?

The int() function converts values to the **int data type**, which stores **whole numbers**. It is useful when you do not need **decimal precision**, such as in **counting** or performing **simple arithmetic**. For example, int(3.8) will convert the value to **3**, ignoring the decimal part. Using int() helps save memory when working with **whole numbers**.

Why is it Important?

The int() function helps save memory by storing **whole numbers**. It is ideal for projects where **precision** is not needed, like **counting** or dealing with **simple operations**. Using int() instead of float() reduces memory usage and improves performance.

Syntax

The syntax for the int () function is

```
int(variable)
```

This converts the variable to an **integer**, ignoring any **decimal places**.

Syntax Explanation

The int () function converts a number or variable into an **integer** by **truncating** the decimal part. For example, using int (4.9) will convert the value to **4**, discarding the **decimal**. This is useful for saving memory when decimals are unnecessary.

Usage

Use int () when you don't need **decimal precision** and want to store **whole numbers**. For instance, when counting events or using **digital inputs**, the int () function is sufficient.

Code Example

Here's an example of converting a **float** to an **int** in an Arduino program:

```
float temperature = 25.67;
int roundedTemperature = int(temperature);
Serial.println(roundedTemperature);
```

This code converts the **float** temperature into an **integer**, truncating the decimal part.

Notes

The int () function is best used when **decimal values** are unnecessary. It saves memory by storing only **whole numbers**.

Warnings

The int() function **truncates** decimal values instead of rounding them. Make sure that you do not need the decimal part before converting.

Troubleshooting Tips

If decimal values are being **cut off**, remember that int() does not round numbers; it simply **truncates** them. If you need **decimal precision**, consider using float() instead.

Quiz: Test Your Understanding of int()

- **What happens to decimal values when you convert them using int()?**
    - They are **truncated**, not rounded.
- **What is the difference between int() and float() conversions?**
    - int() stores **whole numbers**, while float() handles **decimals**.

6. The long() Function

What is long()?

The long() function converts values to the **long data type**, which stores larger **whole numbers** than **int**. The long data type is necessary when dealing with **large integers** that exceed the range of an **int**. For example, **millis()** returns a **long** value representing time in milliseconds. Using long() helps prevent **overflow errors** when storing large numbers.

Why is it Important?

The long() function is essential for storing **large numbers** that go beyond the capacity of **int**. Without long(), numbers would overflow, leading to **errors** in calculations involving **time** or other large values.

Syntax

The syntax for the long() function is:

```
long(variable)
```

This converts the variable to a **long integer**, allowing it to store **large numbers**.

Syntax Explanation

The long() function converts a **numeric value** into a **long integer**. This is used when the number is too large for an **int**. For instance, time values in **milliseconds** from the **millis()** function often require long().

Usage

Use long() when you need to store **large numbers**, such as time intervals in **milliseconds**. This ensures that numbers do not **overflow**, which would lead to errors.

Code Example

Here's an example of using long() to store the **time** in milliseconds:

```
long timeElapsed = millis();
Serial.println(timeElapsed);
```

This code stores the **elapsed time** in a long variable to prevent **overflow**.

Notes

The long() function is essential for handling **large integers**. Use it in projects where **int** cannot store large enough values.

Warnings

Ensure the numbers you store with long() are within the valid **range**. Storing values outside this range can cause **overflow** errors.

Troubleshooting Tips

If you experience **overflow** when dealing with large numbers, check if the **int** type is insufficient. Use long() to handle numbers that exceed the range of **int**.

Quiz: Test Your Understanding of long()

- **Why would you use long() instead of int()?**
  - When you need to store **large integers**.
- **What range of values can long() store?**
  - long can store values from **-2,147,483,648 to 2,147,483,647**.

7. The (unsigned int) Conversion

The (unsigned int) conversion is used in Arduino to handle **non-negative integers**. An unsigned int can store larger positive values compared to a regular int because it does not reserve space for negative numbers. This allows it to represent numbers from **0 to 65,535**, compared to the **-32,768 to 32,767** range of a regular int.

What is `(unsigned int)`?

The `(unsigned int)` conversion is used to store **positive whole numbers** in the range of **0 to 65,535**. Unlike regular integers, which can store both positive and negative numbers, `unsigned int` only stores **non-negative** values. This allows you to store **larger positive numbers** without using extra memory. For instance, `(unsigned int)` is useful when counting **non-negative values**, such as time or distance.

Why is it Important?

The `(unsigned int)` conversion is important when you know that your values will always be **non-negative**. By using `unsigned int`, you can store **larger positive numbers** without needing more memory. This is helpful for projects involving **timing**, **counting**, or storing values that are always positive.

Syntax

The syntax for the `(unsigned int)` conversion is:

```
(unsigned int)(variable)
```

This converts the given variable to an **unsigned integer**, meaning it will store **positive values only**.

Syntax Explanation

The (unsigned int) function converts a **number** or **variable** into an **unsigned integer**. This means that it can only store **positive values** and the range of values increases to **65,535**. For example, (unsigned int) (50000) would convert the number **50,000** to an unsigned integer.

Usage

The (unsigned int) conversion is often used when dealing with values that can't be **negative**, like counting **time intervals** or **sensor readings** that are always positive. Using unsigned int ensures **memory efficiency**.

Code Example

Here's an example of using (unsigned int) to count non-negative values:

```
int count = -5;
unsigned int positiveCount = (unsigned int)(count);
Serial.println(positiveCount);
```

In this example, the negative value **-5** is converted to a **large positive number** due to the limitations of (unsigned int), so you should avoid converting negative values.

Notes

The (unsigned int) function is ideal for storing **positive values**. It's helpful for projects where you know that negative numbers will not be encountered, such as **counting events**.

Warnings

Be careful when converting **negative values** using (unsigned int).
Doing so will result in **incorrect outputs**, as negative numbers are
converted into **large positive values**.

Troubleshooting Tips

If you experience unexpected results when using (unsigned int),
check if negative values are being converted. Converting **negative
numbers** can lead to **incorrect large values**, which can cause
issues. Make sure your data is strictly **non-negative**.

Quiz: Test Your Understanding of (unsigned int)

1. **What happens when a negative value is converted using
   (unsigned int)?**
   - The negative value is converted into a **large positive
     value**.
2. **What is the range of values that (unsigned int) can
   store?**
   - **0 to 65,535.**

---

8. The (unsigned long) Conversion

The (unsigned long) conversion in Arduino is used to store **large
positive numbers**. It is particularly useful in time-related functions
such as **millis()**, which return large values that represent time in
milliseconds. The range of an unsigned long is **0 to
4,294,967,295**, making it ideal for applications requiring very large
numbers.

What is (unsigned long)?

The (unsigned long) conversion allows you to store **large positive numbers** in Arduino, with a range of **0 to 4,294,967,295**. It is useful for applications like **time tracking** or **counters** where the values can become very large. For instance, the function **millis()** returns the number of milliseconds since the program started, which is a large value that fits within an unsigned long.

Why is it Important?

The (unsigned long) conversion is essential when dealing with **large numbers** that exceed the capacity of **unsigned int**. It is especially useful for **time-based calculations** or **counters** where large values need to be stored without risking **overflow** errors.

Syntax

The syntax for the (unsigned long) conversion is:

```
(unsigned long)(variable)
```

This converts the variable to an **unsigned long**, allowing it to store very **large numbers**.

Syntax Explanation

The (unsigned long) function converts a **number** or **variable** into an **unsigned long integer**. This allows you to store much larger values compared to unsigned int. For example, the result of (unsigned long) (1000000) would be a **large positive number**.

Usage

The (unsigned long) conversion is commonly used in time-related functions like **millis()**, which return the time in **milliseconds**. Using (unsigned long) ensures you can store **large numbers** without risking overflow.

Code Example

Here's an example of using (unsigned long) to store time in milliseconds:

```
unsigned long currentTime = millis();
Serial.println(currentTime);
```

In this code, the current time is stored in an unsigned long to handle the **large value** returned by **millis()**.

Notes

The (unsigned long) conversion is essential for storing **large positive values**. It is typically used in **time calculations** or **large counters**.

Warnings

Ensure that the values you store using (unsigned long) do not exceed its **maximum range**. If you exceed this range, it will result in **overflow errors**.

Troubleshooting Tips

If your program starts showing **overflow errors** or incorrect values, check that the numbers you are using are within the valid range for (unsigned long). Make sure that your calculations do not exceed **4,294,967,295**.

Quiz: Test Your Understanding of (unsigned long)

1. **What is the maximum value an** (unsigned long) **can store?**
   - **4,294,967,295**.
2. **How is** (unsigned long) **useful in time tracking or counting?**
   - It allows you to store **large numbers** for **precise time measurements** or large counters.

9. Practical Projects for Mastering Conversion Techniques

9.1 Project 1: Converting Analog Temperature Data to Fahrenheit and Celsius

---

This project demonstrates how to use the **LM35 temperature sensor** with an Arduino to read analog temperature values in **Celsius** and convert them to **Fahrenheit**. You'll learn how to handle **sensor readings** using float () to ensure accurate conversions, and the values will be displayed on the **Serial Monitor**.

Components List:

- **Arduino**
- **LM35 Temperature Sensor**
- **Breadboard**
- **Wires**
- **LCD display** (optional)

Circuit Diagram:

The **LM35 sensor** has three pins:

- **VCC** → Connects to **5V** on the Arduino.
- **GND** → Connects to **ground (GND)** on the Arduino.
- **Output** → Connects to **A0** (analog input pin) on the Arduino.

Circuit Connection:

1. **VCC** pin of the **LM35** connects to **5V** on the Arduino.
2. **GND** pin of the **LM35** connects to **ground (GND)** on the Arduino.
3. **Output** pin of the **LM35** connects to the **analog input pin A0** on the Arduino.

The **LM35** provides an **analog output** proportional to the surrounding temperature. The analog value is read using analogRead(), and **math operations** are performed to convert the value into **Celsius** and **Fahrenheit**, using float() to handle precise calculations.

Code:

```
void setup() {
  Serial.begin(9600);  // Initialize the Serial Monitor at 9600 baud
rate
}

void loop() {
  int sensorValue = analogRead(A0);  // Read the analog value from LM35
  float temperatureC = (sensorValue / 1024.0) * 500.0;  // Convert
analog reading to Celsius
  float temperatureF = (temperatureC * 9.0 / 5.0) + 32.0;  // Convert
Celsius to Fahrenheit

  // Print temperature values to the Serial Monitor
  Serial.print("Temperature in Celsius: ");
  Serial.println(temperatureC);
  Serial.print("Temperature in Fahrenheit: ");
  Serial.println(temperatureF);

  delay(1000);  // Delay for 1 second for readability
}
```

Code Walkthrough:

1. **sensorValue**:
   The analogRead(A0) function reads the **analog value** from
   the **LM35 sensor**, which outputs a value between **0 and
   1023**. This value corresponds to the measured temperature.
2. **temperatureC**:
   The formula (sensorValue / 1024.0) * 500.0 converts the
   analog value to **Celsius**. The **LM35 sensor** outputs **10
   mV/°C**, and this calculation scales the analog reading to
   represent the temperature in Celsius.
3. **temperatureF**:
   The Celsius temperature is converted to **Fahrenheit** using
   the formula (C * 9/5) + 32. This is a standard conversion
   formula to switch from Celsius to Fahrenheit.
4. **Serial Output**:
   The temperatures in both **Celsius** and **Fahrenheit** are
   printed to the **Serial Monitor** for easy monitoring.
5. **Delay**:
   A **1-second delay** (delay(1000)) is added to space out the
   readings and make them more readable on the Serial
   Monitor.

Challenge: Add a Display
Add an **LCD display** using the I2C protocol to show both Celsius and Fahrenheit on the screen. Alternatively, you can use an OLED display for a more modern look.

9.2 Project 2: Mapping Sensor Values Using `int()` and `long()`

This project demonstrates how to use a **potentiometer** as an input to control a **servo motor**. The potentiometer's analog values are read by the Arduino, then mapped using `int()` and `long()` to convert the sensor input into a usable range for controlling the **servo's angle**. This teaches the importance of **data conversion** when working with sensor values and hardware components.

Components List:

- **Arduino**
- **Potentiometer**
- **Servo motor**
- **Breadboard**
- **Wires**

Circuit Diagram:

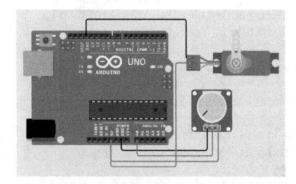

- **Potentiometer**:
  - Connect the **middle pin** (signal) to **A0** on the Arduino.
  - The other two pins go to **5V** and **GND**.

- **Servo Motor**:
  - ○ Connect the **control wire** of the servo to **pin 9** (a PWM pin).
  - ○ Connect the **power pin** of the servo to **5V**.
  - ○ Connect the **GND** pin of the servo to **GND** on the Arduino.

Circuit Connection:

1. **Potentiometer**:
   - ○ The potentiometer acts as a **variable resistor**, providing an analog value between **0-1023**.
   - ○ This value is read by the Arduino and mapped to control the **servo's angle** from **0° to 180°**.
2. **Servo Motor**:
   - ○ The potentiometer's raw value is converted to a servo angle using int () and long () conversions to ensure **precision** in the movement of the servo.

Code:

```
#include <Servo.h>

Servo myServo;   // Create servo object
int potValue;    // Variable to store potentiometer value
int servoAngle;  // Variable to store the calculated servo angle

void setup() {
  myServo.attach(9);   // Attach the servo to pin 9
}

void loop() {
  potValue = analogRead(A0);   // Read the potentiometer value (0-1023)
  servoAngle = map(potValue, 0, 1023, 0, 180);   // Map the value to a
range of 0-180 for the servo
  myServo.write(servoAngle);   // Move the servo to the calculated angle
}
```

Code Walkthrough:

1. **Analog Reading**:
   - The analogRead(A0) function reads the potentiometer's value, which ranges from **0 to 1023**. This represents the potentiometer's current position.
2. **Mapping the Value**:
   - The map() function is used to convert the **potentiometer's range (0-1023)** into a **servo angle range (0°-180°)**.
   - The int type is sufficient to store the **mapped servo angle**, while long could be used for larger ranges, but is not needed in this case.
3. **Servo Control**:
   - The **servo** is then moved to the mapped angle using the myServo.write(servoAngle) function, and the position is adjusted as the **potentiometer** is turned.
   - This allows for real-time control of the **servo motor's angle** by simply turning the **potentiometer**.

Challenge: Add Additional Sensors
Add a second sensor, such as an **LDR (Light Dependent Resistor)**, to control the servo motor based on both **light intensity** and **potentiometer** readings. This requires combining two sensor inputs for multi-variable control.

9.3 Project 3: Timing Events with (unsigned long) and long() for LED Control

---

This project demonstrates how to control **LEDs** based on the duration a **push button** is pressed using the millis() function and the **unsigned long** data type. The time the button is pressed is measured, and different LEDs are turned on depending on how long the button is held down. This project shows the practical use of **timing events** and precise tracking using millis() for controlling LEDs.

Components List:

- **Arduino**
- **3 LEDs**
- **Resistors** (220Ω recommended for each LED)
- **Push button**
- **Breadboard**
- **Wires**

Circuit Diagram:

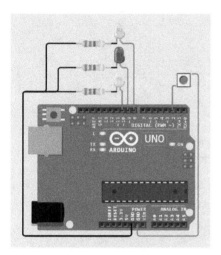

- **LEDs** are connected to digital pins **8, 9, and 10** with **resistors** to limit the current.
- **Push button** is connected to **pin 2** with a **pull-down resistor** to **ground** to avoid floating values when the button is not pressed.

Circuit Connection:

1. **LEDs**:
   - Connect the **positive leg** (anode) of the LEDs to **pins 8, 9, and 10** on the Arduino.
   - Connect a **220Ω resistor** between the **negative leg** (cathode) of each LED and **GND**.
2. **Push Button**:
   - Connect one pin of the **push button** to **pin 2** on the Arduino.
   - Connect the other pin to **GND**.

o   Add a **10kΩ pull-down resistor** between **pin 2** and **GND** to stabilize the signal.

Code:

```
unsigned long pressStartTime = 0;  // Store time when button is pressed
bool buttonPressed = false;        // Track button press state
void setup() {
  pinMode(2, INPUT);     // Button pin
  pinMode(8, OUTPUT);    // LED 1 pin
  pinMode(9, OUTPUT);    // LED 2 pin
  pinMode(10, OUTPUT);   // LED 3 pin (optional for further timing
control)

  digitalWrite(8, LOW);  // Ensure LED 1 is off initially
  digitalWrite(9, LOW);  // Ensure LED 2 is off initially
  digitalWrite(10, LOW); // Ensure LED 3 is off initially
}
void loop() {
  // Check if button is pressed and not already pressed before
  if (digitalRead(2) == HIGH && !buttonPressed) {
    pressStartTime = millis();  // Record time of press
    buttonPressed = true;       // Set button press state to true
  }

  if (buttonPressed) {
    // Turn on LED 1 after 1 second
    if (millis() - pressStartTime > 1000) {
      digitalWrite(8, HIGH);
    }

    // Turn on LED 2 after 3 seconds
    if (millis() - pressStartTime > 3000) {
      digitalWrite(9, HIGH);
    }

    // Turn on LED 3 after 5 seconds (optional)
    if (millis() - pressStartTime > 5000) {
      digitalWrite(10, HIGH);
    }
    // Reset if button is released
    if (digitalRead(2) == LOW) {
      buttonPressed = false;      // Reset button state
      digitalWrite(8, LOW);       // Turn off LED 1
      digitalWrite(9, LOW);       // Turn off LED 2
      digitalWrite(10, LOW);      // Turn off LED 3 (optional)
    }
  }
}
```

Code Walkthrough:

1. **Tracking Time with millis():**
   - When the button is pressed, pressStartTime stores the current time in **milliseconds** using millis(). This is done using **unsigned long** to handle the potentially large numbers generated over time.
2. **LED Control Based on Time:**
   - The millis() function continuously checks how much time has passed since the button was pressed:
     - If **1 second** has passed, **LED 1** turns on.
     - If **3 seconds** have passed, **LED 2** turns on.
     - If **5 seconds** have passed (optional), **LED 3** turns on.
3. **Button Release and Reset:**
   - When the button is released (digitalRead(2) == LOW), the state is reset, and all LEDs turn off, allowing the process to repeat the next time the button is pressed.

Challenge: Add a Buzzer
Include a **buzzer** that sounds if the button is pressed for more than **5 seconds**. You can use similar timing logic to control the buzzer activation.

9.4 Project 4: Converting Sensor Data for Communication with Other Devices

---

In this project, you will read **temperature** and **humidity** data from a **DHT11 sensor** and convert the data for display or transmission to other devices, such as via **I2C** or **Bluetooth**. You will use **int()**, **float()**, and **char()** to format and transmit the sensor values. This project demonstrates how to handle sensor data and prepare it for different communication protocols.

Components List:

- **Arduino**
- **DHT11 sensor**
- **OLED display** (optional) or I2C module

- **Breadboard**
- **Wires**

Circuit Diagram:

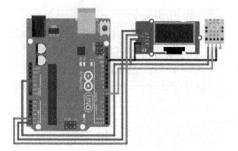

- **DHT11 sensor**:
    - ○ **VCC** → Connect to **5V**.
    - ○ **GND** → Connect to **GND**.
    - ○ **Data pin** → Connect to **digital pin 7**.
- **OLED display** (if using):
    - ○ **SDA** → Connect to **A4** (I2C data).
    - ○ **SCL** → Connect to **A5** (I2C clock).

Circuit Connection:

1. Connect the **DHT11 sensor** to the Arduino:
    - ○ **VCC** to **5V**
    - ○ **GND** to **GND**
    - ○ **Data pin** to **pin 7** on the Arduino.
2. (Optional) **OLED display** via **I2C**:
    - ○ **SDA** to **A4** on the Arduino.
    - ○ **SCL** to **A5** on the Arduino.

Code:

```
#include <DHT.h>
```

```cpp
#define DHTPIN 7          // Pin where the DHT sensor is connected
#define DHTTYPE DHT11     // DHT11 sensor type

DHT dht(DHTPIN, DHTTYPE);  // Initialize DHT sensor

void setup() {
  Serial.begin(9600);   // Start Serial communication
  dht.begin();          // Initialize the DHT sensor
}

void loop() {
  // Reading temperature and humidity
  float humidity = dht.readHumidity();
  float temperature = dht.readTemperature();

  // Check if any readings failed
  if (isnan(humidity) || isnan(temperature)) {
    Serial.println("Failed to read from DHT sensor!");
    return;
  }

  // Print humidity and temperature to Serial Monitor
  Serial.print("Humidity: ");
  Serial.print(humidity);
  Serial.println(" %");

  Serial.print("Temperature: ");
  Serial.print(temperature);
  Serial.println(" *C");

  delay(2000);  // Wait 2 seconds between measurements
}
```

Code Walkthrough:

1. **DHT Sensor Setup**:
   - The **DHT11 sensor** is connected to **pin 7**, and the DHT library is used to read the **temperature** and **humidity** values.
   - The DHT dht(DHTPIN, DHTTYPE) line initializes the sensor with the correct pin and sensor type.
2. **Reading Sensor Data**:
   - dht.readHumidity() and dht.readTemperature() functions are used to retrieve the **humidity** and **temperature** values, which are stored as **float** for precise calculations.

3. **Error Handling**:
    - o The code checks for failed sensor readings using isnan() (which stands for "is not a number"). If any reading fails, an error message is printed to the Serial Monitor.
4. **Displaying Data**:
    - o The temperature and humidity values are displayed on the **Serial Monitor** using Serial.print() and Serial.println().
5. **Delay**:
    - o A **2-second delay** (delay(2000)) is introduced between each reading to avoid flooding the monitor with data and to allow time for the sensor to take new measurements.

Challenge: Add Wireless Communication
Modify the project to send data via **Bluetooth** using an **HC-05** or **ESP8266** Wi-Fi module. This allows the sensor data to be monitored remotely through a mobile app.

10. Common Troubleshooting and Debugging Tips

10.1 Common Errors and How to Fix Them

What are common errors?
Common errors in Arduino programming involve issues like **overflow** when converting large values, **truncation** of decimal numbers, or using the wrong data type for a specific operation. For instance, converting a floating-point number into an integer without understanding that decimals will be truncated can lead to incorrect results. Using unsigned int for potentially negative values can also result in large, unexpected positive numbers.

Why do they happen?
These errors often happen because of incorrect data type usage, such as using int when a **float** or **long** is required. Overflow occurs when the value exceeds the data type's capacity, while truncation occurs when converting between types like float() to int(). Lack of proper understanding of the conversion processes can lead to inefficient use of **Arduino's limited memory** or processing capabilities.

Use of Serial Monitor for Debugging

The **Serial Monitor** is an essential tool for debugging in Arduino. You can use **Serial.print()** and **Serial.println()** to display variable values, sensor readings, and program flow. For example, print the value before and after conversion to see if it matches your expectations. This allows you to identify where an error might be happening in real-time, making it easier to fix issues quickly.

10.2 Optimizing Conversion Techniques for Performance

What is optimization?

Optimization refers to improving the **efficiency** of your code so that it runs faster and uses less memory. In Arduino, this can mean choosing the correct data type for conversions (e.g., using byte or int instead of long or float when possible). Ensuring efficient memory use and reducing unnecessary calculations is key to **performance optimization**.

Why is it important?

Optimizing conversions is important because Arduino boards have **limited memory** and **processing power**. If too much memory is used, the system may slow down, reset randomly, or crash. By optimizing data types and conversion processes, you ensure your program runs **smoothly** and handles more **complex tasks** without running into performance bottlenecks.

Tips for Performance and Accuracy

- Use smaller data types like byte or int for small values to save memory.
- Avoid frequent float() conversions as they take more processing power.
- Use **Serial Monitor** to track memory usage and adjust as needed.
- When possible, store constants in **PROGMEM** (flash memory) to free up **RAM**.

---

11. Conclusion and Next Steps

11.1 Recap of Conversion Techniques

What have we learned?
Throughout this guide, we've explored how to use various **conversion techniques** in Arduino, such as byte(), int(), float(), long(), and **unsigned types**. Each function serves a unique purpose, whether it's handling small values efficiently or dealing with **large numbers** and **decimals**. You've learned how to convert **analog sensor data**, map values using int() and long(), and optimize performance. Mastering these conversions allows you to handle different **sensors**, **displays**, and **communication protocols**, ensuring your projects run smoothly.

Why is mastering conversions important?
Understanding and mastering conversions is key to building more efficient, accurate, and **memory-optimized** Arduino projects. By using the correct data types and conversion methods, you reduce the risk of **overflow**, **truncation errors**, and **memory leaks** while improving the reliability and performance of your project.

Chapter 15: Characters and Strings

Chapter 15 introduces character and string handling in Arduino programming. Characters represent individual letters, numbers, or symbols, while strings are a collection of characters grouped together. In Arduino, characters are stored as char data types, and strings can either be arrays of characters or String objects. Understanding characters and strings is essential for processing text, managing user inputs, and displaying messages on screens. Functions such as isAlpha(), isDigit(), isPrintable(), and isUpperCase() are crucial for handling and validating text-based data effectively in Arduino projects.

Syntax Table: Arduino Character and String Functions

Topic Name	Syntax	Simple Example

Checking for Letters	isAlpha(char)	if (isAlpha('A')) { ... } // True
Checking for Numbers	isDigit(char)	if (isDigit('5')) { ... } // True
Checking for ASCII Characters	isAscii(char)	if (isAscii('A')) { ... } // True
Checking for Uppercase Letters	isUpperCase(char)	if (isUpperCase('B')) { ... } // True
Checking for Lowercase Letters	isLowerCase(char)	if (isLowerCase('b')) { ... } // True
Validating Printable Characters	isPrintable(char)	if (isPrintable('!')) { ... } // True

1. Introduction to Character and String Functions in Arduino

1.1 What are Characters and Strings in Arduino?

Characters represent individual **letters, numbers**, or symbols, while **strings** are a collection of characters grouped together. In Arduino, a **character** is stored as a single byte (using the **char** data type). A **string** is either an array of characters or an object that stores multiple characters. You can use characters and strings to **process text**, manage user inputs, or display messages on screens. For example, a string can hold the name of a user, and characters can help break down the text to check for specific letters or symbols. Knowing the difference between these two helps you handle **text-based data** in your projects.

Why are they important?
Characters and strings are crucial in **text handling**, user input, and

display functions in Arduino. They allow you to process **names, passwords**, and messages in projects. For example, in a project where users input their name or press keys on a keypad, understanding characters and strings helps ensure the correct text is processed. Without them, it would be difficult to handle **textual data** effectively, making interactive projects harder to create.

1.2 Key Concepts and Terms (Glossary)

What is a Character?
A character is a **single letter, number**, or symbol, stored in a **char** data type, taking up **1 byte** of memory.

Why is it important?
Characters help **break down** strings and work with **individual text elements**, essential in **text processing** tasks like checking input.

What is a String?
A string is a collection of characters, used to store **words, sentences**, or any text. In Arduino, it can be an **array of characters** or a **String object**.

Why is it important?
Strings are important for handling **longer text**, like user inputs, names, and messages in Arduino projects. They simplify **text manipulation**.

1.3 Overview of Core Character and String Functions

What are Core Character and String Functions?
In Arduino, functions like **isAlpha()**, **isDigit()**, and **isPrintable()** help process text effectively. **isAlpha()** checks if a character is a letter, **isDigit()** confirms if it's a number, and **isPrintable()** verifies if a character can be displayed. These functions simplify **input validation** and **text analysis** by breaking down strings into individual characters and analyzing them. For instance, if you want to ensure that a password contains only letters and numbers, these functions can help.

Why are they important?
These functions are critical for **input validation** and **text manipulation** in projects. They allow you to **verify user inputs**,

such as ensuring a user's name contains only letters, or checking that a string has no non-printable characters before displaying it on an LCD. By using functions like **isAlpha()** and **isDigit()**, you can build more reliable and interactive programs that handle text accurately.

Quiz: Test Your Understanding of Characters and Strings

- What is the purpose of **isAlpha()**?
  - o A: To check if a character is a letter.
- How does **isDigit()** work?
  - o A: It checks if a character is a number.

2. Basic Character Validation Functions

2.1 The isAlpha() Function: Checking for Letters

What is isAlpha()?
The isAlpha() function checks whether a character is a **letter** from the alphabet. It identifies both **uppercase and lowercase** letters. You use it in Arduino programs when you need to verify that a specific input or character is a letter. This function helps prevent errors by ensuring the input contains only **alphabetic characters**, which is useful in name fields or text-based interactions.

Why is it important?
Validating input with isAlpha() ensures **text fields** contain only letters. This is essential when working on projects where inputs should not include **numbers** or **symbols**, such as when processing **names** or **words**. It simplifies error-checking and helps avoid invalid entries.

Syntax
isAlpha(char)
This function takes one **character** and returns **true** if it's a letter, or **false** if it's anything else, like a number or symbol.

Syntax Explanation
The function accepts one input, which is a **single character**. If the character is an alphabetic letter (A-Z or a-z), it returns **true**. If the input is not a letter, the function returns **false**.

Usage

isAlpha() is commonly used for **validating text fields** where letters are required, like a **name input**. This function ensures only alphabetic characters are accepted, making the program more reliable.

Code Example

```
char input = 'A';
if (isAlpha(input)) {
  Serial.println("This is a letter.");
} else {
  Serial.println("This is not a letter.");
}
```

In this example, the code checks if the character input is a letter and prints the result to the serial monitor.

Notes

Use isAlpha() to filter **non-letter characters** in projects that require letters only, ensuring **valid input**.

Warnings

The function only works on **individual characters**. If you pass multiple characters or strings, it will return **false**.

Troubleshooting Tips

If isAlpha() returns **false** when you expect **true**, double-check that the input is a **single character** and that there are no hidden spaces or non-printable characters.

2.2 The isDigit() Function: Checking for Numbers

What is `isDigit()`?

The `isDigit()` function checks whether a character is a **number** between 0 and 9. You use this function when you need to confirm that the input contains only **numeric characters**. This is essential when working with **numeric data**, such as validating **PIN codes**, **phone numbers**, or other number-only inputs.

Why is it important?

In many projects, especially those requiring **numeric input**, you need to ensure that the input is only numbers. This function is vital in making sure **invalid characters** like letters or symbols don't disrupt your program.

Syntax

```
isDigit(char)
```

The function takes one **character** and checks if it is a **digit** (0-9), returning **true** or **false**.

Syntax Explanation

The function works by accepting a **single character** input. If this character is a digit from 0 to 9, the function returns **true**. Otherwise, it returns **false**.

Usage

`isDigit()` is used when validating inputs that need to be **numbers**, such as when creating a **PIN code** field or a **phone number** input. It ensures the input is purely numeric.

Code Example

```
char input = '5';
if (isDigit(input)) {
  Serial.println("This is a digit.");
} else {
  Serial.println("This is not a digit.");
}
```

This example checks if the input character is a digit and prints the result to the serial monitor.

Notes

Use isDigit() when **numeric validation** is necessary, especially in **input fields** where only numbers should be accepted.

Warnings

The function only checks **single characters**. If multiple characters are passed, such as in strings or letters, it will return **false**.

Troubleshooting Tips

If the function isn't working, ensure the input is a **single digit** and check for **unexpected spaces** or symbols that could cause isDigit() to fail.

2.3 The isAscii() Function: Checking for ASCII Characters

What is isAscii()?

The isAscii() function checks whether a character belongs to the **ASCII** character set, which includes most **standard symbols, numbers, and letters**. It's useful when working with text inputs that should be **displayed** on screens or processed within systems that only support ASCII characters.

Why is it important?

Some systems, especially **displays** or **serial monitors**, only support **ASCII characters**. This function helps ensure input data is in the correct **ASCII range** (0-127), avoiding **display errors**.

Syntax

```
isAscii(char)
```

It checks if a **character** is part of the **ASCII set**, returning **true** or **false**.

Syntax Explanation

The function takes a **single character** as input and returns **true** if the character is within the **ASCII range** (0-127). If the character is outside this range, it returns **false**.

Usage

Use `isAscii()` when validating **inputs** for systems like **LCD screens** or **serial monitors** to ensure only ASCII characters are processed and displayed correctly.

Code Example

```
char input = 'A';
if (isAscii(input)) {
  Serial.println("This is an ASCII character.");
} else {
  Serial.println("This is not an ASCII character.");
}
```

This example checks if input is an ASCII character and prints the result.

Notes

Use this function when working with **displays** or systems that require **ASCII-compliant characters**.

Warnings

If non-ASCII characters are input, they may cause **errors** or display incorrectly on **limited displays** like LCD screens.

Troubleshooting Tips

Ensure that input characters are within the **ASCII range** (0-127). If the function returns **false**, the character is likely outside this range.

Quiz: Check Your Understanding of Basic Character Validation Functions

1. What does the `isAlpha()` function check for?
   - A: Letters only.
2. How does `isDigit()` work?
   - A: It checks if the input is a numeric character (0-9).
3. When would you use `isAscii()`?
   - A: When validating input to ensure it contains only ASCII characters.

3. Advanced Character and String Functions

3.1 The isUpperCase() Function: Checking for Uppercase Letters

What is isUpperCase()?
The isUpperCase() function checks if a character is an **uppercase letter** (A-Z). It is commonly used when case-sensitive input is required, such as validating **passwords** or formatting **output** text. This function ensures that input is properly capitalized where necessary.

Why is it important?
In case-sensitive applications, such as passwords, specific formatting rules often require **uppercase letters**. The isUpperCase() function ensures compliance with these rules by validating input.

Syntax
isUpperCase(char)
This function accepts a **single character** as input and returns **true** if it is an uppercase letter, or **false** if it's not.

Syntax Explanation
The function checks if the input is an uppercase letter. If the character is between **A-Z**, the function returns **true**. Otherwise, it returns **false**.

Usage
Use isUpperCase() when validating inputs that must be **capitalized**, such as in case-sensitive forms, ensuring that users provide the correct input.

Code Example
```
char input = 'B';
if (isUpperCase(input)) {
  Serial.println("This is an uppercase letter.");
} else {
  Serial.println("This is not an uppercase letter.");
}
```

This code checks whether the character is uppercase.

Notes
Use isUpperCase() to ensure that text fields requiring **capitalization** are validated before processing.

Warnings
This function does not validate entire strings; it checks **only one character** at a time.

Troubleshooting Tips
Ensure that the input is a **single character**. If the function isn't working, check for extra characters or spaces in the input.

3.2 The isLowerCase() Function: Checking for Lowercase Letters

What is isLowerCase()?
The isLowerCase() function checks if a character is a **lowercase letter** (a-z). It helps ensure proper formatting where **lowercase input** is required, such as in **usernames** or passwords that are case-sensitive.

Why is it important?
This function is essential for ensuring that **lowercase** letters are properly validated in input fields, particularly when case sensitivity is enforced, such as in password fields.

Syntax

```
isLowerCase(char)
```

It accepts one character as input and returns **true** if the character is lowercase, or **false** otherwise.

Syntax Explanation
The function checks if the input is a lowercase letter. If the character falls within **a-z**, the function returns **true**. Otherwise, it returns **false**.

Usage
Use isLowerCase() when validating **user input** where lowercase characters are required, such as in **usernames** or **passwords** that enforce case sensitivity.

Code Example

```
char input = 'b';
if (isLowerCase(input)) {
  Serial.println("This is a lowercase letter.");
} else {
  Serial.println("This is not a lowercase letter.");
}
```

This code validates whether the input is a lowercase letter.

Notes
This function is particularly helpful in **case-sensitive applications** where **lowercase letters** are necessary for validation.

Warnings
isLowerCase() only checks **one character** at a time. It will not validate entire strings or words.

Troubleshooting Tips
Ensure that the input is **just one character** and not a string. Check for **hidden spaces** or characters that could cause issues.

3.3 The isPrintable() Function: Validating Printable Characters

What is isPrintable()?
The isPrintable() function checks if a character is **printable**, meaning it can be displayed on a screen or **printed** to the serial monitor. This includes **letters, numbers**, and **symbols**, but excludes control characters.

Why is it important?
isPrintable() ensures that text output can be properly **displayed** or printed on **monitors** or screens. Non-printable characters can cause errors or **display issues**, making this function vital for clean outputs.

Syntax

```
isPrintable(char)
```

It checks if a character can be displayed and returns **true** if it's printable, or **false** otherwise.

Syntax Explanation
The function checks if the input character is **printable**, meaning it falls within a valid range for display. If it does, the function returns **true**.

Usage
Use isPrintable() when validating text before **displaying** it on screens, ensuring that the characters will render correctly on **LCDs** or serial monitors.

Code Example

```
char input = 'A';
if (isPrintable(input)) {
  Serial.println("This is a printable character.");
} else {
  Serial.println("This is not a printable character.");
}
```

This example checks if the input character is printable.

Notes
Use this function to avoid **errors** when printing to displays or **monitors** that may not support non-printable characters.

Warnings
If non-printable characters are displayed, they can cause **output errors** or garbled text on **LCD screens**.

Troubleshooting Tips
Ensure that the input character is **within the printable range**. Non-printable characters like control symbols should be avoided when using isPrintable().

Quiz: Test Your Advanced Character Functions Knowledge

1. What does isUpperCase() check for?

- o   A: Uppercase letters only.
2. How does `isLowerCase()` work?
    - o   A: It checks if a character is a lowercase letter (a-z).
3. When should you use `isPrintable()`?
    - o   A: To ensure that the character can be displayed on screens or monitors.

4. Practical Projects for Mastering Character and String Functions

4.1 Project 1: Validating User Input

Validating User Input focuses on checking user inputs using character validation functions like `isAlpha()`, `isDigit()`, and `isPrintable()` and displaying the results on the **Serial Monitor**. The project simulates input validation for systems that require specific character types, such as in **password entry** or **login forms**.

Why is it important?
Input validation ensures that user input is correct and secure. This is vital in real-world applications like **form validations** or **login systems**, where only specific characters (letters, numbers, or special characters) should be accepted. This project helps you understand how to enforce **input restrictions** to prevent errors or security vulnerabilities.

Components List:

- **Arduino**
- **Push button**
- **Resistor** (10kΩ pull-down resistor)
- **Wires**
- **Breadboard**

Circuit Diagram:
The **push button** is used to simulate input, and the **Serial Monitor** displays the validation result.

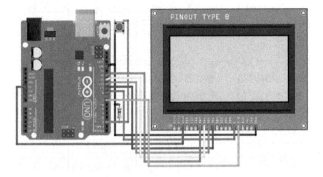

Circuit Connection:

1. **Push button**:
   - One side of the button is connected to **pin 2** on the Arduino.
   - The other side is connected to **ground**.
   - A **10kΩ pull-down resistor** is connected between **pin 2** and **ground** to ensure a stable input state.

Code:

```
char input = 'A';  // Simulate user input

void setup() {
  Serial.begin(9600);  // Initialize serial communication
}

void loop() {
  // Simulated input (you can replace this with actual input logic)
  input = 'A';  // Example character

  // Validate the input and print the result to the Serial Monitor
  if (isAlpha(input)) {
    Serial.println("Valid letter input");
  } else if (isDigit(input)) {
    Serial.println("Valid digit input");
  } else if (isPrintable(input)) {
    Serial.println("Valid special character");
  } else {
    Serial.println("Invalid input");
  }

  delay(2000);  // Wait for 2 seconds before the next validation
}
```

Code Walkthrough:

1. **Serial Communication Setup**: The Serial.begin(9600) command initializes the **Serial Monitor** for displaying validation results.
2. **Simulated Input**: The code simulates a user input ('A' in this case). In real-world applications, this input could be captured from a **keypad** or another input device.
3. **Input Validation**:
     - isAlpha() checks if the input is a **letter** (A-Z, a-z).
     - isDigit() checks if the input is a **number** (0-9).
     - isPrintable() checks if the input is a **printable special character** (such as !, @, #).
4. **Serial Output**: Depending on the validation result, a corresponding message is printed to the **Serial Monitor** (e.g., "Valid letter input" or "Invalid input").
5. **Loop**: The process repeats after a 2-second delay, simulating continuous input validation.

This project simulates **real-time validation** and displays the results on the **Serial Monitor**, making it a useful tool for learning about input validation in embedded systems or form-based applications.

Challenge: Add Support for Special Characters
Expand the project by adding support for **special characters** using isPrintable(). Modify the code to detect special characters like !, @, or #, ensuring that users can enter complex inputs for cases like **password validation** or **custom message systems**.

4.2 Project 2: Formatting and Displaying Text

In this project, we connect a **4x4 keypad** to the **Arduino** to capture user input, which is then formatted and displayed on the **Serial Monitor**. Below are the complete details for wiring the keypad to the Arduino, along with the components and code.

Components List:

- **Arduino Uno**
- **4x4 Keypad**
- **Wires**
- **Breadboard** (optional)

Circuit Connection

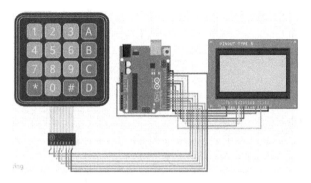

The **keypad** consists of **16 buttons** arranged in **4 rows** and **4 columns**. When you press a button, a circuit is completed between one row and one column. The **8 pins** of the keypad correspond to these rows and columns.

- **Pins 1-4** correspond to the **4 rows**.
- **Pins 5-8** correspond to the **4 columns**.

Pin Mapping:

Keypad Pins	Arduino Pins
Row 1 (Pin 1)	D3
Row 2 (Pin 2)	D4
Row 3 (Pin 3)	D5
Row 4 (Pin 4)	D6
Column 1 (Pin 5)	D7

Column 2 (Pin 6)	D8
Column 3 (Pin 7)	D9
Column 4 (Pin 8)	D10

Steps:

1. **Connect the Row Pins:**
   - Pin 1 → **D3** (Row 1)
   - Pin 2 → **D4** (Row 2)
   - Pin 3 → **D5** (Row 3)
   - Pin 4 → **D6** (Row 4)
2. **Connect the Column Pins:**
   - Pin 5 → **D7** (Column 1)
   - Pin 6 → **D8** (Column 2)
   - Pin 7 → **D9** (Column 3)
   - Pin 8 → **D10** (Column 4)
3. **Power the Arduino**: Connect the **USB cable** to the Arduino for power and to use the **Serial Monitor**.
4. **Optional**: Add **pull-down resistors** (10kΩ) between row/column pins and **ground** if necessary to stabilize input readings.

Code:

```cpp
#include <Keypad.h>
// Define the Keypad layout
const byte ROWS = 4;   // Four rows
const byte COLS = 4;   // Four columns
char keys[ROWS][COLS] = {
  {'1','2','3','A'},
  {'4','5','6','B'},
  {'7','8','9','C'},
  {'*','0','#','D'}
};

byte rowPins[ROWS] = {3, 4, 5, 6};   // Row pin connections
byte colPins[COLS] = {7, 8, 9, 10}; // Column pin connections

Keypad keypad = Keypad(makeKeymap(keys), rowPins, colPins, ROWS, COLS);

String input = "";   // Store user input
```

```
void setup() {
  Serial.begin(9600);  // Initialize Serial Monitor
  Serial.println("Enter Text:");
}

void loop() {
  char key = keypad.getKey();  // Get key press

  if (key) {
    // '*' clears the input, '#' submits the input
    if (key == '*') {
      input = "";  // Clear input
      Serial.println("Input cleared.");
    } else if (key == '#') {
      Serial.println("Final input: " + input);  // Display final input
      input = "";  // Reset after submission
    } else {
      input += key;  // Add key to input string
      Serial.println("Current input: " + input);  // Show input
    }
  }

  delay(100);  // Short delay to avoid multiple inputs from a single
press
}
```

Code Explanation:

- **Keypad Setup:** The **keypad layout** is defined, with rows and columns connected to the Arduino's digital pins. The **Keypad library** handles the row and column scanning.
- **Serial Communication:** The program uses `Serial.begin(9600)` to initialize the **Serial Monitor** for displaying input.
- **Handling Key Input:**
  - ✱ **clears** the input.
  - # **submits** the input and displays it.
  - Any other key is **appended** to the input string and displayed in real-time.
- **Delays:** A short delay ensures **debouncing** and avoids multiple keypresses from a single button press

Challenge: Add a Text Editor Feature
Expand the project by adding **text editing** functionality. Allow users to delete characters, move the cursor, or reformat text before

displaying it on the LCD. This creates a simple **text editor** for modifying input before confirming the final output.

4.3 Project 3: Creating a Password Input System

This project simulates a **password entry system** where the user inputs a password using a **keypad** and validates the password via **string comparison**. The result (correct or incorrect) is displayed on the **Serial Monitor**. This project teaches how to handle **input validation** and **security checks** in Arduino projects.

Components List:

- **Arduino Uno**
- **4x4 Keypad**
- **Buzzer** (for wrong password feedback)
- **Resistors** (for pull-down configuration if needed)
- **Wires**
- **Breadboard**

Circuit Connection:

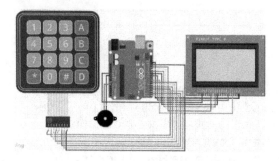

1. **Keypad**:
    - Wire the **keypad** to **digital pins 2-9** on the Arduino.
        - **Pins 2-5** for rows.
        - **Pins 6-9** for columns.
2. **Buzzer**:
    - Connect the **buzzer** to **pin 11** on the Arduino for sound feedback during wrong password attempts.
3. **Power and Ground**:
    - Ensure connections for **5V** and **GND** for all components.

Code:

```
#include <Keypad.h>

// Keypad setup
const byte ROWS = 4;
const byte COLS = 4;
char keys[ROWS][COLS] = {
  {'1','2','3','A'},
  {'4','5','6','B'},
  {'7','8','9','C'},
  {'*','0','#','D'}
};
byte rowPins[ROWS] = {2, 3, 4, 5};  // Row pins of the keypad
byte colPins[COLS] = {6, 7, 8, 9};  // Column pins of the keypad
Keypad keypad = Keypad(makeKeymap(keys), rowPins, colPins, ROWS, COLS);

String password = "Arduino123";  // **Pre-set password**
String input = "";  // **Store user input**

void setup() {
  Serial.begin(9600);  // **Initialize Serial Monitor**
  Serial.println("Enter Password:");  // **Prompt user for password**
}

void loop() {
  char key = keypad.getKey();  // **Read key from keypad**

  if (key) {
    if (key == '*') {  // Clear input if * is pressed
      input = "";
      Serial.println("Input cleared");
    }
    else if (key == '#') {  // **Submit password when # is pressed**
      if (input == password) {
        Serial.println("Access Granted");  // **Correct password**
      } else {
        Serial.println("Access Denied");  // **Incorrect password**
        tone(11, 1000, 200);  // **Buzzer feedback for wrong password**
      }
      input = "";  // Reset input after submission
    }
    else {
      input += key;  // **Append the pressed key to input**
      Serial.print("*");  // Display a * for each key pressed
    }
  }
}
```

Code Explanation:

- **Keypad Setup**: The keypad is initialized with row and column pins connected to digital pins 2-9 on the Arduino.

- **Serial Monitor**: The code uses Serial.begin(9600) to print messages and receive feedback in the **Serial Monitor**.
- **Handling Key Input**:
  - ∗ **key** clears the input.
  - # **key** submits the input and checks if the entered password matches the **pre-set password**.
  - If the password is correct, **"Access Granted"** is displayed; otherwise, **"Access Denied"** is shown, and the **buzzer** sounds for wrong password attempts.
- **Password Masking**: Each key press is masked with an asterisk (∗) in the **Serial Monitor** for privacy.

Challenge: Add Masking for Password
Modify the code to hide the password as it's entered by displaying ∗ characters on the **LCD** instead of the actual keys.

4.4 Project 4: Serial Monitor Data Entry and Validation

This project allows the user to enter text through the **serial monitor**, with the Arduino checking for valid characters using functions like **isAlpha()** and **isPrintable()**. It demonstrates how to handle and validate user input from the serial monitor.

Why is it important?

Serial monitor input is a common method for **debugging** and **receiving input** in Arduino projects. By learning to validate this input, you can ensure that **received data** is valid, reducing the risk of errors in further processing.

Components List:

- **Arduino**
- **USB connection** for serial communication

Circuit Diagram:

No additional hardware is needed, just the **Arduino board** connected to your computer via USB.

Circuit Connection:

No physical wiring is required. All interaction occurs via the **serial monitor**.

Code:

```
String input = "";

void setup() {
  Serial.begin(9600);   // Initialize Serial Monitor communication
  Serial.println("Enter text:");
}

void loop() {
  // Check if there is data available in the Serial Monitor
  if (Serial.available() > 0) {
    input = Serial.readString();   // Read input from the Serial Monitor

    // Loop through each character of the input string
    for (int i = 0; i < input.length(); i++) {
      // Check if each character is printable
      if (!isPrintable(input[i])) {
        Serial.println("Invalid character in input");   // Alert if an
invalid character is found
        break;
      }
    }

    // Display the validated input
    Serial.println("Valid input: " + input);
  }
}
```

Code Walkthrough:

1. **Serial Communication Setup**: The **Serial Monitor** is initialized with Serial.begin(9600) to allow communication at a **9600 baud rate**.
2. **Reading Serial Input**: The Serial.available() function checks if any data is present in the **Serial Monitor**. If so, Serial.readString() reads the input.
3. **Validation of Input**: The program loops through each character of the input string, checking if it is **printable** using isPrintable(). If an invalid character is found, the program prints an error message and stops further validation.
4. **Displaying Valid Input**: If all characters are valid, the program prints the entire string to the **Serial Monitor**.

Challenge: Add Validation for Numbers

To expand this project, you can add **numeric validation** using the **isDigit()** function to ensure only valid numeric characters are processed. This would be useful in applications requiring numeric input, such as entering PIN codes or numerical data.

4.5 Project 5: Data Logger with Validated Input

This project demonstrates how to build a **data logging system** where the user inputs data via a **keypad** or **serial monitor**, validates the input, and stores it in an **SD card**. It covers key topics such as **input validation**, **data processing**, and **data storage**.

Why is it important?

Data logging is essential in many applications, such as environmental monitoring, user input logging, and sensor data collection. Ensuring that data is **validated** before being logged prevents incorrect or invalid data from being stored, which is critical for maintaining **data integrity** in long-term projects.

Components List:

- **Arduino**
- **Keypad** or **Serial Monitor**
- **SD card module**
- **Resistors**
- **Wires**
- **Breadboard**

Circuit Diagram:

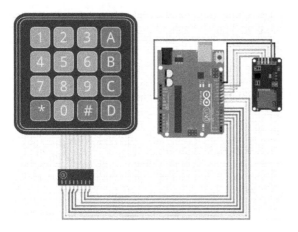

- The input device (**keypad** or **serial monitor**) is used to collect data.
- The **SD card module** is connected to the **SPI pins** on the Arduino (pins 10-13) for data storage.

Circuit Connection:

1. **SD Card Module**:
   - Connect the **SD card module** to the Arduino's **SPI pins**:
     - **MOSI (pin 11)** → SD card module's **MOSI**
     - **MISO (pin 12)** → SD card module's **MISO**
     - **SCK (pin 13)** → SD card module's **SCK**
     - **CS (pin 10)** → SD card module's **CS**
     - **5V** and **GND** for power and ground.
2. **Keypad or Serial Monitor**:
   - For **serial input**, no extra wiring is required, just the **USB connection**.
   - For a **keypad**, connect the **row** and **column pins** to the Arduino's digital pins, similar to earlier keypad projects.

Code:

```
#include <SD.h>

File dataFile;  // File object to handle SD card writing
String input = "";

void setup() {
  Serial.begin(9600);  // Start serial communication
  if (!SD.begin(10)) {  // Initialize SD card module on pin 10 (CS)
    Serial.println("SD card initialization failed!");
    return;
  }
  Serial.println("SD card initialized.");
}

void loop() {
  if (Serial.available()) {
    input = Serial.readString();  // Read input from Serial Monitor

    // Validate the input
    if (validateInput(input)) {
      // Open file for writing
      dataFile = SD.open("log.txt", FILE_WRITE);
      if (dataFile) {
        dataFile.println(input);  // Write data to file
        dataFile.close();  // Close the file
        Serial.println("Data logged: " + input);  // Feedback
      } else {
        Serial.println("Error opening file.");
      }
    } else {
      Serial.println("Invalid input.");
    }
  }
}

// Function to validate input
bool validateInput(String input) {
  for (int i = 0; i < input.length(); i++) {
    if (!isPrintable(input[i])) return false;  // Check if character is
printable
  }
  return true;
}
```

Code Walkthrough:

1. **SD Card Initialization**: The **SD.begin(10)** function initializes
   the **SD card module** using **pin 10** as the **chip select (CS)**
   pin. If initialization fails, an error message is displayed.

2. **Input from Serial Monitor**: The program reads the user's input from the **serial monitor** using `Serial.readString()` and stores it in the `input` variable.
3. **Input Validation**: The `validateInput()` function checks if each character in the input is **printable** (i.e., valid). If any character fails this check, the function returns **false**.
4. **Logging to SD Card**: If the input is valid, the program opens the **log.txt** file in **write mode**, logs the input, and closes the file.
5. **Feedback**: The program provides feedback to the user, confirming whether the data was successfully logged or if an error occurred.

Challenge: Add Multiple Data Fields

To extend this project, you can add multiple data fields (e.g., **temperature**, **humidity**, etc.) and validate each field individually. You can then store these fields in a structured format (e.g., CSV format) on the **SD card**. Each field could be logged with a **timestamp** or in separate lines, depending on the data's nature.

5. Common Troubleshooting and Debugging Tips

5.1 Common Errors and How to Fix Them

What are common errors?
Common errors when handling characters and strings in Arduino include using the wrong **input types**, such as mixing **characters** and **strings**, or failing to properly validate input using functions like `isAlpha()` or `isDigit()`. Other typical mistakes involve **incorrect character indexing**, such as accessing elements outside the valid range of a string, which can cause program crashes.

Why do they happen?
These issues often arise from incorrect handling of character types. For instance, trying to perform string operations on individual **characters** or passing a full string to a function designed for **single character validation**. Errors also occur when developers misunderstand the difference between **char arrays** and **String objects**, leading to **memory allocation problems**.

Use of Serial Monitor for debugging

The **Serial Monitor** is an essential tool for debugging character and string functions. Using Serial.print(), you can output intermediate values of variables, helping identify where input validation fails. For instance, you can print the value of characters during **input processing** or track incorrect index values when accessing a string. This provides real-time feedback on how the code handles inputs.

5.2 Optimizing Code for Efficient Character and String Handling

What is code optimization for character handling?
Optimizing code involves ensuring that character and string operations run **efficiently**. In Arduino, it's important to minimize the number of **string manipulations** to conserve memory. Instead of frequently concatenating strings, you can use **char arrays** or avoid unnecessary conversions between characters and strings. Efficient use of string functions like substring() or indexOf() also prevents **performance bottlenecks**.

Why is it important?
Arduino boards have limited **memory and processing power**, so optimizing string operations ensures the program runs **smoothly** without consuming too much RAM. Inefficient handling of large strings can lead to **program slowdowns** or even crashes due to **memory overflow**. Efficient code helps keep the program lightweight, especially in projects involving real-time **data processing** or **input validation**.

Tips for performance and accuracy
Use **char arrays** instead of String objects where possible, and avoid repetitive string concatenation. Reduce unnecessary memory allocations by reusing variables. When handling large inputs, process data in **small chunks** instead of operating on the entire string at once. Finally, use functions like isAlphaNumeric() or isPrintable() to simplify validation rather than writing custom checks.

---

6. Conclusion and Next Steps

6.1 Recap of Key Character and String Functions

What have we learned?
In this chapter, we've covered essential character and string functions like `isAlpha()`, `isDigit()`, and `isPrintable()`. These functions help you validate input, ensuring that **letters**, **numbers**, and **special characters** are correctly processed in your Arduino projects. You've learned how to use these functions in real-world scenarios such as validating user inputs, formatting text, and troubleshooting common issues. By mastering these functions, you can create more **reliable** and **interactive** Arduino applications.

Chapter 16: Arithmetic and Compound Operators

In this chapter, we cover **Arithmetic Operators** and **Compound Operators**, which are essential for performing mathematical operations in programming.

- **Arithmetic Operators** are used for basic mathematical tasks such as addition, subtraction, multiplication, division, and modulus. These operators enable programmers to perform calculations on variables and data, which is crucial for tasks like managing sensor data, controlling devices, and processing numbers within a program.
- **Compound Operators** simplify arithmetic operations by combining them with assignment. Examples include +=, -=, *=, /=, and %=. These operators help make the code more concise and readable, especially when used in loops or to update values repeatedly.

Both arithmetic and compound operators are important in programming as they allow precise control over variables, calculations, and data manipulation, contributing to efficient and clean code execution.

Syntax Table

Topic Name	Syntax	Simple Example
Addition	result = value1 + value2;	int total = 5 + 3; // result = 8
Subtraction	result = value1 - value2;	int difference = 10 - 4; // result = 6
Multiplication	result = value1 * value2;	int product = 5 * 3; // result = 15
Division	result = value1 / value2;	int result = 20 / 4; // result = 5
Modulus	result = value1 % value2;	int remainder = 10 % 3; // result = 1
Compound Addition	value += increment;	total += 5; // total = total + 5
Compound Subtraction	value -= decrement;	counter -= 2; // counter = counter - 2
Compound Multiplication	value *= multiplier;	value *= 3; // value = value * 3
Compound Division	value /= divisor;	value /= 2; // value = value / 2
Compound Modulus	value %= divisor;	value %= 4; // value = value % 4

1. Introduction to Arithmetic and Compound Operators

1.1 What are Arithmetic and Compound Operators?

What are Arithmetic Operators?
Arithmetic operators perform **basic mathematical calculations** like addition (+), subtraction (−), multiplication (∗), division (/), and modulus (%). These operators are used in **programming** to manipulate numbers. For example, using + adds two values together, while / divides one number by another. In programming tasks like **sensor data calculations** or controlling **robot movements**, arithmetic operators are used to handle numbers efficiently. They are foundational to all programming languages and critical in performing **basic math operations** on data.

What are Compound Operators?
Compound operators are shortcuts that combine arithmetic operators with assignment. For instance, += adds a value to a variable and then assigns the result back to that variable. Other compound operators include −=, ∗=, /=, and %=. These operators simplify code, reduce repetition, and make it more readable. For example, instead of writing x = x + 5, you can write x += 5. This makes compound operators helpful in **loops** and other repetitive tasks where calculations and updates happen frequently.

1.2 Key Concepts and Terms (Glossary)

What is an Arithmetic Operator?
An **arithmetic operator** is used for **basic math operations** like addition, subtraction, multiplication, and division. These operators are fundamental to manipulating numbers in any programming language.

What is a Compound Operator?
A **compound operator** is a shorthand form that combines an **arithmetic operation and assignment** into one step. For example, += adds and assigns the result to the variable in one command.

Common Operators and their roles:

- + (Addition)
  The + **operator** adds two numbers together. For example, 3 + 2 gives 5. It is used to increase values in **mathematical operations**.
- − (Subtraction)
  The − **operator** subtracts one number from another. For example, 5 − 2 gives 3. This operator reduces values in **programming calculations**.
- ∗ (Multiplication)
  The ∗ **operator** multiplies two numbers. For instance, 3 ∗ 4 results in 12. Multiplication is crucial for tasks like **scaling values** in programs.
- / (Division)
  The / **operator** divides one number by another. For example, 10 / 2 results in 5. Division is used for **splitting values** into equal parts.
- += (Compound Addition)
  The += **operator** adds a value to a variable and assigns the new value back to the same variable. For example, x += 2 is the same as x = x + 2.

1.3 Overview of Core Arithmetic and Compound Operators

Core Operators
The core arithmetic operators are +, −, ∗, /, and %, while the core compound operators include +=, −=, ∗=, /=, and %=. These operators perform basic calculations like **adding, subtracting, multiplying, dividing**, and **finding remainders**. Compound operators are shortcuts that help save time in coding by combining arithmetic and assignment in one step. They are especially useful in **loops** and **decision-making** where variables are constantly updated, ensuring efficient and cleaner code.

Importance
Arithmetic and compound operators are essential in programming because they allow **precise calculations** and **value updates**. In Arduino programs, these operators are used to control sensor data, manage loops, and make calculations that guide devices like motors or LEDs. By using **compound operators**, you save time and create more **concise** and **readable code**. Mastering these operators

ensures that you can write effective programs that run smoothly and efficiently, even in **memory-constrained** environments.

Quiz: Test Your Understanding of Arithmetic and Compound Operators

- What is the role of the + operator?
  A) Multiplication
  B) Subtraction
  C) Addition
  Answer: C
- How does the += operator function in an arithmetic operation?
  The += operator adds a value to a variable and updates the variable with the new value.

2. Core Arithmetic Operators

2.1 The + (Addition) Operator

What is +?
The + **operator** adds two numbers together. It's used for basic **addition** in programming. For example, 3 + 2 gives 5. This operator is crucial in calculations such as **accumulating totals**, managing **sensor data**, or updating variables in loops. Whether you're adding constant values or variables, the + operator simplifies these tasks in every **programming language**.

Syntax:

```
result = value1 + value2;
```

Syntax Explanation:
The syntax shows how the + operator adds two values, value1 and value2, and stores the sum in result. It's commonly used in **mathematical expressions** and **data processing**, where two or more values need to be combined.

Usage:
The + operator can be used for **accumulating sensor readings**, **increasing counters**, or combining user inputs. For example, in an Arduino program, you might use + to sum data from multiple sensors to get a total value.

Code Example:

```
int sensor1 = 5;
int sensor2 = 7;
int total = sensor1 + sensor2;
Serial.println(total);  // Outputs 12
```

This code adds two sensor readings together. The result, 12, is printed to the Serial Monitor.

Notes:
The + operator works with integers, floats, and doubles, allowing flexible **addition** across different data types.

Warnings:
Be careful of **integer overflow** when adding large numbers, as the result might exceed the size of the variable type.

Troubleshooting Tips:
If the result of an addition is not as expected, check the **data types** involved. For example, adding an **integer** and a **float** may cause unexpected results if the variable types are not properly declared.

2.2 The − (Subtraction) Operator
What is −?
The − **operator** subtracts one number from another. For instance, 5 − 2 gives 3. It's used in programming to decrease values, such as **reducing counters** or computing **differences** between sensor readings. The − operator is essential in calculations where numbers need to be decreased or where differences between values are needed.

Syntax:

```
result = value1 - value2;
```

Syntax Explanation:
The syntax shows how the – operator subtracts value2 from value1, with the result stored in result. This is commonly used to reduce values, like **decrementing counters** or measuring differences in **sensor data**.

Usage:
Use the – operator to **decrease values** or **find differences**. For instance, subtracting two temperature readings can show how much the temperature has dropped.

Code Example:

```
int value1 = 10;
int value2 = 4;
int difference = value1 - value2;
Serial.println(difference);  // Outputs 6
```

This code subtracts 4 from 10, printing the result 6 to the Serial Monitor.

Notes:
Subtraction can be used to calculate changes over time, like measuring temperature changes or decreasing a counter.

Warnings:
Watch out for **negative results** when subtracting smaller numbers from larger ones. In unsigned variables, this can cause errors.

2.3 The * (Multiplication) Operator

What is *?
The *** operator** multiplies two numbers. For example, 3 * 4 gives 12. Multiplication is crucial in scaling values, such as **adjusting sensor inputs** or **performing calculations** on data. Whether you're

multiplying constants or variables, the ∗ operator simplifies complex calculations.

Syntax:

```
result = value1 * value2;
```

Syntax Explanation:
The ∗ operator multiplies value1 by value2 and stores the result in result. It's commonly used in calculations where **scaling** or **adjusting values** is needed.

Usage:
The ∗ operator is used in **calculating area**, **scaling sensor data**, or **increasing values**. It's frequently applied when multiplying numbers for **sensor adjustments** or performing **loop iterations**.

Code Example:

```
int value1 = 5;
int value2 = 3;
int product = value1 * value2;
Serial.println(product);  // Outputs 15
```

This code multiplies 5 by 3, resulting in 15.

Notes:
Multiplication can quickly scale values, which is useful for **increasing** or **amplifying** results.

Warnings:
Be aware of **overflow** when multiplying large numbers. Use larger data types when needed.

Troubleshooting Tips:
If results are incorrect, check for overflow and ensure **correct data types** are being used. For example, multiplying large numbers might require **long integers** or **doubles** to avoid losing precision.

2.4 The / (Division) Operator

What is /?
The **/ operator** divides one number by another. For example, 10 /
2 gives 5. It is essential in calculations where values need to be **split**
or **averaged**.

Syntax:

```
result = value1 / value2;
```

Syntax Explanation:
The value1 is divided by value2, and the result is stored in result.
It's commonly used in **averaging values** or **splitting data**.

Usage:
Use the / operator to find **averages** or **divide** values. For example,
dividing total sensor readings by the number of sensors to find the
average reading.

Code Example:

```
int value1 = 20;
int value2 = 4;
int result = value1 / value2;
Serial.println(result);   // Outputs 5
```

This code divides 20 by 4, resulting in 5.

Notes:
Division is critical in **finding averages** or **reducing values**
proportionally.

2.5 The % (Remainder) Operator

What is %?
The **% operator** finds the remainder of a division. For example, 10 %
3 gives 1. It's used to **determine divisibility** or when only the
remainder is important.

Syntax:

```
result = value1 % value2;
```

Syntax Explanation:
The % operator divides value1 by value2 and stores the **remainder** in result.

Usage:
Use the % operator to find **remainders**, which is useful for **checking divisibility** or creating **patterns** in loops.

Code Example:

```
int value1 = 10;
int value2 = 3;
int remainder = value1 % value2;
Serial.println(remainder);  // Outputs 1
```

This code calculates the remainder of 10 / 3, which is 1.

Troubleshooting Tips:
If results are incorrect, ensure you're not trying to use % with floating-point numbers, as it only works with integers.

Quiz: Check Your Understanding of Arithmetic Operators

Sample Questions:

- What does the % operator do?
  A) Adds numbers
  B) Divides numbers
  C) Finds the remainder
  Answer: C
- How does the / operator handle division of floating-point numbers?

Answer: It divides floating-point numbers accurately, returning a float result.

FAQ: Common Questions about Arithmetic Operators

What happens when dividing by zero in Arduino?
Dividing by zero will cause an error or undefined behavior. Arduino cannot handle this operation.

Can the % operator be used with floating-point numbers?
No, the % operator only works with **integer values**.

3. Core Compound Operators

3.1 The += (Compound Addition) Operator

What is +=?
The **+= operator** is used to **add** a value to a variable and then store the **new result** back in that same variable. For example, x += 5 is shorthand for x = x + 5. This operator simplifies the code, making it easier to write and read when adding values to a variable repeatedly, such as in **loops** or **accumulating totals**.

Syntax:

```
value += increment;
```

Syntax Explanation:
The **+= operator** adds the value of increment to value, then stores the result back in value. It is equivalent to writing value = value + increment, but in a more **concise** form, especially helpful in **iterative** code.

Usage:
Use the **+= operator** when **accumulating** values over time, such as **adding sensor readings** or increasing a counter. For example, in

an Arduino program, you can continuously add sensor data at regular intervals using +=.

Code Example:

```
int total = 0;
int sensorValue = 5;
total += sensorValue;   // total = total + sensorValue
Serial.println(total);  // Outputs 5
```

In this code, the sensor value is added to the total using the += operator, accumulating the data.

Notes:
The **+= operator** works with both **integers** and **floating-point numbers**, making it flexible in **sensor data** or **loop iterations**.

3.2 The −= (Compound Subtraction) Operator

What is −=?
The **−= operator** subtracts a value from a variable and assigns the result back to that variable. For example, x −= 3 is shorthand for x = x − 3. This operator simplifies the code for **decreasing values**, especially when you need to **subtract repeatedly**, such as in **countdowns** or **loop counters**.

Syntax:

```
value -= decrement;
```

Syntax Explanation:
The **−= operator** subtracts decrement from value and stores the result in value. This is a **concise** way to write value = value − decrement, especially useful in **loops** where values are **decremented** repeatedly.

Usage:
Use the **−= operator** when **reducing** values, such as **counting**

down or **decreasing sensor values** over time. It is helpful in **loops** where counters are **decreased** at each iteration.

Code Example:

```
int counter = 10;
counter -= 2;  // counter = counter - 2
Serial.println(counter);  // Outputs 8
```

In this code, the counter is decremented by 2 using the -= operator, simplifying the subtraction.

3.3 The *= (Compound Multiplication) Operator

What is *=?
The *= **operator** multiplies a variable by a value and assigns the result back to the variable. For example, x *= 4 is shorthand for x = x * 4. This operator simplifies code when **scaling values**, such as in **sensor data** adjustments or **loop iterations** where multiplication is needed.

Syntax:

```
value *= multiplier;
```

Syntax Explanation:
The *= **operator** multiplies value by multiplier and stores the result in value. This is equivalent to writing value = value * multiplier, making the code **more concise** for **repeated multiplications**.

Usage:
Use the *= **operator** to **scale values**, such as when **increasing sensor readings** or **adjusting calculations** in loops where multiplication is needed frequently.

Code Example:

```
int value = 3;
value *= 4;  // value = value * 4
Serial.println(value);  // Outputs 12
```

In this example, value is multiplied by 4 using the *= operator, making the code simpler.

3.4 The /= (Compound Division) Operator

What is /=?
The /= **operator** divides a variable by a value and assigns the result back to the variable. For example, x /= 2 is shorthand for x = x / 2. This operator simplifies **division operations**, especially when continuously **dividing** values in a program.

Syntax:

```
value /= divisor;
```

Syntax Explanation:
The /= **operator** divides value by divisor and stores the result in value. It's shorthand for value = value / divisor, making **division** easier to implement in loops or repeated calculations.

Usage:
Use the /= **operator** to **reduce** values, such as **scaling down sensor data** or **calculating averages** in repeated division operations.

Code Example:

```
int value = 20;
value /= 4;  // value = value / 4
Serial.println(value);  // Outputs 5
```

This example divides value by 4 using the /= operator, simplifying the division process.

4. Using Arithmetic and Compound Operators in Projects

4.1 Project 1: LED Brightness Control with Compound Operators

This project focuses on controlling the **brightness of an LED** using **compound operators** such as += and −=. The LED's brightness is adjusted based on a **potentiometer's** input, which allows for gradual and smooth brightness transitions. By modifying the **PWM (Pulse Width Modulation)** signal on the LED pin, you can incrementally increase or decrease the LED's brightness, achieving a fading effect that cycles between full brightness and full dimness.

Why is it important?

This project demonstrates the practical use of **PWM** for controlling analog devices like LEDs, fans, or motors, in **embedded systems**. By employing **compound operators**, it simplifies the code for adjusting the brightness of the LED, resulting in smoother control over time. This project is crucial for learning how to handle **analog control** in a **digital system** using **PWM signals** and how to implement **efficient coding techniques** to manipulate values incrementally.

Components List:

- **Arduino**: Microcontroller to control the LED brightness.
- **LED**: A basic light-emitting diode used to visualize brightness changes.
- **Potentiometer**: Analog sensor used to adjust the brightness manually.
- **Resistor**: Limits current to the LED, preventing damage.
- **Breadboard**: For easy connections of components.
- **Jumper wires**: For connecting components to the Arduino.

Circuit Diagram:

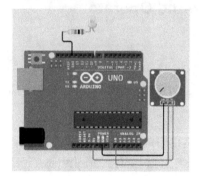

Here's how the components are connected:

1. **LED Circuit:**
   - **Positive leg (anode)** of the LED is connected to **PWM pin 9** of the Arduino.
   - **Negative leg (cathode)** of the LED is connected to **ground (GND)** through a **current-limiting resistor**.
2. **Potentiometer Circuit:**
   - The **middle pin** of the potentiometer is connected to **analog pin A0**.
   - One outer pin of the potentiometer is connected to **5V** on the Arduino, and the other is connected to **GND**.

This setup allows the Arduino to read the potentiometer value from **A0** and adjust the LED brightness using PWM on **pin 9**.

Circuit Connection:

- The **LED** is controlled by the **PWM signal** generated by the Arduino. As the PWM value changes, the brightness of the LED changes proportionally.
- The **potentiometer** acts as a variable resistor, providing an **analog input** to the Arduino. This input can later be used to adjust the brightness manually, though in this code, the brightness is automated with **compound operators**.

Code:

```
int potValue = 0;        // Potentiometer value (to be used for analog
control)
int ledBrightness = 0;   // LED brightness level (0 to 255)
int increment = 5;       // Step value for brightness adjustment

void setup() {
  pinMode(9, OUTPUT);    // Set pin 9 as output for LED
}

void loop() {
  // Read the potentiometer value (currently unused in this example)
  potValue = analogRead(A0);

  // Increase or decrease the LED brightness
  ledBrightness += increment;

  // Check boundaries (0 to 255) and reverse the direction if needed
  if (ledBrightness >= 255 || ledBrightness <= 0) {
    increment = -increment;   // Reverse the direction of brightness
change
  }

  // Apply the brightness to the LED using PWM
  analogWrite(9, ledBrightness);

  // Delay to control the speed of brightness change
  delay(50);   // 50ms delay for smooth transition
}
```

Code Walkthrough:

1. **Variable Declaration**:
   o potValue: Stores the potentiometer reading, which is
     an analog value between 0 and 1023.
   o ledBrightness: Represents the current **brightness
     level** of the LED, ranging from **0** (off) to **255** (full
     brightness).
   o increment: Determines the step size for how fast the
     LED brightness will increase or decrease. In this
     case, the brightness changes in steps of **5**.
2. **Setup Function**:
   o The LED is connected to **pin 9**, which is set as an
     output pin using pinMode(9, OUTPUT).
3. **Loop Function**:
   o **Reading Potentiometer**: The potentiometer value is
     read using analogRead(A0), which could be used later

to control the brightness interactively. However, in this code, the potentiometer reading is just stored but not used.

- ○ **Brightness Adjustment**: The brightness of the LED is adjusted using the += operator. Each loop increases the brightness by the value of increment (initially set to **5**).
- ○ **Boundary Check**: When the **brightness** reaches its maximum (255, full brightness) or minimum (0, off), the direction of the brightness change is reversed. This is achieved by flipping the sign of increment using increment = -increment;. This results in a smooth **oscillating** brightness pattern.
- ○ **PWM Signal**: The analogWrite(9, ledBrightness) function sends a **PWM signal** to pin 9, setting the brightness of the LED. The ledBrightness variable controls the **duty cycle** of the PWM signal, which ranges from 0 (off) to 255 (full brightness).
- ○ **Delay**: A small delay of **50 milliseconds** is added at the end of each loop cycle using delay(50). This delay controls how fast the LED fades in and out, making the brightness transition smooth and visible to the human eye.

Challenge:
Add a **push button** that resets the brightness to 50% when pressed. Use a **digital input** for the button and modify the code to handle the reset function.

4.2 Project 2: Servo Motor Angle Control with Arithmetic Operators

This project involves controlling the **angle** of a **servo motor** using **arithmetic operators**. A **potentiometer** is used to adjust the angle of the servo motor, allowing it to move smoothly between **0 and 180 degrees**. The potentiometer outputs a value between **0 and 1023** which is then converted to a corresponding **servo angle** using **arithmetic operations** like multiplication and division, handled by the map() function in the code.

Why is it important?

This project demonstrates how to use **arithmetic operators** to convert sensor input into usable control signals for devices like a **servo motor**. It's a great example of how to translate a wide **input range** (0-1023 from the potentiometer) into a specific **output range** (0-180 degrees for the servo). This concept is important for building systems that require real-time input-to-output mapping, such as **robotics**, **automation**, or **remote-controlled devices**.

Components List:

- **Arduino**: Microcontroller to process input and control the servo motor.
- **Servo motor**: A small motor with the ability to rotate between 0 and 180 degrees.
- **Potentiometer**: Analog sensor used to adjust the angle of the servo.
- **Jumper wires**: For making connections between components and the Arduino.

Circuit Diagram:

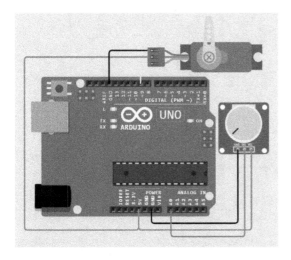

- **Servo Motor**:
  - Connect the **control wire** of the servo motor to **digital pin 9** on the Arduino.
  - Connect the **power wire** of the servo motor to the **5V pin**.
  - Connect the **ground wire** of the servo motor to **GND**.
- **Potentiometer**:
  - Connect the **middle pin** of the potentiometer to **analog pin A0**.
  - Connect one outer pin of the potentiometer to **5V** and the other to **GND**.

Circuit Connection:

- The **potentiometer** provides a **variable resistance**, producing an **analog signal** between **0 and 1023**.
- This value is read by the **Arduino** through **analog pin A0**, and **mapped** to control the **servo motor**, which moves between **0 and 180 degrees** based on the potentiometer's position.

Code:

```
#include <Servo.h>

Servo myServo;  // Create servo object to control a servo motor
int potValue = 0;  // Store potentiometer value (0 to 1023)
int servoAngle = 0; // Store calculated servo angle (0 to 180)

void setup() {
  myServo.attach(9);  // Attach the servo motor to pin 9
}

void loop() {
  potValue = analogRead(A0);  // Read the potentiometer value
  servoAngle = map(potValue, 0, 1023, 0, 180);  // Map the value to a
servo angle
  myServo.write(servoAngle);  // Move the servo to the calculated angle
  delay(50);  // Short delay for stability
}
```

Code Walkthrough:

1. **Library Import**:
   - ○ The Servo.h library is included to simplify the control of the **servo motor**. It provides a simple interface for attaching the servo to a pin and moving it to a specific angle.
2. **Variable Declarations**:
   - ○ potValue: Holds the **analog value** read from the potentiometer, ranging from **0 to 1023**.
   - ○ servoAngle: Stores the **mapped angle** for the servo motor, ranging from **0 to 180 degrees**.
3. **Setup Function**:
   - ○ The servo motor is attached to **pin 9** of the Arduino using the myServo.attach(9) function. This establishes communication between the Arduino and the servo motor.
4. **Loop Function**:
   - ○ The **potentiometer value** is read using analogRead(A0) and stored in potValue. This value will range from **0 to 1023**, depending on the potentiometer's position.

The map() function is used to convert the potentiometer's range (**0 to 1023**) into the servo's range (**0 to 180 degrees**). This is where **arithmetic operators** come into play. Internally, the map() function uses **multiplication** and **division** to scale the input value proportionally to the desired output range:

```
servoAngle = map(potValue, 0, 1023, 0, 180);
```

   - ○ Here, **potValue** is mapped from its natural range (0-1023) to the angle range (0-180) that the **servo motor** can handle.
   - ○ The myServo.write(servoAngle) command then moves the servo to the calculated angle.
   - ○ A **50 ms delay** is added at the end of the loop to ensure stable servo movements.

How Arithmetic Operators Work in the map () Function:

The map () function performs the following calculation internally:

```
servoAngle = (potValue - 0) * (180 - 0) / (1023 - 0) + 0;
```

- The **difference** between the potentiometer's minimum and maximum values (1023 − 0) is used to calculate the **scaling factor**.
- The difference between the servo motor's minimum and maximum angles (180 − 0) is multiplied by the scaled potentiometer value to determine the **servo angle**.
- **Division** is used to normalize the potentiometer's value into the corresponding angle range.

4.3 Project 3: Automated Fan Speed Control with Compound Operators

This project automatically adjusts the **speed of a DC fan** based on temperature readings from a **temperature sensor**. By using **compound operators** like += and −=, the fan's speed is adjusted **dynamically** as the temperature fluctuates. As the temperature rises, the fan speeds up, and as the temperature falls, the fan slows down. This project utilizes **real-time sensor data** to control the fan's speed smoothly.

Why is it important?

This project illustrates the use of **compound operators** for **real-time control** in systems that require dynamic behavior. In **embedded systems**, it's crucial to respond to **changing sensor inputs** by adjusting output devices like motors or fans. This approach saves processing time and simplifies code while allowing precise control over the **fan's speed** based on **temperature changes**. This is especially useful in applications such as **cooling systems**, **HVAC systems**, and **automated environmental controls**.

Components List:

- **Arduino**: Microcontroller to control the fan and read temperature data.
- **Temperature sensor** (e.g., LM35): Used to measure temperature.
- **DC fan**: Controlled based on temperature data.
- **Motor driver** (e.g., L298N): To control the speed of the fan motor.
- **Resistors**: Used to protect the components.
- **Jumper wires**: For making the connections.

Circuit Diagram:

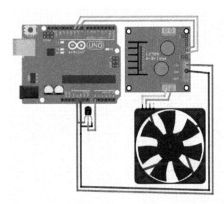

- **Temperature Sensor**:
  - The **output pin** of the temperature sensor is connected to **analog pin A0** on the Arduino.
  - The **VCC** and **GND** pins of the temperature sensor are connected to **5V** and **GND**, respectively.
- **DC Fan**:
  - The **fan motor** is connected to the **motor driver** (e.g., L298N), which acts as an interface between the fan and the Arduino.
  - The **control pins** of the motor driver are connected to **two PWM pins** on the Arduino (e.g., **pins 9 and 10**), which allows for precise control of the fan speed via PWM.

Circuit Connection:

- The **temperature sensor** reads the current **temperature** and sends an **analog signal** to the Arduino.
- The **motor driver** controls the **DC fan** based on the **PWM signal** received from the Arduino, which adjusts the fan speed according to the temperature.
- The fan's speed is controlled by **varying the PWM signal** on **pin 9** of the Arduino.

Code:

```
int tempValue = 0;      // Temperature sensor value
int fanSpeed = 0;       // Fan speed value
int increment = 10;     // Speed adjustment step

void setup() {
  pinMode(9, OUTPUT);   // Set pin 9 for fan control as output
}

void loop() {
  // Read the temperature sensor value from analog pin A0
  tempValue = analogRead(A0);

  // Map the temperature sensor value (0-1023) to a fan speed (0-255)
  fanSpeed = map(tempValue, 0, 1023, 0, 255);

  // Increase the fan speed gradually
  fanSpeed += increment;

  // Ensure the fan speed stays within valid limits (0-255)
  if (fanSpeed >= 255) {
    fanSpeed = 255;   // Limit fan speed to max value
  } else if (fanSpeed <= 0) {
    fanSpeed = 0;   // Limit fan speed to min value
  }

  // Write the calculated fan speed to pin 9 (PWM control)
  analogWrite(9, fanSpeed);

  // Small delay to stabilize fan speed control
  delay(100);
}
```

Code Walkthrough:

1. **Variable Declaration**:
   - tempValue: Holds the **analog input** from the temperature sensor. The range of values from the sensor will be **0 to 1023**.
   - fanSpeed: The value representing the **fan's speed**, mapped to a range of **0 to 255** for PWM control.
   - increment: Determines how fast the fan speed will increase or decrease each time the loop runs.
2. **Setup Function**:
   - **Pin 9** is configured as an **output pin** using pinMode(9, OUTPUT), which will send the **PWM signal** to the motor driver controlling the fan.
3. **Loop Function**:
   - **Reading the temperature**: The analog value from the temperature sensor is read using analogRead(A0) and stored in tempValue.

Mapping the temperature: The map() function is used to scale the **temperature sensor's range** of **0-1023** to a PWM range of **0-255**. This allows the temperature sensor's value to control the fan speed proportionally:

```
fanSpeed = map(tempValue, 0, 1023, 0, 255);
```

Adjusting fan speed: The compound operator += is used to gradually **increase the fan speed** by the step value stored in increment:

```
fanSpeed += increment;
```

   - **Limiting fan speed**: To prevent the fan speed from exceeding the valid range of **0 to 255**, the code checks for boundary conditions:
     - If fanSpeed exceeds **255**, it's capped at **255**.
     - If fanSpeed drops below **0**, it's set to **0**.
   - **Sending the PWM signal**: The calculated **fanSpeed** value is written to **pin 9** using analogWrite(9, fanSpeed). This PWM signal adjusts the speed of the fan based on the temperature.

- Delay: A short delay of **100 milliseconds** is added to ensure the fan speed adjusts smoothly and to prevent rapid fluctuations in speed.

Challenge:
Modify the system to **turn off the fan** when the temperature falls below a certain threshold, using a simple i f condition to detect low temperatures and halt the fan's operation.

5. Common Troubleshooting and Debugging Tips

5.1 Common Errors with Arithmetic and Compound Operators

Common Errors:
Arithmetic errors often include **division by zero**, which causes runtime errors. **Compound operator errors** might arise from incorrect syntax, such as x + = 5 instead of x += 5. These mistakes lead to unexpected results or compilation errors. Another common issue is **overflow**, where calculations exceed the variable's storage capacity.

Why they happen:
Errors can occur due to **misunderstanding of syntax**, **mistakes in operator usage**, or **incorrect assumptions** about variable ranges. For example, mixing up += with + can lead to logical errors, while division by zero usually happens when inputs are not validated. Overflow happens when large values are not managed correctly.

How to fix:
To fix these errors, always **validate inputs** to avoid division by zero. Ensure correct syntax for compound operators, and use **debugging tools** to track variable changes. To handle overflow, **use appropriate data types** and check for values before performing arithmetic operations. Reviewing error messages carefully can also help identify the source of the problem.

5.2 Preventing Overflow and Underflow in Arithmetic Calculations

What is overflow/underflow?

Overflow occurs when a calculation produces a value larger than the maximum limit of the data type, causing unexpected results. **Underflow** happens when a calculation produces a value smaller than the minimum limit. For example, in an 8-bit integer, values greater than 255 or less than 0 can cause overflow or underflow.

Why is it important to avoid them?

Avoiding overflow and underflow is crucial to ensure **program stability** and **correct results**. These issues can lead to **data corruption**, **crashes**, or **erroneous outputs**, affecting the reliability of your program. Proper management of data types and bounds ensures that calculations are performed within expected ranges and maintain the integrity of results.

Tips to prevent overflow/underflow:

To prevent these issues, **choose appropriate data types** that can handle the expected range of values. Use **range checks** before performing arithmetic operations, and implement **error handling** to catch potential overflow or underflow conditions. Consider using libraries or tools that handle large numbers if your calculations involve very large values.

6. Conclusion and Next Steps

6.1 Recap of Key Arithmetic and Compound Operators

What have we learned?

We explored fundamental **arithmetic operators** like +, −, *, and /, which perform basic math operations. We also covered **compound operators** such as +=, −=, *=, and /=, which simplify code by combining arithmetic operations with assignment. These operators are essential in programming for tasks such as **data manipulation**, **loop control**, and **variable updates**. Understanding their proper usage helps streamline code and reduce errors.

Why is it important?

Mastering arithmetic and compound operators is crucial for effective programming. They enable **efficient calculations**, **dynamic data adjustments**, and **simplified code**. By understanding these operators, programmers can write **more concise**, **readable**, and **efficient code**, enhancing the overall performance and reliability of their software applications.

Chapter 17: Arduino with Displays

In this chapter, we explore the different types of displays used with
Arduino, such as LCD (Liquid Crystal Display), OLED (Organic Light
Emitting Diode), and TFT (Thin-Film Transistor) screens. These
displays are essential for visualizing data, interacting with users, and
monitoring system status in real-time. Each display type has its
strengths: LCDs are ideal for simple text-based outputs, OLEDs
offer better contrast and energy efficiency, and TFT screens are
perfect for graphics and high-resolution images. Understanding how
to interface with these displays will enhance your Arduino projects
by providing important feedback and user interaction capabilities.

Syntax Table

Topic Name	Syntax	Simple Example
LCD Initializatio n	lcd.begin(columns, rows);	lcd.begin(16, 2); // Initialize 16x2 LCD
Displaying Text on LCD	lcd.print(text);	lcd.print("Hello, Arduino!");
OLED Initializatio n	oled.begin(SSD1306_S WITCHCAPVCC, 0x3C);	oled.begin(SSD1306_SWITC HCAPVCC, 0x3C);
Displaying Graphics on OLED	oled.drawRect(x, y, width, height, color);	oled.drawRect(10, 10, 50, 30, WHITE);
TFT Initializatio n	tft.begin();	tft.begin();
TFT Touch Input	tft.getTouch(&x, &y);	if (tft.getTouch(&x, &y)) { tft.fillCircle(x, y, 5, RED); }

Custom Fonts on TFT	`tft.setFont(&customF ont);`	`tft.setFont(&FreeSansBol d12pt7b);`
Animation s on TFT	`tft.drawCircle(x, y, radius, color);`	`tft.drawCircle(i, i, 10, WHITE);`

1 Introduction to Arduino Display Systems

What is Arduino Display System?

An Arduino display system refers to using different **types of displays** like **LCD (Liquid Crystal Display), OLED (Organic Light Emitting Diode)**, and **TFT (Thin-Film Transistor)** screens with Arduino to show information. **LCDs** are great for simple, text-based output, while **OLEDs** offer better contrast and visibility in low-light conditions, with lower power consumption. **TFT** displays are ideal for projects that require **graphics** and **high-resolution images**. Each type has its **strengths** and **limitations** based on your project needs.

Why is it Important?

Displays are essential for **real-time data visualization** and **user interaction** in Arduino projects. They provide **feedback** from sensors, allow users to **navigate through menus**, and help monitor system status without needing a computer connection. Whether it's showing temperature, humidity, or system messages, using displays can improve the **overall experience** and **functionality** of your project.

2 Key Concepts and Terms (Glossary)

LCD (Liquid Crystal Display)

LCD is a flat-panel display that uses liquid crystals to show text and simple images. It's widely used for **cost-effective**, low-power, text-based projects.

Why is it Important?
LCDs are crucial in projects like **clocks**, **calculators**, or basic weather stations where simple text displays are needed.

OLED (Organic Light Emitting Diode)
OLED is a display technology where each pixel emits light, offering **better contrast** and visibility without a backlight, making it energy-efficient.

Why is it Important?
OLEDs are great for **low-power**, **portable** projects and are often used in **wearables**, **small devices**, or **battery-powered projects**.

TFT (Thin-Film Transistor)
TFT displays provide **full-color, high-resolution** output. They are commonly used for **graphical user interfaces (GUIs)** or projects requiring **detailed visuals** like images or animations.

Why is it Important?
TFT displays are ideal for **graphic-heavy applications**, such as control panels, gaming devices, or **dashboards** in smart devices.

---

3 Overview of Display-Related Functions

What are Core Display Functions?
Arduino libraries provide easy-to-use functions to control displays. For **LCDs**, you use functions like `lcd.print()` to show text or numbers on the screen. In **OLEDs**, functions like `oled.draw()` are used to display graphics. For **TFT displays**, you can use `tft.fillScreen()` to color the screen or `tft.drawPixel()` to create graphics. These functions simplify interaction with different types of displays, making it easier to control and show information.

Why are They Important?
Core display functions allow you to interact with your project's **visual output** quickly and easily. They enable you to provide **important feedback** to users, such as **sensor readings**, **warnings**, or system **status updates**. By understanding these basic functions, you can make your project more **user-friendly** and **interactive**.

---

4 Using LCD with Arduino

4.1 LCD Initialization and Basic Displaying Functions

What is LCD Initialization?

LCD initialization prepares the **LCD screen** for use with Arduino. It includes setting up the display's size (number of rows and columns) and ensuring the correct connection between the Arduino and the LCD. The function lcd.begin() is used to start communication with the LCD and specify its dimensions. Without initialization, the LCD cannot display any information.

Why is it Important?

Before sending any text or data to an LCD, initialization is necessary. It ensures that the LCD is correctly set up for your project and avoids **display errors** or **communication issues**.

Syntax and Usage

The syntax to initialize an LCD is:

```
lcd.begin(columns, rows);
```

For example, to set up a **16x2 LCD**, you would write:

```
lcd.begin(16, 2);
```

This function prepares the display for printing.

Code Example

```
#include <LiquidCrystal.h>
LiquidCrystal lcd(12, 11, 5, 4, 3, 2);
void setup() {
  lcd.begin(16, 2);
  lcd.print("Hello, Arduino!");
}
void loop() {}
```

This code initializes a 16x2 LCD and displays "Hello, Arduino!".

Real-Life Application
Use an LCD to display real-time **sensor data** like **temperature** or **humidity** for home automation or weather projects.

Practical Exercise
Task: Initialize your **LCD** and display your **name** on the screen. Experiment by changing the display position and text.

Troubleshooting Tips
Check for **incorrect wiring**, use the correct **pin connections**, and ensure the **LCD library** is included in your sketch.

4.2 Displaying Sensor Data on LCD

What is Sensor Data Display?
Displaying sensor data on an **LCD** involves capturing real-time data from a sensor (e.g., temperature or humidity) and showing it on the screen. You can use lcd.print() to update the LCD with the sensor values in real time.

Why is it Important?
Displaying sensor data allows users to **visualize** important **readings** from sensors instantly, helping in projects like weather stations or home automation where data monitoring is essential.

Syntax and Usage
You can display sensor data using lcd.print() in the loop to constantly refresh the values. For example:

```
lcd.print(sensorValue);
```

This function shows the sensor reading on the LCD.

Code Example

```
int sensorPin = A0;
int sensorValue;

void setup() {
```

```
  lcd.begin(16, 2);
}

void loop() {
  sensorValue = analogRead(sensorPin);
  lcd.setCursor(0, 0);
  lcd.print("Temp: ");
  lcd.print(sensorValue);
  delay(1000);
}
```

This code displays a temperature sensor reading on the LCD.

Real-Life Application
Use an LCD to show **real-time sensor readings** in a **weather station** project or monitor environmental conditions.

Practical Exercise
Display **two sensor readings** (e.g., temperature and humidity) on two separate rows of the LCD.

Troubleshooting Tips
Ensure the **sensor is calibrated** properly, and format the data correctly for the LCD.

5 Using OLED with Arduino

5.1 OLED Initialization and Basic Displaying Functions

What is OLED Initialization?
OLED initialization is the process of setting up an **OLED (Organic Light Emitting Diode)** display with Arduino. The display must be **powered** and **connected** properly before it can show any data. Functions like `oled.begin()` are used to start communication between the **Arduino** and the **OLED display**. Initialization sets the **screen size** and ensures that the display is ready to show text, graphics, or images.

Why is it Important?
Without proper initialization, the **OLED screen** won't work correctly, leading to **blank screens** or **errors**. Initialization ensures that the **screen dimensions** are set and that the **Arduino** can send data to the **OLED** for display.

Syntax and Usage
The syntax for initializing an OLED screen is typically:

```
oled.begin(SSD1306_SWITCHCAPVCC, 0x3C);
```

This initializes an OLED with the **SSD1306 driver** and the **0x3C** I2C address. The oled.display() function can be used to update the screen after printing text or graphics.

Code Example

```
#include <Adafruit_SSD1306.h>
Adafruit_SSD1306 oled(128, 64);
void setup() {
  oled.begin(SSD1306_SWITCHCAPVCC, 0x3C);
  oled.clearDisplay();
  oled.setTextSize(1);
  oled.setTextColor(WHITE);
  oled.setCursor(0, 0);
  oled.print("Hello, OLED!");
  oled.display();
}
void loop() {}
```

This code initializes the OLED and displays the text **"Hello, OLED!"**.

Practical Exercise
Initialize your **OLED display** and display your **favorite quote**. Adjust the **text size** and **position** to fit on the screen.

5.2 Displaying Graphics on OLED

What is OLED Graphics Display?
An **OLED graphics display** allows you to show **shapes**, **lines**, and **images** on the OLED screen. Unlike an **LCD**, which is mainly for text, OLEDs can display **complex visuals** such as charts, icons, and dynamic graphs. Functions like oled.drawRect() and oled.drawLine() allow for **custom graphical interfaces**.

Why is it Important?
OLEDs offer **high contrast** and **sharp graphics**, making them

perfect for projects that need **visual feedback**, such as showing **sensor data trends** or creating a **user interface**. They enhance the user experience by making data **visually engaging**.

Syntax and Usage

To display graphics, you can use functions like `oled.drawRect()` to draw a rectangle or `oled.drawCircle()` for a circle. For example:

```
oled.drawRect(x, y, width, height, color);
```

This command draws a **rectangle** at position **(x, y)** with a given width, height, and color.

Code Example

```
void setup() {
  oled.begin(SSD1306_SWITCHCAPVCC, 0x3C);
  oled.clearDisplay();
  oled.drawRect(10, 10, 50, 30, WHITE);   // Draw a rectangle
  oled.drawLine(0, 0, 128, 64, WHITE);    // Draw a line
  oled.display();
}
void loop() {}
```

This code draws a **rectangle** and a **diagonal line** on the OLED screen.

Real-Life Application

Use OLED to display **dynamic graphs** or **icons** for battery levels, environmental data, or sensor outputs. This is useful for **wearable devices** or **real-time data monitoring**.

Practical Exercise

Draw a **battery level indicator** on the OLED. As you simulate power changes, update the battery level dynamically using **rectangles** or **bars**.

Troubleshooting Tips

Ensure that the **OLED connections** (SDA, SCL) are correct. If graphics aren't appearing, try refreshing the display with `oled.display()` after drawing.

18.6 Using TFT with Arduino

6.1 TFT Initialization and Touch Input

What is TFT Initialization?
TFT (Thin-Film Transistor) displays are **full-color displays** that are perfect for showing **graphics**, **images**, and **interfaces**. Initializing a **TFT** involves setting up its **dimensions** and **pin connections** with functions like `tft.begin()`. TFT screens often support **touch input**, which allows users to **interact** directly with the display, making them ideal for creating **interactive dashboards**.

Why is it Important?
TFT displays require proper initialization to display **graphics** and **read touch input**. Without setting up the display and its **touch sensitivity**, your project won't respond to **user actions**, making the interface non-functional.

Syntax and Usage
To initialize a TFT, use:

```
tft.begin();
tft.setRotation(1);   // Optional: Set screen orientation
```

Touch input is usually read with a function like:

```
tft.getTouch(x, y);   // Get touch coordinates
```

These functions allow you to set up the display and capture **touch events**.

Code Example

```
#include <Adafruit_GFX.h>
#include <Adafruit_TFTLCD.h>

void setup() {
```

```
  tft.begin();
  tft.setRotation(1);
  tft.fillScreen(BLACK);
  tft.setCursor(0, 0);
  tft.print("Touch Screen Ready");
}

void loop() {
  int x, y;
  if (tft.getTouch(&x, &y)) {
    tft.fillCircle(x, y, 5, RED);   // Draw a red circle where touched
  }
}
```

This code initializes the **TFT display** and draws a **circle** at the point of touch.

Real-Life Application
Use TFT touch screens to create **control panels, smart home interfaces,** or **game controllers** where users can **interact** with the device using touch input.

Practical Exercise
Create a **touch-controlled interface** where you can toggle between different displays by pressing buttons on the TFT screen.

Troubleshooting Tips
If the **touch input** isn't working, check the **pin assignments** for the touch controller and ensure the correct **library** is installed.

18.7 Advanced Display Functions

7.1 Custom Fonts and Animations

What are Custom Fonts and Animations?
Custom fonts and animations enhance the **visual appeal** of your project. **Custom fonts** allow you to display text in various styles, while **animations** enable you to create **moving elements** on the screen. These features can make your display more **engaging** and **interactive** for users, improving the **user experience**.

Why is it Important?
Using **custom fonts** and **animations** makes your project look more

professional and can convey information more **effectively**. They are especially useful in **user interfaces**, **dashboards**, and **entertainment devices**.

Syntax and Usage
To use custom fonts, include them in your code with:

```
tft.setFont(&customFont);
```

For animations, you can use a loop to update the screen frequently:

```
for (int i = 0; i < 100; i++) {
  tft.drawCircle(i, i, 10, WHITE);
  delay(50);
  tft.fillScreen(BLACK);
}
```

This creates a moving circle animation.

Code Example

```
void setup() {
  tft.begin();
  tft.setFont(&FreeSansBold12pt7b);
  tft.setCursor(0, 30);
  tft.print("Custom Font Example");
  for (int i = 0; i < 100; i++) {
    tft.drawCircle(i, i, 10, WHITE);
    delay(50);
    tft.fillScreen(BLACK);
  }
}

void loop() {}
```

This code displays text in a **custom font** and animates a moving circle.

Real-Life Application
Use custom fonts and animations for creating **interactive menus**, **game interfaces**, or an **animated clock** display.

Practical Exercise
Create an **animated clock** on your **TFT display** using moving elements to show the **current time**.

Troubleshooting Tips
If **fonts** or **animations** are slow or laggy, reduce the complexity of the graphics or use **smaller fonts** for better performance.

18.8 Practical Projects for Display Mastery

8.1 Project 1: Simple Temperature and Humidity Monitor

What is this project about?
This project involves displaying real-time **temperature** and **humidity** data on an **LCD** or **OLED** display. Using a **DHT11** or **DHT22 sensor**, the system continuously monitors the environment and shows updated data on the display. It's a great project for **weather monitoring** or **home automation** systems.

Why is it Important?
Displaying **sensor data** is crucial in many **Arduino projects**. This project allows users to **visualize real-time information** without needing a computer, making it ideal for **independent systems** like home temperature control or environmental monitoring in smart homes.

Components, Circuit Diagram, and Code Walkthrough
Components:

- Arduino board
- DHT11/DHT22 sensor
- LCD or OLED display
- Resistors and jumper wires

Circuit Diagram:
Connect the **DHT sensor** to an **analog pin** on the Arduino and the **display** to the **I2C pins** (for OLED) or designated **digital pins** (for LCD). Make sure the sensor is powered properly and grounded.

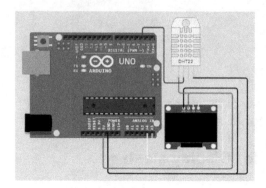

Code Walkthrough:

```
#include <DHT.h>
#include <LiquidCrystal.h>

DHT dht(2, DHT11);   // Sensor on pin 2
LiquidCrystal lcd(12, 11, 5, 4, 3, 2);

void setup() {
  dht.begin();
  lcd.begin(16, 2);
}

void loop() {
  float temperature = dht.readTemperature();
  float humidity = dht.readHumidity();

  lcd.setCursor(0, 0);
  lcd.print("Temp: ");
  lcd.print(temperature);
  lcd.print(" C");

  lcd.setCursor(0, 1);
  lcd.print("Humidity: ");
  lcd.print(humidity);
  lcd.print(" %");

  delay(2000);
}
```

This code reads data from the **DHT sensor** and displays **temperature** and **humidity** values on the **LCD**.

Challenge
Enhance the project by adding a **CO2 sensor** to monitor air quality. Display the **CO2 levels** along with temperature and humidity on the **LCD** or **OLED display**. This creates a more comprehensive environmental monitoring system.

8.2 Project 2: Touch-Controlled RGB LED Matrix

What is this project about?
This project involves controlling an **RGB LED matrix** using a **TFT touchscreen display**. The user can touch different areas of the **TFT screen** to change the **colors** of the **LED matrix**. It's an excellent way to learn **touch interfaces** and **visual feedback** with Arduino.

Why is it Important?
The combination of **touch control** and **RGB LEDs** offers a **hands-on experience** for building **custom interfaces** and **color control** systems. This type of project is useful for creating **interactive art**, **smart lighting systems**, or **entertainment devices**.

Components, Circuit Diagram, and Code Walkthrough
Components:

- Arduino
- 8x8 RGB LED matrix
- TFT touchscreen
- Resistors and jumper wires

Circuit Diagram:
Connect the **TFT display** to the Arduino's **SPI pins** and wire the **RGB LED matrix** to the **PWM pins**. The **TFT** will act as the **interface**, and touching different areas will control the **RGB LEDs**.

Code Walkthrough:

```
#include <Adafruit_GFX.h>
#include <Adafruit_TFTLCD.h>
#include <Adafruit_NeoPixel.h>

#define PIN 6  // Pin for LED matrix
Adafruit_TFTLCD tft(A3, A2, A1, A0, A4);
Adafruit_NeoPixel strip = Adafruit_NeoPixel(64, PIN, NEO_GRB +
NEO_KHZ800);

void setup() {
  tft.begin();
  tft.setRotation(1);
  strip.begin();
  strip.show();
}
void loop() {
```

```
  int x, y;
  if (tft.getTouch(&x, &y)) {
    int color = strip.Color(random(0, 255), random(0, 255), random(0,
255));
    strip.setPixelColor(map(x, 0, 240, 0, 63), color);  // Map touch to
LED matrix
    strip.show();
  }
}
```

This code sets up the **TFT** to detect touch inputs and changes the **RGB color** of the corresponding **LEDs** in the **matrix**.

Challenge
Add additional touch controls, like a **brightness slider** on the **TFT display**, to allow users to adjust the **LED brightness** dynamically.

18.9 Advanced Display Functions

9.1 Project 3: Dynamic Sensor Data Visualization with OLED

What is this project about?
This project uses an **OLED display** to create a **dynamic graph** that shows real-time sensor data, such as **temperature** or **light intensity**. As the sensor readings change, the graph updates, providing users with a **visual representation** of data trends. It's a great project for learning **data visualization** using **graphics**.

Why is it Important?
Visualizing data dynamically is crucial in many **monitoring systems**, where users need to **see changes** over time. This project helps in creating **more engaging displays** and allows users to **quickly interpret** sensor data, making it useful for **home automation**, **weather monitoring**, and **scientific experiments**.

Components, Circuit Diagram, and Code Walkthrough
Components:

- Arduino
- OLED display
- Light or temperature sensor (e.g., LDR or DHT22)
- Resistors and jumper wires

Circuit Diagram:
Connect the **OLED** to the **I2C pins** of the Arduino, and wire the
sensor to one of the **analog inputs**. The display will show a **graph**
that updates in real time.

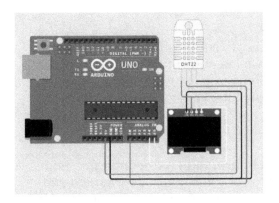

Code Walkthrough:

```
#include <Adafruit_SSD1306.h>
#include <Adafruit_GFX.h>
#define SCREEN_WIDTH 128
#define SCREEN_HEIGHT 64
Adafruit_SSD1306 oled(SCREEN_WIDTH, SCREEN_HEIGHT, &Wire, -1);
int sensorPin = A0;
int sensorValue;

void setup() {
  oled.begin(SSD1306_SWITCHCAPVCC, 0x3C);
  oled.clearDisplay();
}

void loop() {
  sensorValue = analogRead(sensorPin);
  oled.drawLine(0, 63, map(sensorValue, 0, 1023, 0, 127), 63,
WHITE);   // Draw graph
  oled.display();
  delay(1000);
  oled.clearDisplay();   // Clear screen before next draw
}
```

This code reads data from a **light sensor** and updates the **graph** on
the **OLED screen** to reflect the changes in light intensity.
Challenge
Modify the project to track **multiple sensor readings** (e.g.,
temperature and humidity) and plot them as two separate lines on
the **OLED graph**. This will give you a more complex visual
representation.

9.2 Project 4: Animated Weather Dashboard with TFT

What is this project about?
This project uses a **TFT display** to create an animated **weather dashboard**. The display shows the **current temperature**, **humidity**, and **weather status** (e.g., sunny, cloudy) using animated **icons** and text. It provides a **user-friendly interface** for viewing real-time weather data.

Why is it Important?
Animated displays can make **information more engaging** and **easy to understand**. This project combines both **graphics** and **real-time data** to create a visually appealing weather station that can be used in **smart homes** or **weather monitoring systems**.

Components, Circuit Diagram, and Code Walkthrough
Components:

- Arduino
- TFT display
- DHT22 sensor (or similar for temperature and humidity)
- Resistors and jumper wires

Circuit Diagram:
Connect the **TFT** to the **SPI pins** on the Arduino and wire the **DHT sensor** to an **analog pin**. The TFT screen will display weather icons and sensor data.

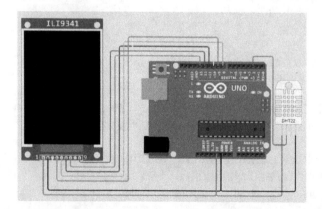

Code Walkthrough:

```cpp
#include <Adafruit_GFX.h>
#include <Adafruit_TFTLCD.h>
#include <DHT.h>
#define DHTPIN 2
#define DHTTYPE DHT22
DHT dht(DHTPIN, DHTTYPE);
Adafruit_TFTLCD tft(A3, A2, A1, A0, A4);

void setup() {
  tft.begin();
  dht.begin();
  tft.fillScreen(BLUE);
}

void loop() {
  float temp = dht.readTemperature();
  float hum = dht.readHumidity();

  tft.setCursor(10, 10);
  tft.setTextColor(WHITE);
  tft.setTextSize(2);
  tft.print("Temp: "); tft.print(temp); tft.print("C");

  tft.setCursor(10, 40);
  tft.print("Humidity: "); tft.print(hum); tft.print("%");

  // Draw weather icon (e.g., sun)
  tft.fillCircle(100, 100, 20, YELLOW);  // Sun icon
  delay(2000);
}
```

This code displays **temperature** and **humidity** readings on a **TFT screen** along with an animated **sun icon**.

Challenge
Add **cloud** and **rain icons** to represent different weather conditions dynamically. You can use sensor inputs or randomize the weather icons to simulate various weather conditions.

9.3 Project 5: Custom Fonts and Animation in OLED

What is this project about?
This project demonstrates how to use **custom fonts** and simple **animations** on an **OLED display**. It involves displaying a **custom message** in a unique font while animating an object like a **moving**

bar or **icon**. This project focuses on making the display **visually engaging**.

Why is it Important?
Using **custom fonts** and **animations** enhances the **user experience** by making the display more **dynamic** and **aesthetically pleasing**. It is especially useful in creating **user interfaces** for projects like **clocks**, **status displays**, or **interactive systems**.

Components, Circuit Diagram, and Code Walkthrough
Components:

- Arduino
- OLED display
- Jumper wires

Circuit Diagram:
Connect the **OLED** to the **I2C pins** of the Arduino. The display will show **custom text** and **animations** such as a moving bar or shape.

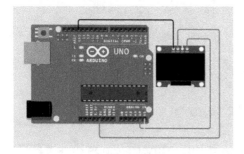

Code Walkthrough:

```
#include <Adafruit_SSD1306.h>
#include <Fonts/FreeMonoBoldOblique12pt7b.h>

Adafruit_SSD1306 oled(128, 64, &Wire, -1);

void setup() {
  oled.begin(SSD1306_SWITCHCAPVCC, 0x3C);
  oled.setFont(&FreeMonoBoldOblique12pt7b);  // Use custom font
  oled.setTextSize(1);
  oled.setCursor(0, 30);
  oled.print("Custom Font");
  oled.display();
}

void loop() {
  for (int i = 0; i < 128; i++) {
```

```
    oled.clearDisplay();
    oled.drawRect(i, 20, 10, 10, WHITE);   // Animate a moving square
    oled.display();
    delay(50);
  }
}
```

This code displays **custom text** using a **custom font** and animates a moving **square** across the OLED screen.

Challenge
Create an **animated clock** with custom fonts, where the **second hand** is a moving line on the OLED. Use **timing functions** to update the display every second.

---

10 Conclusion and Next Steps

Recap of Key Points
In this chapter, we explored using **LCD**, **OLED**, and **TFT displays** with Arduino. We covered how to initialize each type of display, how to print text and graphics, and how to integrate them into real-life projects like **weather stations**, **data visualizations**, and **interactive systems**. You also learned about more advanced features like **touch input** on TFT displays, **animations**, and using **custom fonts**. Mastering these display functions allows you to **enhance** the user experience in your projects by making them more **interactive** and **visually engaging**.

Next Steps
The next step is to explore more **advanced projects** using **multiple displays** or **combining sensor data** with **animations** for a more interactive experience. You can also look into **smart displays** with **Wi-Fi** integration to show **online data** or notifications.

The END

www.ingramcontent.com/pod-product-compliance
Lightning Source LLC
La Vergne TN
LVHW051426050326
832903LV00030BD/2937